中国古代文学

双语读物

Ancient Chinese Literature

熊晓雪 / 主　编
Robert Orth / 审　校

图书在版编目（CIP）数据

中国古代文学双语读物 ：汉英对照 / 熊晓雪主编
. -- 贵阳 ：贵州大学出版社，2022.1
ISBN 978-7-5691-0538-4

Ⅰ. ①中… Ⅱ. ①熊… Ⅲ. ①英语－汉语－对照读物
②中国文学－古典文学－介绍 Ⅳ. ①H319.4：I

中国版本图书馆CIP数据核字（2022）第005995号

中国古代文学双语读物

ZHONGGUO GUDAI WENXUE SHUANGYU DUWU

主　　编：熊晓雪

出 版 人：闵　军
策 划 人：葛静萍
责任编辑：高佩佩
装帧设计：陈　艺　方国进

出版发行：贵州大学出版社有限责任公司
地址：贵阳市花溪区贵州大学北校区出版大楼
邮编：550025　电话：0851-88291180
印　　刷：贵州思捷华彩印刷有限公司
开　　本：889 毫米×1194 毫米　1/32
印　　张：10.5
字　　数：256千字
版　　次：2022年1月　第1版
印　　次：2022年1月　第1次印刷

书　　号：ISBN 978-7-5691-0538-4
定　　价：32.00元

“用外语讲述中国故事”系列丛书

编委会

总　　序

在习近平总书记“讲好中国故事，传播好中国声音”的重要指导下，在展示中华文化独特魅力、塑造良好国家形象的进程中，从事外语教学及研究的学者应主动担当，奋力作为，增强文化自觉、文化自信，提高国家文化软实力，参与推动中华文化走向世界的宏伟工程，为不断提升中国的国际话语权和世界影响力贡献力量。

贵州大学外国语学院创立于 1942 年，名师荟萃，人才辈出。历经 80 年风雨，学院已成为贵州省重要的高层次外语人才培养基地之一，为国家和贵州省经济社会发展输送了近万名具有扎实专业知识、较高综合素质的复合型优秀外语人才。目前，学院拥有英语、日语、法语、俄语、德语、西班牙语、韩语、缅甸语、泰语等语种师资，建设了外国语言文学一级学科硕士点、翻译硕士和汉语国际教育硕士两个专业学位硕士点。英语专业是首批国家级一流本科专业建设点；日语专业入选贵州省省级一流本科专业建设点；缅甸语专业于 2020 年开始招生，2021 年获得教育部首批新文科研究与改革实践项目立项，外国语言文学学科进入发展的黄金时期。

为服务中国文化“走出去”战略及“一带一路”建设，展示外国语言文学学科专业建设成效，我们组织学院中青年教师，着力打造了一系列体现学科教学成果与科研成果的图书。“用外语讲述中国故事”系列丛书是近期推出的第一批代表性成果，包含中国传统节日、中国民间故事、中国神话故事、中国成语故事等中国优秀传统文化的英语、日语、缅甸语等语种读物。这些书既可以作为外国读者了解中国文化的普通读物，也可以作为在校大学生的通识文化类教材或外语类课程教材。这套丛书既可以增强中国学生用外语讲述中国故事的能力，又可以向外国读者介绍中华优秀传统文化，助力中华优秀传统文化“走出去”，让优秀传统文化散发出新的时代魅力。

本套丛书是贵州大学外国语学院国家级一流本科专业（英语专业）、省级一流专业（日语专业）以及教育部首批新文科研究与改革实践项目“‘全人’教育理念下的西部高校英语专业人才培养创新与实践 ”的建设成果。在编写过程中，得到了贵州大学教务处向嵩处长、贵州大学出版社闵军社长、龚晓康副社长的关心和指导，贵州大学出版社教材编辑室的编辑们提出了很好的意见和建议，特此一并致谢。

本丛书的编写，编委会希望尽最大努力做到在内容上有内涵、有深度，在形式上做到语言风格统一。但由于存在各种主客观因素，只能部分达到这些要求。书中难免有差错，希望广大读者不吝赐教，以匡不逮。

丛书编委会

2021 年 12 月

前　　言

中华传统文化源远流长、博大精深，凝聚着中华民族的道德情感，蕴藏着深厚的文化内涵，闪耀着人文思想的理性光芒。中国古代经典著作更是中国传统文化的奇葩。早在两千多年前，中国就出现了优美的《诗经》和《楚辞》；之后，又有了灿烂的唐诗和宋词；接下来，还有家喻户晓的四大名著……这些经典著作在塑造和构成中华民族精神文化方面有着极其重要的意义。在教育全球化的背景下，这些作品既是连接所有中国人思想、情感的文化纽带，也是中国文化和中国民族精神走向世界的重要桥梁。

作为贵州大学外国语言文学学科建设成果的“用外语讲述中国故事”系列丛书之一，本书选取了十本古代经典著作，《诗经》《论语》《史记》《水浒传》《三国演义》《西游记》《红楼梦》等，对作者、作品进行了介绍，并选取其中广为流传的内容作为阅读文本进行欣赏。全书中英文对照，原文翻译均选取许渊冲、大卫·霍克斯等名家的译本，可以让中国学生在欣赏名著的同时学习英语，欣赏优美的译文；而国外的读者也可以通过阅读该书了解中国优秀的经典文化著作和传统文化。因此，该书可以作为英语学习者的拓展阅读文本及教材，也适用于希望了解中国文化的海外留学生和外国读者。

越是民族的，就越是世界的。笔者愿中国读者通过阅读这本书，更加热爱祖国的传统文化，更加振奋民族精神，将来为中国文化、世界文化再添瑰宝，真正成为一个刻有民族烙印的中国人，一个走向世界的中国人！同时，也希望海外的读者通过阅读这本书，对中国的文化有更深刻的理解，愿意走入中国进行更多的文化交流！

最后，感谢贵州大学外国语学院领导们的信任、鼓励和支持，笔者在编译此书过程中收获颇丰，对于中国的文化瑰宝有了更深刻的认识和理解。同时，感谢外籍老师 Robert Orth 审校本书时所付出的心血和劳动。正是有了大家的支持，本书才能顺利出版！

熊晓雪

目　录

CONTENTS

第一章 《诗经》

1. 作品介绍

《诗经》，是中国古代诗歌开端，最早的一部诗歌总集，收集了西周初年至春秋中叶（前11世纪至前6世纪）的诗歌共311篇，其中6篇为笙诗，即只有标题，没有内容。产生地域以黄河流域为中心，南到长江北岸，分布在陕西、甘肃、山西、山东、河北、河南、安徽、湖北等地。

《诗经》是中国最早的现实主义文学。按照韵律，《诗经》分为三个部分："风"（民谣的部分），"雅"（节日歌曲的部分），"颂"（赞美诗的部分）。

2. 作者介绍

《诗经》的作者佚名，绝大部分已经无法考证，传为尹吉甫采集、孔子编订。《诗经》在先秦时期称为《诗》，或取其整数称《诗三百》。西汉时被尊为儒家经典，始称《诗经》，并沿用至今。

相传周代设有采诗之官，每年春天，他们摇着木铎深入民间收集民间歌谣，把能够反映人民欢乐、疾苦的作品，整理后交给太师（负责音乐之官）谱曲，演唱给周天子听，作为施政的参考。这些没有记录姓名的民间作者的作品，占据诗经的多数部分，如十五国风。

周代贵族文人的作品构成了诗经的另一部分。《尚书》记载，《豳风·鸱鸮》为周公旦所作。2008 年入藏清华大学的一批战国竹简（简称清华简）中的《耆夜》篇叙述的是武王等在战胜黎国后庆功饮酒的事情。其间周公旦即席所作的诗《蟋蟀》，内容与现存《诗经·唐风》中的《蟋蟀》一篇有密切关系。

3. 经典赏析

（1）周南

关雎

关关雎鸠，在河之洲；
窈窕淑女，君子好逑。

参差荇菜，左右流之；
窈窕淑女，寤寐求之。

求之不得，寤寐思服；
悠哉悠哉，辗转反侧。

参差荇菜，左右采之；
窈窕淑女，琴瑟友之。

岑差荇菜，左右芼之；
窈窕淑女，钟鼓乐之。

樛木

南有樛木，葛藟累之。
乐只君子，福履绥之！

南有樛木，葛藟荒之。
乐只君子，福履将之！

南有樛木，葛藟萦之。
乐只君子，福履成之！

桃夭

桃之夭夭，灼灼其华。
之子于归，宜其室家。

桃之夭夭，有蕡其实。
之子于归，宜其家室。

桃之夭夭，其叶蓁蓁。
之子于归，宜其家人。

（2）王风

采葛

彼采葛兮，一日不见，如三月兮。

彼采萧兮，一日不见，如三秋兮。

彼采艾兮，一日不见，如三岁兮。

（3）郑风

风雨

风雨凄凄，鸡鸣喈喈。
既见君子，云胡不夷！

风雨潇潇，鸡鸣胶胶。
既见君子，云胡不瘳！

风雨如晦，鸡鸣不已。
既见君子，云胡不喜！

子衿

青青子衿，悠悠我心。
纵我不往，子宁不嗣音？

青青子佩，悠悠我思。
纵我不往，子宁不来？

挑兮达兮，在城阙兮。
一日不见，如三月兮！

（4）魏风

硕鼠

硕鼠硕鼠，无食我黍！
三岁贯女，莫我肯顾。
逝将去女，适彼乐土。
乐土乐土，爰得我所。

硕鼠硕鼠，无食我麦！
三岁贯女，莫我肯德。
逝将去女，适彼乐国。
乐国乐国，爰得我直。

硕鼠硕鼠，无食我苗！
三岁贯女，莫我肯劳。
逝将去女，适彼乐郊。
乐郊乐郊，谁之永号。

（5）唐风

蟋蟀

蟋蟀在堂，岁聿其莫。
今我不乐，日月其除。
无已大康，职思其居。
好乐无荒，良士瞿瞿。

蟋蟀在堂，岁聿其逝。
今我不乐，日月其迈。
天已大康，职思其外。
好乐无荒，良士蹶蹶。

蟋蟀在堂，役车其休。
今我不乐，日月其慆。
天已大康，职思其忧。
好乐无荒，良士休休。

绸缪

绸缪束薪，三星在天。
今夕何夕？见此良人。
子兮子兮，如此良人何！

绸缪束刍，三星在隅。
今夕何夕？见此邂逅。
子兮子兮，如此邂逅何！

绸缪束楚，三星在户。
今夕何夕？见此粲者。
子兮子兮，如此粲者何！

（6）秦风

蒹葭

蒹葭苍苍，白露为霜。
所谓伊人，在水一方。
溯洄从之，道阻且长。
溯游从之，宛在水中央。

蒹葭凄凄，白露未晞。
所谓伊人，在水之湄。
溯洄从之，道阻且跻。
溯游从之，宛在水中坻。

蒹葭采采，白露未已。
所谓伊人，在水之涘。
溯洄从之，道阻且右。
溯游从之，宛在水中沚。

（7）陈风

月出

月出皎兮，佼人僚兮。
舒窈纠兮，劳心悄兮！

月出皓兮，佼人懰兮，
舒忧受兮，劳心慅兮。

月出照兮，佼人燎兮。
舒夭绍兮，劳心惨兮！

（8）曹风

蜉蝣

蜉蝣之羽，衣裳楚楚。
心之忧矣，于我归处。

蜉蝣之翼，采采衣服。
心之忧矣，于我归息。

蜉蝣掘阅，麻衣如雪。
心之忧矣，于我归说。

（9）豳风

七月

七月流火，九月授衣。
一之日觱发，二之日栗烈。
无衣无褐，何以卒岁？
三之日于耜，四之日举趾。
同我妇子，馌彼南亩；
田畯至喜。

七月流火，九月授衣。

春日载阳，有鸣仓庚。
女执懿筐，遵彼微行，
爰求柔桑。
春日迟迟，采蘩祁祁。
女心伤悲，殆及公子同归。

七月流火，八月萑苇。
蚕月条桑，取彼斧斨，
以伐远扬，猗彼女桑。
七月鸣鵙，八月载绩。
载玄载黄，我朱孔阳，
为公子裳。

四月秀葽，五月鸣蜩。
八月其获，十月陨萚。
一之日于貉，取彼狐狸，
为公子裘。
二之日其同，载缵武功。
言私其豵，献豜于公。

五月斯螽动股，
六月莎鸡振羽，
七月在野，八月在宇，
九月在户，
十月蟋蟀入我床下。
穹窒熏鼠，塞向墐户。

嗟我妇子，
曰为改岁，入此室处。

六月食郁及薁，
七月亨葵及菽，
八月剥枣，十月获稻，
为此春酒，以介眉寿。
七月食瓜，八月断壶，
九月叔苴，
采荼薪樗，食我农夫。

九月筑场圃，十月纳禾稼，
黍稷重穋，禾麻菽麦。
嗟我农夫！
我稼既同，上入执宫功；
昼尔于茅，宵尔索绹。
亟其乘屋，其始播百谷。

二之日凿冰冲冲，
三之日纳于凌阴，
四之日其蚤，献羔祭韭。
九月肃霜，十月涤场。
朋酒斯飨，曰杀羔羊，
跻彼公堂，称彼兕觥，
万寿无疆！

（10）小雅

鸳鸯

鸳鸯于飞，毕之罗之。
君子万年，福禄宜之。

鸳鸯在梁，戢其左翼。
君子万年，宜其遐福。

乘马在厩，摧之秣之。
君子万年，福禄艾之。

乘马在厩，秣之摧之。
君子万年，福禄绥之。

Chapter I The Book of Songs

1. Introduction of the Work

Chinese literature begins with *ShiJing* (*The Book of Songs*), the earliest anthology of songs, poems, and hymns. It consists of three hundred and eleven poems (six without text, named Sheng poems) dating from the Zhou Dynasty (1027-771 BC) to the Spring & Autumn Period (770-476 BC). Geographically, these poems were collected from the area which is now central China and the lower HuangHe (Yellow River) Valley of north China where Chinese civilization began and flourished. The area covers what are today ShanXi, GanSu, ShanXi, ShanDong , HeBei, HeNan, AnHui and HuBei provinces.

The Book of Songs was the earliest realistic literature in China. In the light of the rhythms, the anthology was divided into three sections: the "Feng" section (the section of ballads), the "Ya" section (the section of festival songs), and the "Song" section (the section of praises).

2. Introduction of the Author

The author of *The Book of Songs* is anonymous, and most stories about the individuals cannot be verified. The songs were collected by Yin

Jifu and edited by Confucius. “The Book of Songs” in the pre-Qin period was known as “Poems”, or called “Poetry 300”. It was regarded as a Confucian classic in the Western Han dynasty—first known as “*The Book of Songs*” and still known by that name today.

It is said that during the Zhou Dynasty there were officials who collected poems. Every Spring, they went to different places in the country, rang bells to attract people’s attention and collected folk songs. Then they sorted out the works which could reflect people’s joy and sufferings for the TaiShi (officials responsible for music) to set to music. These songs were then sung for the emperor in the Zhou Dynasty as a reference for his administration. The works of these anonymous folk writers comprise most parts of *The Book of Songs*, such as The Fifteen Nations’Styles.

The works of the aristocratic literati of the Zhou Dynasty constitute another part of *The Book of Songs*. *The Book of History* records that “Bin Feng Chi Xiao” was written by Zhou Gongdan. Within a batch of bamboo slips from the Warring States period, in the collection at Tsinghua University in 2008, there is a song named Qi Ye. It recounts how the emperor of Zhou and others drank after the victory over the state of Li. Zhou Gongdan wrote a poem named “The Cricket” during the feast, whose content is closely related to the existing song “The Cricket” in Tang Feng.

3. Appreciation

(1) The Songs of Zhou Nan

Cooing and Wooing

By riverside a pair, Of turtledoves are cooing; There is a maiden fair, whom a young man is wooing.

Water flows left and right, Of cresses here and there; The youth yearns day and night, For the maiden so fair.

His yearning grows so strong, He cannot fall asleep, But tosses all night long, So deep in love, so deep!

Now gather left and right, Cress long or short and tender! O lute, play music light, For the fiancée so slender!

Feast friends at left and right, On cresses cooked tender! O bells and drums, delight. The birds so sweet and slender!

Married Happiness

Up crooked Southern trees, Are climbing creepers'vines; On lords whom their wives please, Quiet happiness shines.

The crooked Southern trees, Are covered by grapevines; On lords whom their wives please, Greater happiness shines.

Round crooked Southern trees, Are twining creepers'vines; On lords whom their wives please, Perfect happiness shines.

The Newly-Wed

The peach tree beams so red; How brilliant are its flowers! The maiden's getting wed, Good for the nuptial bowers.

The peach tree beams so red; How plentiful its fruit! The maiden's getting wed; She's the family's root.

The peach tree beams so red; Its leaves are lush and green. The maiden's getting wed; On household she'll be keen.

(2) The Emperor's Style

One Day When I See Her Not

To gather vine goes she. I miss her whom I do not see, One day seems longer than months three.

To gather reed goes she. I miss her whom I do not see, One day seems long as seasons three.

To gather herbs goes she. I miss her whom I do not see, One day seems longer than years three.

(3) The Style of the State of Zheng

To a Scholar

Student with collar blue, How much I long for you! Though to see you I am not free, O why don't you send word to me?

Scholar with belt-stone blue, How long I think of you! Though to see you I am not free, O why don't you come to see me?

I'm pacing up and down, On the wall of the town. When to see you I am not free, One day seems like three months to me.

Wind and Rain

The wind and rain are chill; The crow of cocks is shrill. When I've seen my man best, Should I not feel at rest?

The wind whistles with showers; the cocks crow dreary hours. When I've seen my dear one, With my ill could I not have done?

Gloomy wind and rain blend; the cocks crow without end. When I've seen my dear, How full I feel of cheer!

(4) The Style of the State of Wei

Large Rat

Large rat, large rat, Eat no more millet we grow! Three years you have grown fat; No care for us you show.

We'll leave you now, I swear, For a happier land, A happier land where, we may have a free hand.

Large rat, large rat, Eat no more wheat we grow! Three years you have grown fat; No kindness for us you show.

We'll leave you now, I swear, For a happier state, A happier state where, we can decide our fate.

Large rat, large rat, Eat no more rice we grow! Three years you have grown fat; No rewards to our labor go.

We'll leave you now, I swear, For a happier plain, A happier plain where, None will groan or complain.

(5) The Style of the State of Tang

The Cricket

The cricket chirping in the hall, The year will pass away.

The present not enjoyed at all, We'll miss the passing day.

Do not enjoy to excess, But do our duty with delight!

We'll enjoy ourselves none the less, If we see those at left and right.

The cricket chirping in the hall, The year will go away.
The present not enjoyed at all, We'll miss the bygone day.
Do not enjoy to excess, But only to the full extent!
We'll enjoy ourselves none the less, If we are diligent.
The cricket chirping in the hall, Our cart stands unemployed.
The year will be no more, With the days unenjoyed.
Do not enjoy to excess, But think of hidden sorrow!
We'll enjoy ourselves none the less, If we think of tomorrow.

A Wedding Song

The firewood's tightly bound, When in the sky three stars appear.
What evening's coming round, For me to find my bridegroom hero!
O he is here! O he is here! What shall I not do with my dear!
The day is tightly bound, When o'er the house three stars appear.
What night is coming round, To find this couple here!
O they are here! O they are here! How lucky to see this couple dear!
The thorns are tightly bound, When o'er the door three stars appear.
What midnight's coming round, For me to find my beauty here!
O,she is here! O,she is here! What shall I not do with my dear!

(6) The Style of the State of Qin

Where is She?

Green, green the reed, Frost and dew gleam. Where's she I need? Beyond the stream.

Upstream I go; The way's so long. And downstream, lo! She's there among.

White, white the reed, Dew not yet dried. Where's she I need? On the other side.

Upstream I go; Hard is the way. And downstream, lo! She's far away.

Bright, bright the reed, With frost dews blend. Where's she I need? At river's end.

Upstream I go; The way does wind. And downstream, lo! She's far behind.

(7) The Style of the State of Chen

The Moon

The moon shines bright; My love's snow-white.
She looks so cute. Can I be mute?
The bright moon gleams; My dear love beams.
Her face so fair, Can I not care?
The bright moon turns; With love she burns.
Her hands so fine, Can I not pine?

(8) The Style of the State of Cao

The Ephemera

The ephemera's wings, Like morning robes are bright.
Grief to my heart it bring; Where will it be at night?
The ephemera's wings, Like rainbow robes are bright.
Grief to my heart it bring; Where will it rest by night?
The ephemera's hole, Like robe of hemp snow-white.
It brings grief to my soul; Where may I go tonight?

(9) The Style of the State of Bin

Life of Peasants

In seventh moon, Fire Star west goes; In ninth to make dress we are told.

In eleventh moon the wind blows; In Twelfth the weather is cold.

We have no warm garments to wear. How can we get through the year?

In the first moon we mend our plough with care.

In the second our way afield we steer.

Our wives and children take the food, to southern fields; the overseer says, "Good!"

In seventh moon, Fire Star west goes; In ninth we make dress all day long.

By and by warm spring grows, And golden orioles sing their song.

The lasses take their baskets deep, And go along the small pathways,

To gather tender mulberry leaves in heap.

When lengthen vernal days, They pile in heaps the southernwood.

They are in gloomy mood. For they will say adieu to maidenhood.

In seventh moon, Fire Star west goes; In eighth we gather rush and reed.

In silkworm month with axe's blow, We cut mulberry springs with speed.

We lop off branches long and high, And bring young tender

leaves in.

In seventh moon we hear shrikes cry; In eighth moon we begin to spin.

We use a bright red dye, And a dark yellow one, To color robes of our lord's son.

In fourth moon grass begins to seed; In fifth cicadas cry.

In eighth moon to reap we proceed; In tenth down come leaves dry.

In eleventh moon we go in chase, For wild cats and foxes fleet, To make furs for the son of noble race.

In the twelfth moon we meet, And maneuver with lance and sword.

We keep the smaller boars for our reward, And offer larger ones o'er to our lord.

In fifth moon locusts move their legs; In sixth the spinner shakes its wings.

In seventh the cricket lays its eggs; In eighth under the eaves it sings.

In ninth it moves indoors when chilled; In tenth it enters under the bed.

We clear the corners, chinks are filled, We smoke the house and rats run in dread.

We plaster northern window and door, And tell our wives and lad and lass;

The old year will soon be no more. Let's dwell inside, alas!

In sixth moon we've wild plums and grapes to eat;

In seventh we cook beans and mallows nice.

In eighth moon down the dates we beat; In tenth we reap the rice,

And brew the vernal wine, A cordial for the oldest-grown.

In seventh moon we eat melon fine; In eighth moon the gourds are cut down.

In ninth we gather the hemp-seed; Of fetid tree we make firewood;

We gather lettuce to feed, Our husbandmen as food.

In ninth moon we repair the threshing-floor; In tenth we bring in harvest clean;

The millet sown early and late are put in store, And wheat and hemp, paddy and bean.

There is no rest for husbandmen: Once harvesting is done, alas!

We're sent to work in lord's house then. By day for thatch we gather reed and grass;

At night we twist them into ropes, Then hurry to mend the roofs again,

For we should not abandon the hopes, Of sowing in time our fields with grain.

In the twelfth moon we hew our ice; In the first moon we store it deep.

In the second we offer early sacrifice, Of garlic, lamb and sheep.

In ninth moon frosty is the weather; In tenth we sweep and clear the threshing-floor.

We drink two bottles of wine together, And kill a lamb before the door.

Then we go up To the hall where, We raise our buffalo horn cup,

And wish our lord to live fore'er.

(10) Xiao Ya

The Love-Birds

Flying love-birds need rest, When large and small nets spread. May you live long and blest, Wealthy and happily wed!

On the dam love-birds stay, In left wing hid the head. May you live safe for aye, Duly and happily wed!

Four horses in the stable, With grain and forage fed. May you live long and stable, For you're happily wed.

Four horses in the stable, With grain and forage fed. May you live comfortable, For you're happily wed.

第二章 《论语》

1. 作品介绍

《论语》是一部记录孔子及其弟子言论和事迹的著作。

自汉代以来，儒家第一经典就是“五经”(《周易》《尚书》《诗经》《礼记》《春秋》)，但《论语》和《孝经》也同样受到推崇。前汉的昭帝、宣帝、元帝在很小的时候就学习过《论语》和《孝经》,《论语》的学习属于当时的基础教育。随着经书研究的深入，后汉的郑玄将《论语》与其他经书放在一起，试图对整个经书做出统一的解释。魏朝的何晏等人的《论语集解》是引用前人的解释编撰而成的。在此基础上，梁朝的皇侃编撰《论语义疏》,接着，在北宋时更是出现了官方注释的《论语正义》。到了南宋，随着朱子学的兴起，与“五经”一样，“四书”(《论语》《孟子》《大学》《中庸》)也愈发受到重视，其作用也更加突出。朱熹撰写了《论语集注》，从朱子学的立场对《论语》进行了新的解释。到了清代，考证兴起，刘宝楠的《论语正义》也试图从经验的角度对《论语》进行解释。

《论语》共10卷，有20篇文章。前10篇被称为“上论”，后10篇被称为“下论”。章节的名称(“子曰”除外)，各篇篇名取自每篇的前2个（或3个）字，每章讲述不同的内容。

2. 作者介绍

孔子（前552年或前551～前479）是春秋时期的思想家和哲学家。他是儒家学派的创始人，姓孔，名丘，字仲尼。孔子是尊称。在欧洲，他以拉丁化的名字“Confucius”（“孔夫子”的音译，夫子是对老师的尊称）闻名。孔子与释迦牟尼、耶稣和苏格拉底并列四圣。

他出生在周朝末年的鲁国，当时强大的王公贵族正朝着领土国家的方向发展，由于人口的流动和功利主义的猖獗，基于旧城邦的氏族共同体的秩序正在被瓦解。孔子的弟子们以孔子的思想为核心形成了一个儒家学派。战国时期，儒家成了诸子百家之一。《论语》是儒家学派的经典著作之一，由孔子的弟子及再传弟子编撰而成。

孔子大约有3000名弟子，特别是七十子，他们“精通六艺”。其中，最杰出的弟子被称为儒家十哲，他们根据天赋分为四类（因此也被称为四家十哲）。这些人是德行（根据《论语》，德行包括言论、政治和文学）领域的颜回、闵子骞、冉伯牛和仲弓，政治领域的冉有和子路，以及文学领域的子游和子夏。其他的人包括曾参（曾子），他以践行孝道而闻名，是《孝经》的作者，他的弟子子思是孔子的孙子，也是《中庸》的作者。

孔子去世后，儒家学派被分为八个流派。其中，孟轲（孟子）主张性善说，主张实行仁政。荀况（荀子）提倡性恶说，主张礼治。儒家六经是《诗》《书》《礼》《易》《乐》《春秋》。《春秋左氏传》《春秋公羊传》《春秋谷梁传》同为解说《春秋》的三传。

孔子死后，孟子和荀子继承了孔子的学说，但从战国时期到汉初，他们的影响力不大，然而，在整个西汉时期，它的力量逐渐增强，并被统治者所推崇。从那时起，儒家思想一直是中国思想的基本组成部分。

3. 经典赏析

(1)《论语·学而》

①子曰：“学而时习之，不亦说乎？有朋自方来，不亦乐乎？人不知而不愠，不亦君子乎？”

②子禽问于子贡曰：“夫子至于是邦也，必闻其政，求之与，抑与之与？”子贡曰：“夫子温、良、恭、俭、让以得之。夫子之求之也，其诸异乎人之求之与？”

(2)《论语·为政》

①子曰：“吾十有五而志于学，三十而立，四十而不惑，五十而知天命，六十而耳顺，七十而从心所欲，不逾矩。”

②子曰：“温故而知新，可以为师矣。”

③子曰：“人而无信，不知其可也。大车无輗，小车无軏，其何以行之哉？”

(3)《论语·八佾》

哀公问社于宰我。宰我对曰：“夏后氏以松，殷人以柏，周人以栗，曰使民战栗。”子闻之曰：“成事不说，遂事不谏，既往不咎。”

(4)《论语·里仁》

①子曰：“富与贵是人之所欲也，不以其道得之，不处也；贫与贱是人之所恶也，不以其道得之，不去也。君子去仁，恶乎成名？君子无终食之间违仁，造次必于是，颠沛必于是。”

②子曰：“我未见好仁者，恶不仁者。好仁者，无以尚之；恶不仁者，其为仁矣，不使不仁者加乎其身。有能一日用其力于

仁矣乎？我未见力不足者。盖有之矣，我未之见也。”

（5）《论语・公治长》

孟武伯问：“子路仁乎？”子曰：“不知也。”又问。子曰：“由也，千乘之国，可使治其赋也，不知其仁也。”“求也何如？”子曰：“求也，千室之邑，百乘之家，可使为之宰也，不知其仁也。”“赤也何如？”子曰：“赤也，束带立于朝，可使与宾客言也，不知其仁也。”

（6）《论语・乡党》

食不厌精，脍不厌细。食饐而餲，鱼馁而肉败，不食。色恶，不食。臭恶，不食。失饪，不食。不时，不食。割不正，不食。不得其酱，不食。肉虽多，不使胜食气。惟酒无量，不及乱。沽酒市脯不食。不撤姜食。不多食。

（7）《论语・颜渊》

①颜渊问仁。子曰：“克己复礼为仁。一日克己复礼，天下归仁焉。为仁由己，而由人乎哉？”颜渊曰：“请问其目。”子曰：“非礼勿视，非礼勿听，非礼勿言，非礼勿动。”颜渊曰：“回虽不敏，请事斯语矣。”

②季康子问政于孔子曰：“如杀无道，以就有道，何如？”孔子对曰：“子为政，焉用杀？子欲善而民善矣。君子之德风，小人之德草。草上之风，必偃。”

Chapter II The Analects of Confucius

1. Introduction of the Work

The Analects of Confucius is a record of the words and deeds of Confucius and his disciples.

Since the Han Dynasty, the first Confucian classic had been the "Five classics" (*The Book of Changes*, *The Book of Documents*, *The Book of Songs*, *The Book of Rites* and *Spring and Autumn Annals*), but *The Analects of Confucius* and *The Book of Filial Piety* were highly praised by the public. In the early Han Dynasty, Emperor Zhao, Emperor Xuan, and Emperor Yuan studied *The Analects of Confucius* and *The Book of Filial Piety* at their young age, the study of *The Analects* was part of the basic education at that time. With the further study of the classics, Zheng Xuan of the later Han Dynasty combined the studies on *The Analects of Confucius* together with other classics, trying to make a unified interpretation of the whole book. *The Analects of Confucius* by He Yan and others in the Wei Dynasty was compiled from the explanations of their predecessors. On that basis, Huang Kan of the Liang Dynasty compiled *The Semantic Thinning of The Analects of Confucius*. Afterwards, in the Northern Song Dynasty, there was an official interpretation of *The Rectification of Notes of the Analects of Confucius*. In the southern Song Dynasty, with the rise of Zhu Xi Studies, like the "Five Classics", the "Four Books" (*The Analects of Confucius*, *Mencius*, *Great Learning* and *The Doctrine of the Mean*) have been paid more attention and their functions have become more prominent. Zhu Xi wrote *The Collective Commentaries on the Analects of Confucius* and gave a new interpretation from the standpoint of Zhu Xi's theory. In the Qing Dynasty, with the rise of textual research, Liu Baonan's The Rectification of Notes of The Analects tried to explain The Analects of Confucius empirically.

There are ten volumes and twenty articles in The Analects of Confucius. The first ten articles are also called "The Upper Part of the Theory", and the last ten articles are called "The Lower Part of the Theory". The name of each chapter (except "Confucius Said") is named after the first two (or three) words of each, which introduces the content.

2. Introduction of the Author

Confucius (552 or 551B.C. ～ 479 B.C) was a thinker and philosopher of the Spring and Autumn Period in China. He, whose surname is Kong, the given name is Qiu, and his courtesy name is Confucius, is the founder of the Confucian School, Confucius is a courtesy title. In Europe, he was known by his Latin name, Confucius (transliteration of "Kong Fuzi, Fuzi is the honorific title for teachers). Confucius was one of the Four Saints, along with Gautama Buddha, Christ and Socrates.

He was born in the State of Lu at the end of the Zhou Dynasty, when powerful kings and nobles were moving toward a territorial state and the order of the clan community based on the Old City state was being disrupted by population movements and rampant utilitarianism. Confucius's disciples formed a Confucian school based on Confucius's ideas. During the Warring States period, Confucianism became part of the Hundred Schools of Thought. Around four hundred years after Confucius's death, his disciples codified his teachings in *The Analects of Confucius*.

Confucius had about three thousand disciples, especially the seventy disciples, who were proficient in "the Six Arts". Among them, the most outstanding disciples are called the ten philosophers of Confucianism, and they are divided into four groups according to their talents (hence also known as the ten philosophers of four schools). They are Yan Hui, Min Ziqian, Ran Boniu and Zhong Gong of the field of virtue (according to the Analects, virtue includes speech, politics and literature); Ran You and Zi Lu of the field of politics, and Zi You and Zi Xia as literary scholars. Others include Zeng Shen(Zeng Zi), known for practicing filial piety, who is the author of *The Book of Filial Piety*, and his disciple Zi Si, who is Confucius's grandson and the author of *The Doctrine of the Mean*.

After Confucius's death, Confucianism was divided into eight schools. Among them, Mencius (Meng Zi) maintained the idea of goodness of nature, he also advocated the idea of morality and justice. Xun Kuang (Xun Zi) advocated the opinion of evil nature and the rule of propriety. The six Confucian classics are *The Book of Songs*, *The Book of History*, *The Book of Rites*, *The Book of Changes*, *The Book of Music and The Spring and Autumn Annals*. *The Spring and*

Autumn Annals of the Zuo Family, *Biography of Gong Yang in Spring and Autumn* and *Biography of Gu Liang in Spring and Autumn* are the explanation of *The Spring and Autumn Annals*.

After Confucius's death, he was succeeded by Mencius and Xun Zi, but their influence was limited during the Warring States period through to the early Han Dynasty. But throughout the Western Han Dynasty, their power gradually increased, and was respected by the rulers. Since then, Confucianism has been a fundamental part of Chinese thought, though it has fluctuated from time to time.

3. Appreciation

(1) The Analects of Confucius. Learning

① Is it not a delight, said the Master, to acquire knowledge and put it into practice? Is it not a pleasure to meet friends coming from afar? Is he not an intelligent man, who is careless alike of being known or unknown?

② Zi You said to Zi Gong, "When our Master comes to a country, he would make inquiry into the way how the state is governed. Is the inquiry made on invitation or on his own initiative?" Zi Gong said, "Our Master makes inquiry in good way, moderate and temperate, modest and humble. Is it not different from other ways of inquiry? What matters if it is made on invitation or on his own initiative?"

(2)The Analects of Confucius. Politics

① At fifteen, said the Master, I was fond of learning. At thirty, I was established. At forty, I did not waver. At fifty, I knew my sacred mission. At sixty, I had a discerning ear. At seventy, I could do what I would without going beyond what is right.

② One who can learn something new while reviewing what he has learned, said the Master, is fit to be a teacher.

③ "How can an untrustworthy man be employed?" said the Master, "Could a large cart go without a yoke-bar or small cart without a cross-bar?"

(3) The Analects of Confucius. Eight Teams

When Duke Ai asked Zai Wo what symbol was used in the altar, Zai Wo replied, "The Xia rulers used the pine, the Yin rulers used the cypress, and the Zhou rulers used the chestnut, which means to chase the people off their nut." Hearing of this, the Master said, "What is done cannot be undone; what is accomplished need not be criticized, what is bygone need not be blamed."

(4)The Analects of Confucius. Good Neighborhood

① Wealth and rank, said the Master, are what men desire. If they could be attained only in an improper way, they should be relinquished. Poverty and obscurity are what men dislike, if they could be avoided only in an improper way, they should be endured. If a man had no virtue, how could he be worthy of his fame? A cultured man cannot do anything contrary to virtue even for the shortest time of a meal. He must do nothing contrary to virtue even in haste or in distress.

② I have not seen anyone, said the Master, who really loves virtue and abhors vice. If one really loves virtue, how could anyone else be better than he? If one abhors vice, it is because he is afraid that vice would do harm to him. Is there anyone who has practiced virtue with all his might all the day long? I have not seen one. Perhaps there are some, but I have seen none.

(5)The Analects of Confucius. GongYe Chang

Meng Wu asked whether Zi Lu was a man of men. The Master said, "I do not know." When asked again, he said, "In a country of a thousand chariots, Zi Lu might serve in the military field, but I do not know how he could be a man of men." When asked about Ran Qiu, the Master said, "In a city of a thousand families or baronial house of a hundred chariots, Qiu might serve as an administrator, but I do not know how he could be a man of men." When asked about Gongxi Chi, the Master said, "Standing at court with a sash around the waist, Chi might serve in the intercourse with honorable guests, but I do not know how he could be a man of men."

(6)The Analects of Confucius. In Native Village

He did not reject finely cleaned rice or minced meat. He did not eat rice affected by weather or turned sour, not rotten fish and putrid flesh, nor discolored or bad-smelling meat. He did not eat over-or under-cooked food, nor vegetables out of season or improperly cut, nor meat or food without its proper sauce. He must not eat more meat than rice. There was no limit for wine, but he must not get drunken. He must not buy wine or dried meat in the market. He might eat ginger food, but not much.

(7)The Analects of Confucius. Yan Yuan

① Yan Yuan asked about benevolence. The Master said, "A benevolent man will control himself in conformity with the rules of propriety. Once every man can control himself in conformity with the rules of propriety, the world will be in good order. Benevolence depends on oneself, not on others.” Yan Yuan asked about the details. The Master said, “Do not look at anything nor listen to anything nor speak of anything nor do anything against the rules of propriety.” Then Yan Yuan said, “Dull as I am, I would put your instruction into practice.”

② Asking about the art of ruling, Ji Kang Zi said to Confucius, “What do you think of killing the evil-doer to protect the good people?” Confucius replied, “Why should you kill to rule? If you rule in the right way, people will be good. The relation between the ruler and the ruled is like that between the wind and the grass. When the wind blows, the grass will bend down.”

第三章 《道德经》

1. 作品介绍

《道德经》又称《老子》，是中国古代先秦诸子分家前的一部著作，为其时诸子所共仰，传说是春秋时期的老子李耳撰写的，是道家哲学思想的重要来源。《道德经》分上、下两篇，原文上篇《德经》、下篇《道经》，不分章，后改为《道经》在前，《德经》在后，并分为81章，全文共约5000字，是中国历史上首部完整的哲学著作。

《道德经》常会被归属为道教学说。其实哲学上的道家和宗教上的道教是不能混为一谈的，但《道德经》作为道教基本教义的重要构成之一，被道教视为重要经典，其作者老子也被道教视为至上的三清尊神之一道德天尊的化身，又称太上老君，所以应该说道教吸纳了道家思想，道家思想完善了道教。《道德经》提出了“无为而治”的主张。“无为而治”是道家的基本思想，也是其修行的基本方法。

《道德经》并不像一般人所理解的那样，是一部论述道德的著作。事实上，道、德二字各有不同的概念。《道德经》前37章讲道，后44章言德，简单说来，道是体，德是用，二者不能等同。

2. 作者介绍

老子，姓李名耳，字聃，春秋末期人，生卒年不详，出生于春秋时期陈国，籍贯也多有争议。中国古代思想家、哲学家、文学家和史学家，道家学派创始人和主要代表人物，与庄子并称“老庄”。后被道教尊为始祖，称“太上老君”。在唐朝，被追认为李姓始祖。

老子曾担任周朝守藏室之史，以博学而闻名，孔子曾入周向他问礼。春秋末年，天下大乱，老子欲弃官归隐，遂骑青牛西行。到灵宝函谷关时，受关令尹喜之请著《道德经》。

老子思想对中国哲学发展具有深刻影响，其思想核心是朴素的辩证法。在政治上，主张无为而治、不言之教；在权术上，讲究物极必反之理；在修身方面，讲究虚心实腹、不与人争的修持。

3. 经典赏析

（1）第一章

道，可道也，非恒道也。名，可名也，非恒名也。无，名天地之始；有，名万物之母。故，常无，欲以观其妙；常有，欲以观其徼。此两者，同出而异名。玄之又玄，众妙之门。

（2）第七章

天长地久。天地所以能长且久者，以其不自生，故能长生。是以圣人后其身而身先，外其身而身存。非以其无私邪？故能成其私。

（3）第八章

上善若水，水善利万物而不争。处众人之所恶，故几于道。居善地，心善渊，与善仁，言善信，政善治，事善能，动善时。

夫唯不争，故无尤。

（4）第九章

持而盈之，不如其已。揣而锐之，不可长保。金玉满堂，莫之能守。富贵而骄，自遗其咎。功成身退，天之道也。

（5）第十二章

五色令人目盲；五音令人耳聋；五味令人口爽；驰骋畋猎，令人心发狂；难得之货，令人行妨。是以圣人为腹不为目，故去彼取此。

（6）第十四章

视而不见，名曰夷；听之不闻，名曰希；搏之不得，名曰微。此三者，不可致诘，故混而为一。其上不皦，其下不昧，绳绳兮不可名，复归于无物。是谓无状之状，无物之象，是谓恍惚。迎之不见其首，随之不见其后。执古之道，以御今之有。能知古始，是谓道纪。

（7）第三十三章

知人者智，自知者明。胜人者有力，自胜者强。知足者富，强行者有志。不失其所者久，死而不亡者寿。

（8）第三十七章

道常无为而无不为。侯王若能守之，万物将自化。化而欲作，吾将镇之以无名之朴。镇之以无名之朴，夫将不欲。不欲以静，天下将自正。

（9）第五十六章

知者不言，言者不知。挫其锐，解其纷；和其光，同其尘，是谓玄同。故不可得而亲，不可得而疏；不可得而利，不可得而害；不可得而贵，不可得而贱。故为天下贵。

（10）第八十一章

信言不美，美言不信。善者不辩，辩者不善。知者不博，博者不知。圣人不积，既以为人，己愈有，既以与人，己愈多。天之道，利而不害；圣人之道，为而不争。

Chapter III Tao De Ching

1. Introduction of the Work

Tao De Ching, also called *Lao Tzu*, is a classic of the pre-Qin philosophers in ancient China, which was admired by all the masters at that time. It is believed that the book was written by Lao Tzu (Li Er) in the Spring and Autumn period. It is the foundational work of Taoism and a cornerstone of its philosophy. *Tao De Ching* contains two parts in the original text, *De Ching and Dao Ching* both without chapters. Later, the order was changed, with *Tao Ching* coming first and *De Ching* following. They contain 5,000 words in eighty-one chapters. It is regarded as the first complete work of philosophy in Chinese history.

Tao De Ching is often classified as Taoist doctrine. But in fact, Taoism in philosophy and Taoism in religion cannot be treated as the same thing. As one of the important parts of Taoist Doctrine, *Tao De Ching* is regarded as a classic by Taoists, and its author, Lao Tzu, is also regarded by Taoism as the embodiment of the moral God, one of the supreme three pure deities, named Lord Lao Tzu. So it can be said that Taoism absorbed Taoism, and Taoism perfected Taoism. *Tao De Ching puts* forward the proposition of "Inaction", which is the basic thought of Taoism and the basic method of its practice.

Tao De Ching is not commonly known as a morality work. In fact, there are different concepts for the two words: Tao and De. The first thirty-seven chapters of *Tao De Ching* talk about methods, while the last forty-four chapters speak of virtues. In a word, Tao is the body and De is the usage; they are not equal.

2. Introduction of the Author

Lao Tzu, also Li Erh or Li Dan, was born in the State of Chen in the late Spring and Autumn period. His birth and death dates, as well as his hometown are unknown. He was a thinker, a philosopher, a writer and a historian in Ancient China, who was also the founder and chief representative of the Taoist School. He and Zhuang Tzu are called "Lao Zhuang". Later, he was revered as the founder of Taoism, and was called "Lord Lao Tzu". In the Tang Dynasty, he was posthumously recognized as the ancestor of the Li Family name.

Lao Tzu served as a storeroom keeper in the Zhou Dynasty and was famous for being learned and accomplished. Confucius went to the state of Zhou to show respect to him. In the period of the Spring and Autumn, the world was in chaos. Lao Tzu wanted to abandon his post and retire; he rode on an ox to the West. When he arrived at Ling Bao Han Gu Guan, he was asked to write the book of *Tao De Ching* by the local leader, Yin Xizhi.

His ideas have exerted great influence on the development of Chinese philosophy. The core of them is naive dialectic. In politics, inaction is highly proposed, not in words. In the methods to deal with power, extremity can cause reverse. In self-cultivation, modesty should be paid much attention. The practice of not arguing with others is the first rule of the dual cultivation of Taoist life.

3. Appreciation

(1)Chapter I

The divine law may be spoken of, but it is not the common law.

(Truth can be known, but it may not be the well-known truth or Truth can be known,but it may not be the truth you known.)

Things may be named, but names are not the things.

In the beginning heaven and earth are nameless; When named, all things become known.

So we should be free from desires in order to understand the internal mystery of the divine law;and we should have desires in order to observe its external manifestations.

Internal mystery and external manifestations come from the same origin,

But have different names.

They may be called essence.

The essential of the essence is the key to the understanding of all mysteries.

(2)Chapter VII

Heaven and earth exist for ever.

The reason why they exist so long

is not that they want to exist;

where there is no want,

to be and not to be are one.

Therefore for the sage

The last becomes the first,

The out becomes the in.

As he is selfless, all become his self.

(3)Chapter VIII

The highest good is like water.

Water benefits everything by giving without taking or contending.

It likes the place others dislike,

So it follows closely the divine law.

The place should be the low, the mind broad, the gifts kind,

the speech trustworthy, the rule sound, the deed well-done, the action timely.

Without contention, a man is blameless.

(4)Chapter IX

Don't hold your fill but refrain from excess.

A whetted and sharpened sword cannot be sharp for ever.

A houseful of gold and jade cannot be safeguarded.

Arrogance of wealth and power will bring ruin.

Withdrawal after success conforms to the divine law.

(5)Chapter XII

The five colors may confuse the eye.

The five sounds may deafen the ear.

The five tastes may spoil the palate.

Riding and hunting may madden the mind.

Rare goods may tempt one to do evil.

Therefore the sage satisfies the belly rather than the eye.

He prefers the former to the latter.

(6)Chapter XIV

What cannot be seen is invisible,

What cannot be heard is inaudible,

What cannot be touched is intangible.

These three, unfathomable, blend into one.

Up, it is not bright; down, it is not dark.

Like a nameless endless string, it ends in nothing.

It is a formless form, an image of nothing.

It seems to be and not to be.

Before it, you cannot see its front;

After it, you cannot see its rear.

Ruling over the present with the law of the past,

You can know the beginning of antiquity.

Such is the rule of the divine law.

(7)Chapter XXXIII

It needs observation to know others, but reflection to know oneself.

Physically strong, one can conquer others;

Mentally strong, one can conquer oneself.

Content, one is rich; with strong will, one can preserve.

Staying where one should, one can endure long;

Unforgettable, one is immortal.

(8)Chapter XXXVII

The divine law will not interfere, so there is nothing it cannot do.

If ruler can follow it, everything will be done by itself.

If there is desire to do anything, I shall control it with nameless simplicity.

When controlled by nameless simplicity, there will be no desire.

Without desire, there will be tranquility, and the world will be peaceful by itself.

(9)Chapter LVI

Those who know do not speak; those who speak do not know.

Dull your senses and shut your door;

Blunt the sharp and solve the dispute;

Soften the light and mingle with dust so as to be one with the mysterious law.

Therefore, none could be your friend or your foe;

None could do you good or harm; none could honor you or debase you.

So you are honored by the world.

(10)Chapter LXXXI

Truthful words may not be beautiful; beautiful words may not be truthful.

A good man need not just justify himself;

who justifies himself may not be a good man.

A wise man may not be learned; a learned man may not be wise.

A sage does not keep things for himself.

The more he helps others, the more he still has.

The more he gives, the more he keeps.

The divine law will do all good and no harm.

The way of a sage is to do what he can but contend with none.

第四章 《庄子》

1. 作品介绍

《庄子》为庄子（庄周）所著的道家经典。现存《内篇》7篇，《外篇》15篇，《杂篇》11篇。

现存《庄子》仅有《内篇》为庄周本人所著，大众认为《外篇》和《杂篇》均为后世他人所著。《史记·老子韩非列传》中收录了《庄子》一书的内容十万余字。《汉书·艺文志》显示《庄子》一书中原有52篇。

晋代郭象分析了汉代留存的《庄子》原文，因其中有同庄周思想相悖之处，故删除了三成内容，保留了《内篇》7篇，《外篇》15篇，杂篇11篇，现存33篇。这是现在流通的版本。书中字数约为65000字。郭象也著有《庄子注》一书。

人们普遍认为老、庄之间的思想也存在相融之处，但《内篇》中均为庄子本人思想。淮南王刘安将《老子》和《庄子》合并，《外篇》和《杂篇》中对此有所表示。

另一方面，从《庄子》一书中孔子时常出现便可以看出，庄子阅读过《论语》等儒家经典。但与同时代的孟子似乎并无关联。

列子（列御寇）为道家思想家，是庄子的前辈。《庄子》中列子也时常出现。然而现存《列子》一书中存在较多问题，故人们多不将其当作列子本人的著作。《列子》和《庄子》两书中有相同的故事，《庄子》成书于《列子》之前，《列子》或有参考《庄子》一书。

《庄子》提倡无为自然。其中内容则各不相同。

《杂篇》中有《让王篇》《盗跖篇》《说剑篇》《渔父篇》等内容，显然同庄子的思想并无关联。

同《老子》不同，《庄子》一书出现了较多真实存在的人物，使用了较多专有名词。文中几乎所有的故事均为寓言，无法作为史料，然而通过这些文章可以了解当时的风俗，从这方面来说，《庄子》是极为珍贵的资料。书中孔子及其弟子多次登场，孔子形象幽默，亦备受尊敬。

2. 作者介绍

庄子（约前 369 ～前 286），为战国时代宋国蒙（现菏泽东明县庄寨）人，是《庄子》一书的作者，也是道教的创始人之一。庄氏，名周，字子休。

庄子强调“无为”“顺物自然而无容私焉”。其与老子的思想不同，老子思想中政治色彩较为浓厚，庄子则希望远离世俗，畅游于无为世界之中。其核心思想倾向于价值的无穷相对性，在日常生活中利用反论，来批判“有用”一事。

庄子对孔子持批判态度，但他经常阅读孔子的文章，对孔子十分重视，也有诸多迹象表明庄子阅读了诸多儒家经典。因此自古以来就有学者怀疑庄子原本为儒家学者，苏轼在《庄子祠堂记》中认为庄子思想的内容和本质均属于儒家。

道教汲取了老庄思想，并将老庄作为道教神明来崇拜，老庄思想和道教思想也无法分割。然而，也有人对此持反对意见。

道教作为唐朝国教，庄子也被唐玄宗神化，公元 742 年，唐玄宗诏封庄子为南华真人，亦称为南华老仙。《庄子》一书因此也被称为《南华真经》。《三国演义》故事开头登场的南华老仙即为庄子。

3. 经典赏析

(1)《庄子·内篇·逍遥游第一》

至人无己，神人无功，圣人无名。

北冥有鱼，其名为鲲。鲲之大，不知其几千里也。化而为鸟，其名为鹏。鹏之背，不知其几千里也。怒而飞，其翼若垂天之云。是鸟也，海运则将徙于南冥。南冥者，天池也。

齐谐者，志怪者也。谐之言曰："鹏之徙于南冥也，水击三千里，抟扶摇而上者九万里，去以六月息者也。"野马也，尘埃也，生物之以息相吹也。天之苍苍，其正色邪？其远而无所至极邪？其视下也，亦若是则已矣。

且夫水之积也不厚，则其负大舟也无力。覆杯水于坳堂之上，则芥为之舟，置杯焉则胶，水浅而舟大也。风之积也不厚，则其负大翼也无力。故九万里则风斯在下矣，而后乃今培风；背负青天，而莫之夭阏者，而后乃今将图南。

蜩与学鸠笑之曰："我决起而飞，抢榆枋而止，时则不至，而控于地而已矣，奚以之九万里而南为？"适莽苍者，三餐而反，腹犹果然；适百里者，宿舂粮；适千里者，三月聚粮。之二虫，又何知！

小知不及大知，小年不及大年。奚以知其然也？朝菌不知晦朔，蟪蛄不知春秋，此小年也。楚之南有冥灵者，以五百岁为春，五百岁为秋；上古有大椿者，以八千岁为春，八千岁为秋，此大年也。而彭祖乃今以久特闻，众人匹之，不亦悲乎！

汤之问棘也是已：穷发之北，有冥海者，天池也。有鱼焉，其广数千里，未有知其修者，其名为鲲。有鸟焉，其名为鹏，背若泰山，翼若垂天之云，抟扶摇羊角而上者九万里，绝云气，负青天，然后图南，且适南冥也。斥鴳笑之曰："彼且奚适也！我腾跃而上，不过数仞而下，翱翔蓬蒿之间，此亦飞之至也，而彼且奚适也！"此小大之辩也。

故夫知效一官，行比一乡，德合一君，而征一国者，其自视也，亦若此矣。而宋荣子犹然笑之。且举世誉之而不加劝，举世非之而不加沮，定乎内外之分，辩乎荣辱之境，斯已矣。彼其于世，未数数然也。虽然，犹有未树也。

夫列子御风而行，泠然善也，旬有五日而后反。彼于致福者，未数数然也。此虽免乎行，犹有所待者也。若夫乘天地之正，而御六气之辩，以游无穷者，彼且恶乎待哉！故曰：至人无己，神人无功，圣人无名。

(2)《庄子 · 内篇 · 齐物论第二》

①大知闲闲，小知间间；大言炎炎，小言詹詹。

大知闲闲，小知间间；大言炎炎，小言詹詹。其寐也魂交，其觉也形开，与接为构，日以心斗。缦者，窖者，密者。小恐惴惴，大恐缦缦。其发若机栝，其司是非之谓也；其留如诅盟，其守胜之谓也；其杀若秋冬，以言其日消也；其溺之所为之，不可使复之也；其厌也如缄，以言其老洫也；近死之心，莫使复阳也。喜怒哀乐，虑叹变慹，姚佚启态。

乐出虚，蒸成菌，日夜相代乎前，而莫知其所萌。已乎，已乎！旦暮得此，其所由以生乎！

②天地与我并生，而万物与我为一。

天下莫大于秋毫之末，而太山为小；莫寿乎殇子，而彭祖为天。天地与我并生，而万物与我为一。既已为一矣，且得有言乎？既已谓之一矣，且得无言乎？一与言为二，二与一为三。自此以往，巧历不能得，而况其凡乎！故自无适有，以至于三，而况自有适有乎！无适焉，因是已。

(3)《庄子·内篇·养生主第三》

①吾生也有涯，而知也无涯。以有涯随无涯，殆已。

吾生也有涯，而知也无涯。以有涯随无涯，殆已。已而为知者，殆而已矣！

②为善无近名，为恶无近刑。

为善无近名，为恶无近刑。缘督以为经，可以保身，可以全生，可以养亲，可以尽年。

(4)《庄子·内篇·大宗师第六》

其嗜欲深者，其天机浅。

古之真人，其寝不梦，其觉无忧，其食不甘，其息深深。真人之息以踵，众人之息以喉。屈服者，其嗌言若哇。其耆欲深者，其天机浅。

(5)《庄子·外篇·刻意第十五》

众人重利，廉士重名，贤士尚志，圣人贵精。

夫有干越之剑者，柙而藏之，不敢用也，宝之至也。精神四达并流，无所不及，上际于天，下蟠于地，化育万物，不可为象，其名为同帝。纯素之道，唯神是守。守而勿失，与神为一。一之精通，合于天伦。野语有之曰："众人重利，廉士重名，贤士尚志，圣人贵精。"故素也者，谓其无所与杂也；纯也者，谓其不亏其神也。能体纯素，谓之真人。

(6)《庄子·外篇·秋水第十七》

井蛙不可以语于海者，拘于虚也；夏虫不可以语于冰者，

笃于时也

北海若曰："井蛙不可以语于海者，拘于虚也；夏虫不可以语于冰者，笃于时也；曲士不可以语于道者，束于教也。今尔出于崖涘，观于大海，乃知尔丑，尔将可与语大理矣。天下之水，莫大于海：万川归之，不知何时止而不盈；尾闾泄之，不知何时已而不虚；春秋不变，水旱不知。此其过江河之流，不可为量数。而吾未尝以此自多者，自以比形于天地，而受气于阴阳，吾在天地之间，犹小石小木之在大山也。方存乎见少，又奚以自多！计四海之在天地之间也，不似礨空之在大泽乎？计中国之在海内，不似梯米之在大仓乎？号物之数谓之万，人处一焉；人卒九州，穀食之所生，舟车之所通，人处一焉；此其比万物也，不似豪末之在于马体乎？五帝之所连，三王之所争，仁人之所忧，任士之所劳，尽此矣！伯夷辞之以为名，仲尼语之以为博。此其自多也，不似尔向之自多于水乎？"

（7）《庄子·外篇·田子方第二十一》

夫哀莫大于心死，而人死亦次之。

颜渊问于仲尼曰："夫子步亦步，夫子趋亦趋，夫子驰亦驰；夫子奔逸绝尘，而回瞠若乎后矣！"

夫子曰："回，何谓邪？"

曰："夫子步亦步也，夫子言亦言也；夫子趋亦趋也，夫子辩亦辩也；夫子驰亦驰也，夫子言道，回亦言道也；及奔逸绝尘而回瞠若乎后者，夫子不言而信，不比而周，无器而民蹈乎前，而不知所以然而已矣。"

仲尼曰："恶！可不察与？夫哀莫大于心死，而人死亦次之。日出东方而入于西极，万物莫不比方，有目有趾者，待是而后成功。是出则存，是入则亡。万物亦然，有待也而死，有待也而生。

吾一受其成形而不化以待尽。效物而动，日夜无隙，而不知其所终；薰然其成形，知命不能规乎其前，丘以是日徂。吾终身与汝交一臂而失之，可不哀与？汝殆著乎吾所以著也。彼已尽矣，而汝求之以为有，是求马于唐肆也。吾服，汝也甚忘；汝服，吾也亦甚忘。虽然，汝奚患焉！虽忘乎故吾，吾有不忘者存。”

（8）《庄子·外篇·知北游第二十二》

人生天地之间，若白驹之过郤，忽然而已！

孔子问于老聃曰：“今日晏闲，敢问至道。”

老聃曰：“汝齐戒，疏瀹而心，澡雪而精神，掊击而夫道，窅然难言哉！将为汝言其崖略。

“夫昭昭生于冥冥，有伦生于无形，精神生于道，形本生于精，而万物以形相生。故九窍者胎生，八窍者卵生。其来无迹，其往无崖，无门无房，四达之皇皇也。邀于此者，四肢强，思虑恂达，耳目聪明。其用心不劳，其应物无方。天不得不高，地不得不广，日月不得不行，万物不得不昌，此其道与！

“且夫博之不必知，辩之不必慧，圣人以断之矣！若夫益之而不加益、损之而不加损者，圣人之所保也。渊渊乎其若海，巍巍乎其若山，终则复始也，运量万物而不匮，则君子之道，彼其处与！万物皆往资焉而不匮，此其道与！

“中国有人焉，非阴非阳，处于天地之间，直且为人，将反于宗。自本观之，生者喑醷物也。虽有寿夭，相去几何？须臾之说也，奚足以为尧桀之是非！果蓏有理，人伦虽难，所以相齿。圣人遭之而不违，过之而不守。调而应之，德也；偶而应之，道也。帝之所兴，王之所起也。

“人生天地之间，若白驹之过郤，忽然而已！注然勃然，莫不出焉；油然漻然，莫不入焉。已化而生，又化而死，生物哀之，人类悲之。解其天韬，堕其天袠，纷乎宛乎，魂魄将往，乃身从之，乃大归乎！不形之形，形之不形，是人之所同知也，非将至之所务也，此众人之所同论也。彼至则不论，论则不至。明见无值，辩不若默。道不可闻，闻不若塞。此之谓大得。”

Chapter IV Chuang Tzu

1. Introduction of the Work

Chuang Tzu is a Taoist classic by Zhuang Zi (Zhuang Zhou). There are existing seven articles in the Inner Chapters, fifteen articles in the Outer Chapters, and eleven articles in the Mixed Chapters.

Only The Inner Chapters of *Chuang Tzu* is written by Zhuang Zi, while The Outer Chapters and The Mixed Chapters are believed to have been written by others. More than 100,000 words of *Chuang Tzu* are included in *The Records of the Grand Historian* (Biographies of Lao Tzu and Han Feizi). The Book of Han Dynasty (*Art and Literature Records*) shows that the book of *Chuang Tzu* has fifty-two Chapters in the original version.

In the Jin Dynasty, Guo Xiang analyzed the original text of *Chuang Tzu*, who, because of its contradiction with Zhuang Zi's thought, deleted 30% of the book's contents, retaining seven articles in the inner part, fifteen articles in the outer part, eleven in the mixed part, and thirty-three altogether. This is the current version. The number of words in the book is about sixty-five thousand. Guo Xiang also wrote the book of *Annotations to Chuang Tzu*.

It is generally accepted that there is a convergence of ideas between Lao Zi and Zhuang Zi, but the inner chapters are all from Zhuang Zi himself. Liu An, King of Huainan, combined *The Book of Lao Zi with Chuang Tzu*, which is expressed in the outer chapters and the mixed ones.

On the other hand, the frequent presence of Confucius in *Chuang Tzu* suggests that Zhuang Zi read Confucian classics such as *The Analects*. It doesn't seem to have anything to do with Mencius during the same era.

Lie Zi (Lie Yukou) was a Taoist thinker and a predecessor of Zhuang Zi. Lie Zi also appears frequently in *Chuang Tzu*. However, there are many problems in the extant *Lieh Tzu*, so people do not regard it as Lie Zi's work. There are same stories in both *Lieh Tzu* and *Chuang Tzu*. *Chuang Tzu* was written before *Lieh Tzu*, and *Lieh Tzu* may have a reference to *Chuang Tzu*.

Chuang Tzu advocates natural nonaction. Thus that content is different.

There are "Kings Who Have Wished to Resign the Throne", "The Robber Kih", "Speaking of Swords", "The Old Fisherman", and so on in the mixed chapter, which obviously have nothing to do with Zhuangzi's thought.

Unlike *The Book of Lao Zi*, in the book of *Chuang Tzu*, there are more people who really exist in the world, thus more proper nouns are used. Almost all of the stories in the text are allegorical and cannot be used as historical materials, but through these articles we can know the customs of that time. In this respect, *Chuang Tzu* is extremely valuable. Confucius and his disciples make multiple appearances in the book, and Confucius is both humorous and well respected.

2. Introduction of the Author

Zhuang Zi (about 369B.C.-286 B.C.) was a native of Meng of the Song Dynasty (now the village of Zhuang, Dongming County, Heze City) during the Warring States period. He was the author of the Book of *Chuang Tzu*, and one of the founders of Taoism. The given name of Zhuang Zi is Zhou and his courtesy name is Zi Xiu.

Zhuang Zi stresses "nonaction,"and "following the nature of things without allowing privacy." Unlike Lao Zi, whose core idea was more political, Zhuang Zi wanted to be free from the secular and travel around the world without doing anything. Its core thought tends to the infinite relativity of value, which can be used to criticize the "Useful" by using anti-theory in daily life.

Zhuang Zi was critical of Confucius, but he often read Confucius's writings and attached great importance to Confucius. There were signs that Zhuang Zi had read many Confucian classics. Therefore, since ancient times, some scholars have suspected that Zhuang Zi was originally a Confucian scholar, and Su Shi thought that the content and essence of Zhuang Zi's thought belonged to Confucianism in *Zhuang Zi's Records in Ancestral Hall*.

Taoism absorbed Lao Zi and Zhuang Zi's thought and worshiped them as Taoist Gods, thus their thoughts and Taoist thought could not be separated. However, there are some people who disagree.

Taoism was the state religion of the Tang Dynasty, and so Zhuang Zi was also deified by Emperor Xuanzong of Tang. In the year of 742,

Emperor Xuanzong of the Tang Dynasty gave an imperial order that Zhuang Zi was to be respected as Nanhua Immortal, also known as the Celestial Being of Nanhua. Zhuang Zi is also known as *Nanhua Taoist Scripture*. The story of *Romance of the Three Kingdoms* begins with the appearance of the Celestial Being of Nanhua, Zhuang Zi.

3. Appreciation

(1)Chapter I Chuang Tzu. Inner Chapter. A Happy Excursion

The perfect man ignores self; the divine man ignores achievement; the true Sage ignores reputation.

In the northern ocean there is a fish, called the kun, I do not know how many thousand li in size. This kun changes into a bird, called the peng. Its back is I do not know how many thousand li in breadth. When it is moved, it flies, its wings obscuring the sky like clouds. When on a voyage, this bird prepares to start for the Southern Ocean, the Celestial Lake. And in the Records of Marvels we read that when the peng flies southwards, the water is smitten for a space of three thousand li around, while the bird itself mounts upon a great wind to a height of ninety thousand li, for a flight of six months'duration. There mounting aloft, the bird saw the moving white mists of spring, the dust clouds, and the living things blowing their breaths among them. It wondered whether the blue of the sky was its real color, or only the result of distance without end, and saw that the things on earth appeared the same to it. If there is not sufficient depth, water will not float large ships. Upset a cupful into a hole in the yard, and a mustard-seed will be your boat. Try to float the cup, and it will be grounded, due to the disproportion between water and vessel. So with air. If there is not sufficient a depth, it cannot support large wings. And for this bird, a depth of ninety thousand li is necessary to bear it up. Then, gliding upon the wind, with nothing save the clear sky above, and no obstacles in the way, it starts upon its journey to the south. A cicada and a young dove laughed, saying, "Now, when I fly with all my might, 'tis as much as I can do to get from tree to tree. And sometimes I do not reach, but fall to the ground midway. What then can be the use of going up ninety thousand li to start for the south?" He who goes to the countryside taking three meals with him comes back with his stomach as full as when he started. But he who travels a hundred li must take ground rice enough for an overnight stay. And he who travels a thousand li must supply himself with provisions for three months. Those two little creatures, what should they know? Small knowledge has not the compass of great knowledge any more than a short year has the length of a long year. How can we tell that this is so? The fungus plant of a morning knows not the alternation of day and night. The cicada knows not the alternation of spring and autumn. Theirs are short years. But in the south of Chu there is a mingling (tree) whose spring and autumn are each of five hundred years' duration. And in former days there was a large tree which had a spring and autumn each of eight thousand years. Yet, Peng Tsu is known for reaching a great age and is still, alas! an object of envy to all! It was on this very subject that the Emperor Tang spoke to Chi, as follows: "At the north of Chiungta, there is a Dark Sea, the Celestial Lake. In it there is a fish several thousand li in breadth, and I know not how many in length. It is called the kun. There is also a bird, called the peng, with a back like Mount Tai, and wings like clouds across the sky. It soars up upon a whirlwind to a height of ninety thousand li, far above the region of the clouds, with only the clear sky above it. And then it directs its flight towards the Southern Ocean. "And a lake sparrow laughed, and said: Pray, what may that creature be going to do? I rise but a few yards in the air and settle down again, after flying around among the reeds. That is as much as anyone would want to fly. Now, wherever can this creature be going to?" Such, indeed, is the difference between small and great. Take, for instance, a man who creditably fills some small office, or whose influence spreads over a village, or whose character pleases a certain prince. His opinion of himself will be much the same as that lake sparrow's. The philosopher Yung of Sung would laugh at such a one. If the whole world flattered him, he would not be affected thereby, nor if the whole world blamed him would he be dissuaded from what he was doing. For Yung can distinguish between essence and superficialities, and understand what is true honor and shame. Such men are rare in their generation. But even he has not established himself. Now Liehtse could ride upon the wind. Sailing happily in the cool breeze, he would go on for fifteen days before his return. Among mortals who attain happiness, such a man is rare. Yet although Liehtse could dispense with walking, he would still have to depend upon something. As for one who is charioted upon the eternal fitness of Heaven and Earth, driving before him the changing elements as his team to roam through the realms of the Infinite, upon what, then, would such a one have need to depend? Thus it is said, "The perfect man ignores self; the divine man ignores achievement; the true Sage ignores reputation."

(2)Chapter II Chuang Tzu. Inner Chapter. On Leveling All Things

① Great wisdom is generous; petty wisdom is contentious. Great speech is impassioned, small speech cantankerous.

Great wisdom is generous; petty wisdom is contentious. Great speech is impassioned, small speech cantankerous. For whether the soul is locked in sleep or whether in waking hours the body moves, we are striving and struggling with the immediate circumstances. Some are easy-going and leisurely, some are deep and cunning, and some are secretive. Now we are frightened over petty fears, now disheartened and dismayed over some great terror. Now the mind flies forth like an arrow from a cross-bow, to be the arbiter of right and wrong. Now it stays behind as if sworn to an oath, to hold on to what it has secured. Then, as under autumn and winter's blight, comes gradual decay, and submerged in its own occupations, it keeps on running its course, never to return. Finally, worn out and imprisoned, it is choked up like an old drain, and the failing mind shall not see light again. Joy and anger, sorrow and happiness, worries and regrets, indecision and fears, come upon us by turns, with ever-changing moods, like music from the hollows, or like mushrooms from damp. Day and night they alternate within us, but we cannot tell whence they spring. Alas! Alas! Could we for a moment lay our finger upon their very Cause?

② The universe and I came into being together; I and everything therein are One.

There is nothing under the canopy of heaven greater than the tip of a bird's down in autumn, while the Tai Mountain is small. Neither is there any longer life than that of a child cut off in infancy, while Peng Tsu himself died young. The universe and I came into being together; I and everything therein are One. If then all things are One, what room is there for speech? On the other hand, since I can say the word 'one' how can speech not exist? If it does exist, we have One and speech — two; and two and one — three from which point onwards even the best mathematicians will fail to reach (the ultimate); how much more then should ordinary people fail? Hence, if from nothing you can proceed to something, and subsequently reach there, it follows that it would be still easier if you were to start from something. Since you cannot proceed, stop here.

(3)Chapter III Chuang Tzu. Inner Chapter. The Preservation Of Life

① Human life is limited, but knowledge is limitless. To drive the limited in pursuit of the limitless is fatal.

Human life is limited, but knowledge is limitless. To drive the limited in pursuit of the limitless is fatal; and to presume that one really knows is fatal indeed!

② In doing good, avoid fame. In doing bad, avoid disgrace.

In doing good, avoid fame. In doing bad, avoid disgrace. Pursue a middle course as your principle. Thus you will guard your body from harm, preserve your life, fulfill your duties by your parents, and live your allotted span of life.

(4)Chapter VI Chuang Tzu. Inner Chapter. The Great Supreme

When man's attachments are deep, their divine endowments are shallow.

The true men of old slept without dreams and waked up without worries. They ate with indifference to flavor, and drew deep breaths. For true men draw breath from their heels, the vulgar only from their throats. Out of the crooked, words are retched up like vomit. When man's attachments are deep, their divine endowments are shallow.

(5)Chapter XV Chuang Tzu. Outer Chapter. Rigid and Arrogant

The common people prize profit above all else; the worthy scholar, fame; the wise man, ambition and the sage his essential purity.

To have a sword like Kan Yueh, you must look after it in a special box and hardly dare use it, for this is the greatest of treasures. The spirit emanates in all four directions, without restriction, rising to Heaven and sinking down to enfold the Earth, It changes and nourishes all forms of life yet no one can find its shape. Its title is Harmony in the Supreme. It is only the Tao of true simplicity which guards the spirit; if you are guarded and never lost, you become one with the spirit. In being one you are in communion with the Order of Heaven. Peasant wisdom says, "The common people prize profit above all else; the worthy scholar, fame; the wise man, ambition and the sage his essential purity." Simplicity means no mixing; purity means an unimpaired spirit. The one who manifests simplicity and purity can truly be called the true man.

(6)Chapter XVII Chuang Tzu. Outer Chapter. Autumn Floods

You cannot speak of ocean to a well-frog, which is limited by his abode. You cannot speak of ice to a summer insect, which is limited by his short life.

To this North-Sea Jo (the Spirit of the Ocean) replied, "You cannot speak of ocean to a well-frog, which is limited by his abode. You cannot speak of ice to a summer insect, which is limited by his short life. You cannot speak of Tao to a pedagogue, who is limited in his knowledge. But now that you have emerged from your narrow sphere and have seen the great ocean, you know your own insignificance, and I can speak to you of great principles. There is no body of water beneath the canopy of heaven which is greater than the ocean. All streams pour into it without cease, yet it does not overflow. It is being continually drained off at the Tail-Gate yet it is never empty. Spring and autumn bring no change; floods and droughts are equally unknown. And thus it is immeasurably superior to mere rivers and streams. Yet I have never ventured to boast on this account. For I count myself, among the things that take shape from the universe and receive life from the yin and yang, but as a pebble or a small tree on a vast mountain. Only too conscious of my own insignificance, how can I presume to boast of my greatness? Are not the Four Seas to the universe but like ant-holes in a marsh? Is not the Middle Kingdom to the surrounding ocean like a tare-seed in a granary? Of all the myriad created things, man is but one. And of all those who inhabit the Nine

Continents, live on the fruit of the earth, and move about in cart and boat, an individual man is but one. Is not he, as compared with all creation, but as the tip of a hair upon a horse's body? The succession of the Five Rulers, the contentions of the Three Kings, the concerns of the kind-hearted, the labors of the administrators, are but this and nothing more. Po Yi refused the throne for fame. Chungni (Confucius) discoursed to get a reputation for learning. This over-estimation of self on their part — was it not very much like your own previous self-estimation in reference to water?"

(7)Chapter XXI Chuang Tzu. Outer Chapter. Thien Tsze-Fang

Of all causes for sorrow there is none so great as the death of the mind; —the death of man's (body) is only next to it.

Yen Yüan asked Kung-nî, saying, "Master, when you pace quietly along, I also pace along; when you go more quickly, I also do the same; when you gallop, I also gallop; but when you race along and spurn the dust, then I can only stand and look, and keep behind you." The Master said, "Hui, what do you mean?" The reply was, in saying that "when you, Master, pace quietly along, I also pace along," I mean that when you speak, I also speak. By saying, "When you go more quickly, I also do the same," I mean that when you reason, I also reason. By saying, "When you gallop, I also gallop, I mean that when you speak of the Way, I also speak of the Way; but by saying, "When you race along and spurn the dust, then I can only stare, and keep behind you," I am thinking how though you do not speak, yet all men believe you; though you are no partisan, yet all parties approve your catholicity; and though you sound no instrument, yet people all move on harmoniously before you, while (all the while) I do not know how all this comes about; and this is all which my words are intended to express." Kung-nî said, "But you must try and search the matter out. Of all causes for sorrow there is none so great as the death of the mind;—the death of man's (body) is only next to it. The sun comes forth in the east, and sets in the extreme west; —all things have their position determined by these two points. All that have eyes and feet wait for this (sun), and then proceed to do what they have to do. When this comes forth, they appear in their places; when it sets, they disappear. It is so with all things. They have that for which they wait, and (on its arrival) they die; they have that for which they wait, and then (again) they live. When once I receive my frame thus completed, I remain unchanged, awaiting the consummation of my course. I move as acted on by things, day and night without cessation, and I do not know when I will come to an end. Clearly I am here a completed frame, and even one who (fancies that he) knows what is appointed cannot determine it beforehand. I am in this way daily passing on, but all day long I am communicating my views to you; and now, as we are shoulder to shoulder you fail (to understand me);— is it not matter for lamentation? You are able in a measure to set forth what I more clearly set forth; but that is passed away, and you look for it, as if it were still existing, just as if you were looking for a horse in the now empty place where it was formerly exhibited for sale. You have very much forgotten my service to you, and I have very much forgotten wherein I served you. But nevertheless why should your account this such an evil? What you forget is but my old self; that which cannot be forgotten remains with me."

(8)Chapter XXII Chuang Tzu. Outer Chapter. Knowledge Rambling in the North

Men's life between heaven and earth is like a white colt's passing a crevice, and suddenly disappearing.

Confucius asked Lao Dan, saying, "Being at leisure to-day, I venture to ask you about the Perfect Dao."

Lao Dan replied, "You must, as by fasting and vigil, clear and purge your mind, wash your spirit white as snow, and sternly repress your knowledge. The subject of the Dao is deep, and difficult to describe; — I will give you an outline of its simplest attributes."

"The Luminous was produced from the Obscure; the Multiform from the Unembodied; the Spiritual from the Dao; and the bodily from the seminal essence. After this all things produced one another from their bodily organizations. Thus it is that those which have nine apertures are born from the womb, and those with eight from eggs. But their coming leaves no trace, and their going no monument; they enter by no door; they dwell in no apartment: —they are in a vast arena reaching in all directions. They who search for and find (the Dao) in this are strong in their limbs, sincere and far-reaching in their thinking, acute in their hearing, and clear in their seeing. They exercise their minds without being toiled; they respond to everything aright without regard to place or circumstance. Without this heaven would not be high, nor earth broad; the sun and moon would not move, and nothing would flourish:—such is the operation of the Dao. Moreover, the most extensive knowledge does not necessarily know it; reasoning will not make men wise in it;—the sages have decided against both these methods. However you try to add to it, it admits of no increase; however you try to take from it, it admits of no diminution;—this is what the sages maintain about it. How deep it is, like the see! How grand it is, beginning again when it has come to an end! If it carried along and sustained all things, without being overburdened or weary, that would be like the way of the superior man, merely an external operation; when all things go to it, and find their dependence in it; —this is the true character of the Dao. Here is a man (born) in one of the middle states. He feels himself independent both of the Yin and Yang, and dwells between heaven and earth; only for the present a mere man, but he will return to his original source. Looking at him in his origin, when his life begins, we have (but) a gelatinous substance in which the breath is collecting. Whether his life be long or his death early, how short is the space between them! It is but the name for a moment of time, insufficient to play the part of a good Yao or a bad Jie in. The fruits of trees and creeping plants have their distinctive characters, and though the relationships of men, according to which they are classified, are troublesome, the sage, when he meets with them, does not set himself in opposition to them, and when he has passed through them, he does not seek to retain them; he responds to them in their regular harmony according to his virtue; and even when he accidentally come across any of them, he does so according to the Dao. It was thus that the Dao flourished, thus that the kings arose. Men's life between heaven and earth is like a white colt's passing a crevice, and suddenly disappearing. As with a plunge and an effort they all come forth; easily and quietly they all enter again. By a transformation they live, and by another transformation they die. Living things are made sad (by death), and mankind grieve for it; but it is (only) the removal of the bow from its sheath, and the emptying the natural satchel of its contents. There may be some confusion amidst the yielding to the change; but the intellectual and animal souls are taking their leave, and the body will follow them:—This is the Great Returning home. That the bodily frame came from incorporeity, and will return to the same, is what all men in common know, and what those who are on their way to (know) it need not strive for. This is what the multitudes of men discuss together. Those whose (knowledge) is complete do not discuss it;—such discussion shows that their (knowledge) is not complete. Even the most clear-sighted do not meet (with the Dao);—it is better to be silent than to reason about it. The Dao cannot be heard with the ears;—it is better to shut the ears than to try and hear it. This is what is called the Great Attainment."

第五章 《荀子》

1. 作品介绍

《荀子》是战国末年著名唯物主义思想家、文学家荀子的著作，是儒家学派的重要典籍，是研究荀子思想和先秦各派学说的重要材料。

《荀子》一书，刘向校定为32篇，称《荀卿新书》。《汉书·艺文志》称之为《孙卿子》，唐代杨倞开始为其作注，分为二十卷，改题为《荀子》。

《荀子》内容涵盖哲学、伦理、政治、文学、语言学、教育，乃至经济、军事等，是先秦一大思想宝库。荀子倡导性恶论，认为“人之性恶，其善者伪也”，所以他尤为重视后天学习，《劝学》《修身》等篇多阐述学习、修身。如“吾尝终日而思矣，不如须臾之所学也”（《劝学》），“见善，修然必以自存也；见不善，愀然必以自省也”（《修身》）。

《非十二子》以言简意赅的语言评论诸家思想；《正名》以明晰的逻辑思维方式阐述正名学说与语言理论，发前人之所未发；而用民歌形式所写的韵文《成相》成为后世弹词的起点，《赋》与屈原、宋玉的赋一道被称为汉代辞赋的源头，成为后世赋体的典范。这些都是研究先秦学术思想、语言文学所应当关注的。

荀子的学说，源自孔子而又对孔子思想有所发展，成为儒家思想的重要支流，虽然其精髓是以礼容法，但其思想之广博宏深，内涵之丰富，均为各家思想之大成。荀子善于论辩，谈及问题往往长于推理，善用比喻，表达深刻，说理中肯，值得细细品味。

2. 作者介绍

荀子（约前 313 ～前 238），名况，字卿，时人尊称为“荀卿”，汉代避宣帝讳，称之为孙卿。赵国人，儒家代表人物之一。曾游学于齐，为稷下先生，名望极高。晚年著书授徒，现存《荀子》一书。荀子的思想主要继承了孔子关于“礼”的思想，核心是实行礼治。他把礼由伦理规范上升为一种治国之策。他主张实行“隆礼重法”的“王制”，把礼与维护等级制度的“法”结合起来。礼主要起“化”的作用，法主要起“治”的作用，而礼与法都是为了限制人性之中的恶。在人性理论上，荀子持“性恶论”，他猛烈抨击孟子的“性善论”，主张性伪之分，把人性区分为自然之性和道德之性。自然之性与生俱来，称之为性；道德之性受后天教育熏习而成，称之为伪（伪就是人为的意思）。他否定有天赋之性善，认为人生而有欲望要求，欲望要求无度量分界则发生争夺。因此要靠礼法加以规范限制。所以荀子特别强调人后天的教化和学习，《荀子》的首篇就是《劝学》。在自然观上，荀子否定了天人感应的思想，认为自然界的变化是客观规律作用的结果，“天行有常，不为尧存，不为桀亡”，与人事没有任何关系，这实际上也否定了君权天授的思想。不仅如此，荀子认为就连人类也是自然界的产物，先有了人的形体，即物质实体，然后派生精神作用，“形具而神生”。另一方面，他肯定了人在自然界面前的主导作用和能动作用，尽人事而知天命就能“制天命而用之”，做到人定胜天，这种思想是战国后期人民战天斗地发展生产的反映。

3. 经典赏析

（1）《荀子·劝学》

①君子曰：学不可以已。青，取之于蓝，而青于蓝。

②不登高山，不知天之高也；不临深溪，不知地之厚也；不闻先王之遗言，不知学问之大也。

③锲而舍之，朽木不折；锲而不舍，金石可镂。

（2）《荀子·修身》

见善，修然必以自存也；见不善，愀然必以自省也。

（3）《荀子·不苟》

君子行不贵苟难，说不贵苟察，名不贵苟传，唯其当之为贵。

（4）《荀子·荣辱》

先义而后利者荣，先利而后义者辱；荣者常通，辱者常穷；通者常制人，穷者常制于人；是荣辱之大分也。

（5）《荀子·儒效》

我欲贱而贵，愚而智，贫而富，可乎？

曰：其唯学乎！彼学者，行之，曰士也；敦慕焉，君子也；知之，圣人也。

（6）《荀子·王制》

传曰：君者，舟也；庶人者，水也。水则载舟，水则覆舟。

（7）《荀子·强国》

人之命在天，国之命在礼。人君者，隆礼尊贤而王，重法爱民而霸，好利多诈而危，权谋倾覆幽险而亡。

（8）《荀子·正名》

名无固宜，约之以命，约定俗成谓之宜，异于约则谓之不宜。名无固实，约之以命实，约定俗成，谓之实名。

(9)《荀子·宥坐》

今有其人，不遇其时，虽贤，其能行乎？苟遇其时，何难之有！故君子博学深谋，修身端行，以俟其时。

Chapter V Xun Zi

1. Introduction of the Work

Xun Zi, the significant work of Confucius School, was written by Xun Zi. This book is important for it preserved precious materials that represent the thoughts of both Xun Zi and various schools during the late years of the Warring States Period (475—221 B.C.).

The Han (202 B.C.—220) scholar Liu Xiang (77—6 B.C.) first edited the texts of *Xunzi* and separated them into thirty-two chapters. The book was entitled *New Book of Xun Qing*. In the "Book Catalogue" of *History of Han Dynasty*, the book *Xunzi* was recorded as Sun Qingzi. In the Tang Dynasty (618—907), a scholar named Yang Liang annotated *Xunzi*, and further separated the texts into twenty volumes. The title of the book was changed to *Xunzi*.

The book *Xunzi* covers a wide range of topics: philosophy, ethics, politics, literature, linguistics, education, economy and military issues. No wonder it is regarded as a treasure house of ancient thoughts. Xun Zi advocated the idea that "Human nature is evil; any goodness in humans is acquired by conscious efforts." Therefore, he attached great importance to learning. A number of chapters illustrate the significance of learning and cultivation, such as "Exhortation to Learning" and

"Self Cultivation": "I once spent a whole day in thought, but came to realize that a moment in study was more rewarding"("Exhortation to Learning"). "If a man sees what is good, he should seriously preserve it within himself; if a man sees what is not good, he should apprehensively examine it within himself "("Self Cultivation").

There are a few other chapters that could best represent the thoughts of Xun Zi: "Contra Twelve Philosophers": concise comments on his contemporary philosophers; "Rectify Names": original explication on rectification of names and linguistic theories; "Sing Songs": rhymed folk songs and the predecessor of Tanci (Plucking Verses); "Rhapsody": this chapter together with the rhapsody works of Qu Yuan and Song Yu were regarded as the origin of Han rhapsodies, and classics for rhymed verses in later generation. They are all precious materials for scholars who focus on studying Pre-Qin academic thoughts, linguistics and literature.

Xun Zi was a very important representative of the Confucian School, and his theories were inherited from those of Confucius. However, he also developed new ideas and concepts. While his core theory is relevant to Confucian and Legalist doctrines, its profound depth and rich content represent the essence of thoughts from various schools. Xun Zi's arguments feature perfect logic, reasoning and vivid analogy. His thought-provoking and pertinent words deserve our appreciation.

2. Introduction of the Author

Xun Zi (313 B.C.~238 B.C.), whose given name was Kuang and courtesy name Qing, was a key figure in the Confucius school born in the State of Zhao. When studying in the State of Qi, he became one of the celebrated scholars at the Jixia Academy. In his later years, he dedicated himself in teaching disciples and writing books, one of which is Xun Zi, an epitome of his thoughts. Politically, he inherited the Confucian thought of li (rites) and considers li as not merely a moral standard but a necessity of governing the country. He also called upon the practice of the "royal regulations" which emphasizes li and fa (standards): the purpose of li is to educate while that of fa is to rule. Their combined practice means to restrain evil in human nature. A strong critic to Mencius'claim that human beings are good by nature, Xun Zi held that human beings are born evil but they are perfectible through education. He believed that people are born with a conflicting mixture of desires that if allowed unfettered, would lead to disaster. It is only through the imposition of li and fa that these desires can be well channeled. Therefore, Xun Zi valued moralization and education so much that the very first chapter of Xun Zi was named "Encouraging Learning". On nature, Xun Zi held that the change of the natural world is under the control of objective laws, which have no relation to humanity. He rejected the thought of the existence of a correspondence between humanity and the universe. This, in fact, leads to the denial of an allegation that royal power is divinely bestowed. Furthermore, Xun Zi believed that even human beings are products of nature: born first in physical body, from which spiritual functions derive. On the other hand, he affirmed the dominant and positive power of human beings in nature and put forward the thought of "controlling fatality and making use of it", which can be seen in the thought that reflected the development of production by the people in the late Warring States period.

3. Appreciation

(1) Xun Zi. Exhortation to Learning

① The gentleman says, "Learning should not be left unfinished. Blue dye comes from the indigo plant, but it is bluer."

② You will not know the height of the heaven, if you do not climb a high mountain. You will not know the thickness of the earth, if you do not look down into a deep valley. You will not know the greatness of learning, if you have not heard the words from the ancient kings.

③ If you start carving, but give up halfway, even a rotting piece of wood will stay intact. If you start carving, and never give up, even metal and stone can be engraved.

(2) Xun Zi. Self-Cultivation

If a man sees what is good, he should seriously preserve it within himself; if a man sees what is not good, he should apprehensively examine it within himself.

(3) Xun Zi. Decorum

In his deeds, a gentleman does not value what is indecorous. In his words, a gentleman does not value improper observations. In matters of reputation, a gentleman does not value an unsuitable fame. A gentleman will only esteem the words, deeds and fame which are suitable and decorous.

(4) Xun Zi. Honor and Disgrace

He who prioritizes what is just over what is beneficial is honorable. He who prioritizes what is beneficial over what is just is shameful. The honorable people are always the winners, and the shameful people are invariably the losers. Winners always dominate losers, and losers are always dominated by winners. Such is the great distinction between honor and disgrace.

(5) Xun Zi. Teachings of the Confucianists

Though I was base-born, I wish to be noble. Though I am stupid, I wish to be wise. Though I am poor, I wish to be rich. Would this be possible?

The answer is: it can be achieved only through learning. He who learns knowledge and puts it into practice is called a scholar. He who learns diligently is called a gentleman. He who understands thoroughly what he learns is called a sage.

(6) Xun Zi. Royal Regulation

According to an ancient book, a ruler is like a boat, and his people the water. Water sustains the boat, and water also capsizes the boat.

(7) Xun Zi. Consolidating the State

The fate of men lies with the Heaven, and the fate of a state lies with rituals. If a ruler exalts rituals and respects worthy men, he will become a convincing king; if a ruler values laws and loves people, he will become an overlord; if a ruler is greedy and deceitful, he will be in danger; if a ruler plays politics and risks intrigues, he will be doomed to failure.

(8) Xun Zi. Rectify Names

Names have no intrinsic appropriateness. They are bound to something by agreement in order to name it. When the agreement becomes fixed, the custom is established. It is called appropriate. If a name is different from its agreed name, it is called inappropriate. Names have no intrinsic object. They are bound to some reality by agreement in order to name that object. When the object becomes fixed, the custm is established. It is called the name of that object.

(9) Xun Zi. Warning Vessel

If a man has not met the right time, how could he be able to put his ideas into practice, though he is worthy? If he could meet the right time, what difficulties would he have to achieve great success? Therefore, a gentlemen should broaden his studies, deepen his plans, cultivate his character, and rectify his conduct, so as to wait for his right time.

第六章 《史记》

1. 作品介绍

《史记》，最初称为《太史公书》《太史公记》《太史记》，是西汉史学家司马迁撰写的纪传体史书，是中国历史上第一部纪传体通史，记载了上至上古传说中的黄帝时代，下至汉武帝时期共3000多年的历史，被人们称为“信史”。该著作前后经历了14年才得以完成。共一百三十篇，五十二万六千五百余字，规模巨大，体系完备。被列为“二十四史”之首，与《汉书》《后汉书》《三国志》合称“前四史”，其首创的纪传体编史方法为后来历代“正史”所传承。《史记》还被认为是一部优秀的文学著作，在中国文学史上有重要地位，被鲁迅誉为“史家之绝唱，无韵之《离骚》”，与《资治通鉴》并称为“史学双璧”，有很高的文学价值。

全书包括十二本纪、七十列传、三十世家、十表、八书五部分。“本纪”是全书提纲，以王朝的更替为体，按年月时间记述帝王的言行政绩。其中记载先秦历史的五篇，依次是五帝、夏、殷、周、秦；记载秦汉历史的七篇，依次是秦始皇、楚霸王项羽、汉高祖刘邦、高后吕雉、汉文帝刘恒、汉景帝刘启和汉武帝刘彻。“列传”是帝王诸侯外其他各方面代表人物的生平事迹和少数民族的传记。“世家”记述子孙世袭的王侯封国史迹和特别重要的人物事迹。“表”用表格来简列世系、人物和史事。“书”则记述制度发展，涉及礼乐制度、天文兵律、社会经济、河渠地理等方面内容。本书包罗万象，而又融会贯通，脉络清晰，翔实地记录了上古时期的政治、经济、军事、文化各个方面的发展状况。

《史记》不同于前代史书所采用的以时间为次序的编年体，或以地域为划分的国别体，而是以人物传记为中心来反映历史内容的一种体例。从此以后，从东汉班固的《汉书》到民国初期的《清史稿》，近两千年间历代所修正史，尽管在个别名目上有某些增改，但都无一例外地沿袭了《史记》的本纪和列传两部分，而成为传统。

2. 作者介绍

司马迁（前145~约前86），字子长，生于龙门（今陕西省韩城市，另说今山西省河津市），西汉史学家、散文家。他是司马谈之子，家中历代皆任“太史令”，被后世尊称为“史迁”“太史公”“历史之父”“史圣”。与司马光并称“史界两司马”，与司马相如合称“文章西汉两司马”。

司马迁早年受学于孔安国、董仲舒，漫游各地，了解风俗，采集传闻。初任郎中，奉使西南。二十八岁任太史令，继承父业，著述历史。他以“究天人之际，通古今之变，成一家之言”的史识创作了中国第一部纪传体通史《史记》。《史记》被公认为是中国史书的典范。

3. 经典欣赏

（1）《史记·货殖列传》

天下熙熙，皆为利来；天下攘攘，皆为利往。

(2)《史记·越王勾践世家》

飞鸟尽，良弓藏，狡兔死，走狗烹。敌国破，谋臣亡。

(3)《史记·李将军列传》

桃李不言，下自成蹊。

(4)《史记·汲郑列传》

一死一生，乃知交情；一贫一富，乃知交态；一贵一贱，交情乃见。

(5)《史记·淮阴侯列传》

智者千虑，必有一失；愚者千虑，必有一得。

(6)《史记·屈原贾生列传》

祸兮福所倚，福兮祸所伏。

(7)《史记·张仪列传》

众口铄金，积毁销骨。

(8)《史记·管晏列传》

仓廪实而知礼节，衣食足而知荣辱。

(9)《史记·滑稽列传》

不飞则已，一飞冲天；不鸣则已，一鸣惊人。

(10)《史记·游侠列传》

其言必信，其行必果，已诺必诚。

(11)《史记·司马相如列传》

兴必虑衰，安心思危。

(12)《史记·齐悼惠王世家》

当断不断，反受其乱。

(13)《史记·陈涉世家》

燕雀安知鸿鹄之志哉！

（14）《史记·项羽本纪》

今者项庄拔剑舞，其意常在沛公也。

（15）《史记·报任安书》

人固有一死，或重于泰山，或轻于鸿毛。

（16）《史记·陈涉世家》

王侯将相，宁有种乎。

（17）《史记·留侯世家》

忠言逆耳利于行，良药苦口利于病。

Chapter VI Records of the Grand Historian

1. Introduction of the Work

Records of the Grand Historian, as one of the Twenty-Four Histories, was originally called *The Book of Taishi Gong*, *Records of Taishi Gong or Records of Taishi*. It was written by Sima Qian, a historian of the Western Han Dynasty, and was the first general history of China by chronology. It records the history of more than 3,000 years, including the supreme ancient legend of the Yellow Emperor era, down to the early four years of Emperor Wu of the Han Dynasty, known as the "True History". The work took fourteen years to complete with a complete large-scale system involving a total of one hundred and thirty articles, and more than 526,500 words. It is listed as the first of the "Twenty-Four Histories", and collectively known as "The First Four Historiographies", whose first approach to take *Records of the Grand Historian* chronologically was passed on by subsequent generations to record "official history". *Records of the Grand Historian* is also considered to be an excellent literary work, which has an important position in Chinese literature. It was praised by Lu Xun as "the peak of poetic perfection, the top of picturesque rhythm", and was called "Double Historical Jades" with *Comprehensive Mirror for Aid in Government*, both of which have great literary value.

The book consists of records of twelve "Benji", seventy "Liezhuan", thirty "Shijia", ten "Biao" and eight "Shu". "Benji" is the outline of the book, based on the replacement of the dynasty to record the words and deeds of the emperors according to the months and years. The five chapters record the history of the pre-Qin period including the Five emperors, the Xia, Yin, Zhou and Qin dynasties, and the seven chapters record the history of the Qin and Han Dynasties including the First Emperor of Qin, King Xiang Yu of Chu, Emperor Gaozu of the Han Dynasty, Empress Lü Zhi of the Han Dynasty, Emperor Wen of Han—Liu Heng, Emperor Jing of Han—Liu Qi and Emperor Liu Che of the Han Dynasty. "Liezhuan" are the biographies of the lives and deeds of emperors, princes and other representatives and minor nationalities. "Shijia" are the historical records of hereditary princes and feudal states and the deeds of special important persons. "Biao" uses tables to show lineage, characters, and historical events. "Shu" records the development of different systems, involving the ritual and musical system, astronomical and military laws, socio-economic, geography of rivers and canals and so on. The book is an all-encompassing, digestible, clear and detailed record of the development of ancient politics, economy, military, culture and other aspects.

Records of the Grand Historian differs from the chronological style which takes time as the order, or the national style which takes the region as the division, but it is a style which takes biography as its center to reflect historical content. Since then, although some additions and changes have been made to individual titles, such as Ban Gu's *The History of the Han Dynasty* in the eastern Han Dynasty or The Manuscript of *the History of Qing Dynasty* in the early period of the Republic of China, including the history of successive dynasties for nearly 2,000 years, without exception, all historical books traditionally follow the two parts of the book of *Records of the Grand Historian* –"Benji" and "Liezhuan".

2. Introduction of the Author

Sima Qian, whose courtesy name was Zichang, was born in Longmen (now Hancheng city, Shanxi Province, also known as Hejin city) and was a Western Han Dynasty historian and essayist. He is the son of Sima Tan, whose family had been "the imperial astronomers" for generations. Sima Qian is known as "Shi Qian", "Tai Shi Gong", "The Father of the History" and "History Saint". He is also known with Sima Guang as "Two Sima in the Field of History" and with Sima Xiangru as "Two Sima in the Articles of Western Han".

In his early years, Sima Qian was taught by Kong Anguo and Dong Zhongshu, traveling widely to learn customs and gather stories. At first, he was sent to the southwest as an official. At the age of twenty-eight, he followed in his father's footsteps as the imperial astronomer and recorded histories. He created the first historical record and biography book in China—*Records of the Grand Historian*—by using his historical knowledge "to explore the relationship between the Way of Heaven and the Way of Man, have a thorough understanding of the course of historical development and the changes involved therein, expound my own opinions of the events of the past and present my own system of analysis", which is regarded as the model for Chinese historical books.

3. Appreciation

（1）Records of the Grand Historian. Biographies of Merchants

All the hustle, all for profit, and the world, and all for profit into.

(2)Records of the Grand Historian·Goujian Family of the King of Yue

To put away the bow once the birds are gone,

To boil the hound once the cunning hare is killed.

(3)Records of the Grand Historian. Biography of General Li

The peach and the plum do not speak, yet a path is born beneath them.

(4)Records of the Grand Historian. Biographies of Ji Zheng

To live or to die is to know friends; To be poor or to be rich is to know the state of friendship; to be high or to be low can know where the friends are.

(5) Records of the Grand Historian. Biographies of Marquis Huai Yin

Even the wise is not always free from error. Even the fool may be right for once.

(6)Records of the Grand Historian. Biographies of Qu Yuan and Jia Sheng

Good fortune follows upon disaster；Disaster lurks within good fortune.

(7)Records of the Grand Historian. Biographies of Zhang Yi

Public clamor can melt metals; And accumulated defamation wears the bones.

(8)Records of the Grand Historian. Biographies of Guan Yan

If people have enough food supply stored in granaries, they will pay attention to etiquettes. If people are not short of food and clothes, they will lay stress on the sense of honor and shame.

(9)Records of the Grand Historian. Biographies of Humorous Affairs

Does not fly then already, as soon as flies flush the day; Does not call then, has surprised people.

(10) Records of the Grand Historian. Biographies of Wanderers

Promises must be kept; Action must be resultful; and said it had better be able to.

(11)Records of the Grand Historian. Biographies of Sima Xiangru

When the country is rising, one must think of the possibility of its falling; When the country is stable and peaceful, one must be prepared for possible turbulences.

(12) Records of the Grand Historian. Family of Liu Fei

Be indecisive when decision is needed, one should be disturbed by it.

(13)Records of the Grand Historian. Family of Chen She

How can a sparrow know the will of a swan?

(14)Records of the Grand Historian. Biographic Sketches of Xiang Yu

Xiang Zhuang performed the sword dance as a cover for his attempt on Liu Bang's life—act with a hidden motive.

(15)Records of the Grand Historian. A Reply to Ren An

A man will die someday, or more magnitude than Mountain Tai, or tinier than a feather!

(16)Records of the Grand Historian. Family of Chen She

Do those gentry have blue blood certainly?

(17)Records of the Grand Historian. Family of the Marquis of Liu

It takes blunt advice to put us on the right track; it takes bitter medicine to cure a disease properly.

第七章 《水浒传》

1. 作品介绍

《水浒传》是元末明初施耐庵（现存刊本署名大多有施耐庵、罗贯中两人中的一人，或两人皆有）编著的章回体长篇小说。《水浒传》又名《忠义水浒传》，简称《水浒》，作于元末明初，是中国四大名著之一。问世后，在社会上产生了巨大的影响，成了后世中国小说创作的典范。全书描写北宋末年以宋江为首的一百〇八好汉在梁山泊起义，以及聚义之后接受招安、四处征战的故事。

《水浒传》是一部长篇英雄传奇，是中国古代长篇小说的代表作之一，是以宋江起义故事为线索创作出来的。宋江起义发生在北宋徽宗时期，《宋史》的《徽宗本纪》《侯蒙传》《张叔夜传》等都有记载。从南宋起，宋江起义的故事就在民间流传，《醉翁谈录》记载了一些独立的有关水浒英雄的传说，《大宋宣和遗事》把许多水浒故事连缀起来，和长篇小说已经很接近。元代出现了不少水浒戏，一批梁山英雄作为舞台形象出现。

《水浒传》是宋江起义故事在民间长期流传基础上产生出来的，吸收了民间文学的营养。《水浒传》是我国人民最喜爱的古典长篇白话小说之一。它产生于明代，是在宋元以来有关水浒的故事、话本、戏曲的基础上，由作者加工、整理、创作而成的。

全书以宋江领导的农民起义为主要题材，艺术地再现了中国古代人民反抗压迫、英勇斗争的悲壮画卷。作品充分暴露了封建统治阶级的腐朽和残暴，揭露了当时尖锐对立的社会矛盾和"官逼民反"的残酷现实，成功地塑造了鲁智深、李逵、武松、林冲、阮小七等一批英雄人物形象。小说故事情节曲折，语言生动，人物性格鲜明，具有高度的艺术成就。但作品歌颂、美化宋江，鼓吹"忠义"和"替天行道"，表现出严重的思想局限。

2. 作者介绍

施耐庵，元末明初文学家，本名彦端，汉族，今江苏兴化人。博古通今，才气横溢，辞章、诗歌、天文、地理、医卜、星象等无不精通。施耐庵自幼聪明好学，才气过人，事亲至孝，为人仗义。19 岁时中秀才，28 岁时中举人，36 岁与刘伯温同榜中进士。至顺二年（1331 年）登进士不久任浙江钱塘县尹。后弃官归里，闭门著述，与门下弟子罗贯中一起研究《三国演义》《三遂平妖传》的创作，搜集整理关于梁山泊宋江等英雄人物的故事，最终写成"四大名著"之一的《水浒传》。

有关施耐庵生平事迹材料极少，搜集到的一些记载亦颇多矛盾。说他原籍苏州，后迁淮安，为至顺辛未进士，曾官钱塘二载，以不合当道权贵而弃官归里，闭门著述。为施之常后裔，自幼才气过人，为人仗义。

20 世纪 20 年代以来，在今江苏省兴化、大丰、盐都等地陆续发现了一些有关施耐庵的材料，有《施氏族谱》《施氏长门谱》等，另有《兴化县续志》卷十三补遗载有《施耐庵传》1 篇，卷十四补遗载有明初王道生撰《施耐庵墓志》1 篇。

3. 经典赏析

（1）第 1 回　张天师祈禳瘟疫　洪太尉误走妖魔

话说大宋仁宗天子在位，嘉祐三年三月三日五更三点，天子驾坐紫宸殿，受百官朝贺。……

当有殿头官喝道："有事出班早奏，无事卷帘退朝。"只见班部丛中，宰相赵哲、参政文彦博出班奏曰："目今京师瘟疫盛行，伤损军民甚多。伏望陛下释罪宽恩，省刑薄税，祈禳天灾，救济万民。"天子听奏，急敕翰林院随即草诏：一面降赦天下罪囚，应有民间税赋悉皆赦免；一面命在京宫观寺院，修设好事禳灾。不料其年瘟疫转盛。仁宗天子闻知，龙体不安。复会百官，众皆计议。向那班部中，有一大臣越班启奏。天子看时，乃是参知政事范仲淹。拜罢起居，奏曰："目今天灾盛行，军民涂炭，日夕不能聊生，人遭缧绁之厄。以臣愚意，要禳此灾，可宣嗣汉天师星夜临朝，就京师禁院修设三千六百分罗天大醮，奏闻上帝，可以禳保民间瘟疫。"仁宗天子准奏。急令翰林学士草诏一道，天子御笔亲书，并降御香一炷，钦差内外提点殿前太尉洪信为天使，前往江西信州龙虎山，宣请嗣汉天师张真人星夜来朝，祈禳瘟疫。就金殿上焚起御香，亲将丹诏付与洪太尉，即便登程前去。

洪信领了圣敕，辞别天子，不敢久停。从人背了诏书，金盒子盛了御香，带了数十人，上了铺马，一行部队，离了东京，取路径投信州贵溪县来。

（2）第 3 回　史大郎夜走华阴县　鲁提辖拳打镇关西

且说郑屠开着两间门面，两副肉案，悬挂着三五片猪肉。郑屠正在门前柜身内坐定，看那十来个刀手卖肉。鲁达走到面前，叫声："郑屠！"郑屠看时，见是鲁提辖，慌忙出柜身来唱喏道："提辖恕罪。"便叫副手掇条凳子来，"提辖请坐。"鲁达坐下道："奉着经略相公钧旨，要十斤精肉，切做臊子，不要见半点肥的在上头。"郑屠道："使得，你们快选好的切十斤去。"鲁提辖道："不要那等腌臜厮们动手，你自与我切。"郑屠道："说得是，小人自切便了。"自去肉案上拣了十斤精肉，细细切做臊子。那店小二把手帕包了头，正来郑屠家报说金老之事，却见鲁提辖坐在肉案门边，不敢拢来，只得远远地立住在房檐下望。这郑屠整整的自切了半个时辰，用荷叶包了，道："提辖，教人送去？"鲁达道："送甚么！且住，再要十斤，都是肥的，不要见些精的在上面，也要切做臊子。"郑屠道："却才精的，怕府里要裹馄饨，肥的臊子何用？"鲁达睁着眼道："相公钧旨分付洒家，谁敢问他？"郑屠道："是。合用的东西，小人切便了。"又选了十斤实膘的肥肉，也细细的切做臊子，把荷叶来包了。整弄了一早晨，却得饭罢时候。那店小二那里敢过来，连那正要买肉的主顾也不敢拢来。郑屠道："着人与提辖拿了，送将府里去。"鲁达道："再要十斤寸金软骨，也要细细地剁做臊子，不要见些肉在上面。"郑屠笑道："却不是特地来消遣我！"鲁达听罢，跳起身来，拿着那两包臊子在手里，睁眼看着郑屠说道："洒家特地要消遣你！"把两包臊子劈面打将去，却似下了一阵的肉雨。郑屠大怒，两条忿气从脚底下直冲到顶门，心头那一把无明业火，焰腾腾的按纳不住，从肉案上抢了一把剔骨尖刀，托地跳将下来。鲁提辖早拔步在当街上。众邻舍并十来个火家，那个敢向前来劝？两边过路的人都立住了脚，和那店小二也惊的呆了。

郑屠右手拿刀，左手便来要揪鲁达，被这鲁提辖就势按住左手，赶将入去，望小腹上只一脚，腾地踢倒在当街上。鲁达再入一步，踏住胸脯，提着那醋钵儿大小拳头，看着这郑屠道："洒家始投老种经略相公，做到关西五路廉访使，也不枉了叫做镇关西。你是个卖肉的操刀屠户，狗一般的人，也叫做镇关西！你如何强骗了金翠莲！"扑的只一拳，正打在鼻子上，打得鲜血迸流，鼻子歪在半边，却便似开了个油酱铺，咸的、酸的、辣的，一发都滚出来。郑屠挣不起来，那把尖刀也丢在一边，口里只叫："打得好！"鲁达骂道："直娘贼，还敢应口！"提起拳头来，就眼眶际眉梢只一拳，打得眼棱缝裂，乌珠迸出，也似开了个彩帛铺的，红的、黑的、绛的，都滚将出来。两边看的人，惧怕鲁提辖，谁敢向前来劝？郑屠当不过，讨饶。鲁达喝道："咄！你是个破落户，若是和俺硬到底，洒家倒饶了你。你如何对俺讨饶，洒家偏不饶你！"又只一拳，太阳上正着，却似做了一个全堂水陆的道场，磬儿、钹儿、铙儿一齐响。鲁达看时，只见郑屠挺在地下，口里只有出的气，没了入的气，动弹不得。鲁提辖假意道："你这厮诈死，洒家再打。"只见面皮渐渐的变了。鲁达寻思道："俺只指望痛打这厮一顿，不想三拳真个打死了他。洒家须吃官司，又没人送饭，不如及早撒开。"拔步便走，回头指着郑屠尸道："你诈死，洒家和你慢慢理会。"一头骂，一头大踏步去了。街坊邻舍并郑屠的火家，谁敢向前来拦他？鲁提辖回到下处，急急卷了些衣服盘缠、细软银两，但是旧衣粗重，都弃了。提了一条齐眉短棒，奔出南门，一道烟走了。

（3）第 9 回 柴进门招天下客 林冲棒打洪教头

当下又吃过了五七杯酒，却早月上来了，照见厅堂里面如同白日。柴进起身道："二位教头较量一棒。"林冲自肚里寻思道："这洪教头必是柴大官人师父，不争我一棒打翻了他，须不好看。”柴进见林冲踌躇，便道：“此位洪教头也到此不多时，此间又无对手；林武师休得要推辞，小可也正要看二位教头的本事。”柴进说这话，原来只怕林冲碍柴进的面皮，不肯使出本事来。林冲见柴进说开就里，方才放心。只见洪教头先起身道：“来，来，来！和你使一棒看。”一齐都哄出堂后空地上。庄客拿一束杆棒来，放在地下。洪教头先脱了衣裳，拽扎起裙子，掣条棒使个旗鼓，喝道：“来，来，来！”柴进道：“林武师，请较量一棒。”林冲道：“大官人休要笑话。”就地也拿了一条棒起来道：“师父请教。”洪教头看了，恨不得一口水吞了他。林冲拿着棒，使出山东大擂，打将入来。洪教头把棒就地下鞭了一棒，来抢林冲。两个教头就明月地下交手，真个好看。……

两个教头在明月地上交手，使了四五合棒，只见林冲托地跳出圈子外来，叫一声：“少歇！”柴进道：“教头如何不使本事？”林冲道：“小人输了。”柴进道：“未见二位较量，怎便是输了？”林冲道：“小人只多这具枷，因此，权当输了。”柴进道：“是小可一时失了计较。”大笑着道：“这个容易。”便叫庄客取十两银来，当时将至。柴进对押解两个公人道：“小可大胆，相烦二位下顾，权把林教头枷开了。明日牢城营内但有事务，都在小可身上。白银十两相送。”董超、薛霸见了柴进人物轩昂，不敢违他，落得做人情，又得了十两银子，亦不怕他走了。薛霸随即把林冲护身枷开了。柴进大喜道：“今番两位教师再试一棒。”

洪教头见他却才棒法怯了，肚里平欺他做，提起棒却待要使。柴进叫道：“且住！”叫庄客取出一锭银来，重二十五两。无一时，至面前。柴进乃言：“二位教头比试，非比其他，这锭银子权为利物；若是赢的，便将此银子去。”柴进心中只要林冲把出本事来，故意将银子丢在地下。洪教头深怪林冲来，又要争这个大银子，又怕输了锐气，把棒来尽心使个旗鼓，吐个门户，唤做把火烧天势。林冲想道："柴大官人心里只要我赢他。"也横着棒，使个门户，吐个势，唤做拨草寻蛇势。洪教头喝一声："来，来，来！"便使棒盖将入来。林冲望后一退，洪教头赶入一步，提起棒又复一棒下来。林冲看他步已乱了，被林冲把棒从地下一跳，洪教头措手不及，就那一跳里和身一转，那棒直扫着洪教头臁儿骨上，撇了棒，扑地倒了。柴进大喜，叫快将酒来把盏。众人一齐大笑。洪教头那里挣扎起来？众庄客一头笑着扶了。洪教头羞颜满面，自投庄外去了。

（4）第12回　梁山泊林冲落草　汴京城杨志卖刀

却说牛二抢到杨志面前，就手里把那口宝刀扯将出来，问道："汉子，你这刀要卖几钱？"杨志道："祖上留下宝刀，要卖三千贯。"牛二喝道："甚么鸟刀，要卖许多钱！我三十文买一把，也切得肉，切得豆腐。你的鸟刀有甚好处，叫做宝刀！"杨志道："洒家的须不是店上卖的白铁刀，这是宝刀。"牛二道："怎的唤做宝刀？"杨志道："第一件，砍铜剁铁，刀口不卷；第二件，吹毛得过；第三件，杀人刀上没血。"牛二道："你敢剁铜钱么？"杨志道："你便将来剁与你看。"牛二便去州桥下香椒铺里讨了二十文当三钱，一垛儿将来，放在州桥栏杆上，叫杨志道："汉子，你若剁得开时，我还你三千贯。"那时看的人虽然不敢近前，向远远地围住了望。杨志道："这个直得甚么？"把衣袖卷起，拿刀在手，看的较准，只一刀，把铜钱剁做两半。众人都喝采。牛二道："喝甚么鸟采！你且说第二件是甚么？"杨志道："吹毛得过。若把几根头发望刀口上只一吹，齐齐都断。"牛二道："我不信。"自把头上拔下一把头发，递与杨志："你且吹我看。”杨志左手接过头发，照着刀口上尽气力一吹，那头发都做两段，纷纷飘下地来。众人喝采，看的人越多了。牛二又问：“第三件是甚么？”杨志道：“杀人刀上没血。”牛二道：“怎么杀人刀上没血？”杨志道：“把人一刀砍了，并无血痕，只是个快。”牛二道：“我不信！你把刀来剁一个人我看。”杨志道：“禁城之中，如何敢杀人？你不信时，取一只狗来，杀与你看。”牛二道：“你说杀人，不曾说杀狗！”杨志道：“你不买便罢，只管缠人做甚么！”牛二道：“你将来我看。”杨志道：“你只顾没了当！洒家又不是你撩拨的。”牛二道：“你敢杀我？”杨志道：“和你往日无冤，昔日无仇，一物不成，两物现在。没来由杀你做甚么？”牛二紧揪住杨志说道：“我偏要买你这口刀。”杨志道：“你要买，将钱来。”牛二道：“我没钱。”杨志道：“你没钱，揪住洒家怎地？”牛二道：“我要你这口刀。”杨志道：“我不与你。”牛二道：“你好男子，剁我一刀。”杨志大怒，把牛二推了一交。牛二爬将起来，钻入杨志怀里。杨志叫道：“街坊邻舍，都是证见。杨志无盘缠，自卖这口刀。这个泼皮强夺洒家的刀，又把俺打。”街坊人都怕这牛二，谁敢向前来劝？牛二喝道：“你说我打你，便打杀直甚么？”口里说，一面挥起右手，一拳打来。杨志霍地躲过，拿着刀抢入来，一时性起，望牛二嗓根上搠个着，扑地倒了。杨志赶入去，把牛二胸脯上又连搠了两刀，血流满地，死在地上。

杨志叫道：“洒家杀死这个泼皮，怎肯连累你们！泼皮既已死了，你们都来同洒家去官府里出首。”坊隅众人慌忙拢来，随同杨志，径投开封府出首。正值府尹坐衙。杨志拿着刀，和地方邻舍众人都上厅来，一齐跪下，把刀放在面前。杨志告道：“小人原是殿司制使，为因失陷花石纲，削去本身职役，无有盘缠，将这口刀在街货卖。不期被个泼皮破落户牛二强夺小人的刀，又用拳打小人，因此一时性起，将那人杀死，众邻舍都是证见。”众人亦替杨志告说，分诉了一回。府尹道：“既是自行前来出首，免了这厮入门的款打。”且叫取一面长枷枷了。差两员相官带了仵作行人，监押杨志并众邻舍一干人犯，都来天汉州桥边登场检验了，叠成文案。众邻舍都出了供状，保放随衙听候，当庭发落，将杨志于死囚牢里监守。

（5）第16回　杨志押送金银担　吴用智取生辰纲

只见那七个贩枣子的客人，立在松树傍边，指着这一十五人说道：“倒也，倒也！”只见这十五个人，头重脚轻，一个个面面厮觑，都软倒了。那七个客人从松树林里推出这七辆江州车儿，把车子上枣子都丢在地上，将这十一担金珠宝贝都装在车子内，遮盖好了，叫声：“聒噪！”一直望黄泥冈下推了去。正是：诛求膏血庆生辰，不顾民生与死邻。始信从来招劫盗，亏心必定有缘因。杨志口里只是叫苦，软了身体，挣扎不起。十五人眼睁睁地看着那七个人都把这金宝装了去，只是起不来、挣不动、说不的。

我且问你，这七人端的是谁？不是别人，原来正是晁盖、吴用、公孙胜、刘唐、三阮这七个。却才那个挑酒的汉子，便是白日鼠白胜。却怎地用药？原来挑上冈子时，两桶都是好酒。七个人先吃了一桶，刘唐揭起桶盖，又兜了半瓢吃，故意要他们看着，只是叫人死心塌地。次后，吴用去松林里取出药来，抖在瓢里，只做走来饶他酒吃，把瓢去兜时，药已搅在酒里，假意兜半瓢吃，那白胜劈手夺来，倾在桶里，这个便是计策。那计较都是吴用主张，这个唤做“智取生辰纲。”

原来杨志吃的酒少，便醒得快，爬将起来，兀自捉脚不住。

看那十四个人时，口角流涎，都动不得。正应俗语道："饶你奸似鬼，吃了洗脚水。"杨志愤闷道："不争你把了生辰纲去，教俺如何回去见得梁中书？这纸领状须缴不得，就扯破了。如今闪得俺有家难奔，有国难投，待走那里去？不如就这冈子上寻个死处。"撩衣破步，望着黄泥冈下便跳。

（6）第 23 回　横海郡柴进留宾　景阳冈武松打虎

那一阵风过处，只听得乱树背后扑地一声响，跳出一只吊睛白额大虫来。武松见了，叫声："阿呀！"从青石上翻将下来，便拿那条哨棒在手里，闪在青石边。那个大虫又饥又渴，把两只爪在地下略按一按，和身望上一扑，从半空里撺将下来。武松被那一惊，酒都做冷汗出了。说时迟，那时快，武松见大虫扑来，只一闪，闪在大虫背后。那大虫背后看人最难，便把前爪搭在地下，把腰胯一掀，掀将起来。武松只一躲，躲在一边。大虫见掀他不着，吼一声，却似半天里起个霹雳，振得那山冈也动。把这铁棒也似虎尾倒竖起来，只一剪。武松却又闪在一边。原来那大虫拿人，只是一扑，一掀，一剪，三般提不着时，气性先自没了一半。那大虫又剪不着，再吼了一声，一兜兜将回来。

武松见那大虫复翻身回来，双手抡起哨棒，尽平生气力，只一棒，从半空劈将下来。只听得一声响，簌簌地将那树连枝带叶劈脸打将下来。定睛看时，一棒劈不着大虫。原来打急了，正打在枯树上，把那条哨棒折做两截，只拿得一半在手里。那大虫咆哮，性发起来，翻身又只一扑，扑将来。武松又只一跳，却退了十步远。那大虫恰好把两只前爪搭在武松面前。武松将半截棒丢在一边，两只手就势把大虫顶花皮肐膊地揪住，一按按将下来。那只大虫急要挣扎，早没了气力。被武松尽气力纳定，那里肯放半点儿松宽？武松把只脚望大虫面门上、眼睛里，只顾乱踢。那大虫咆哮起来，把身底下扒起两堆黄泥，做了一个土坑。武松把那大虫嘴直按下黄泥坑里去。那大虫吃武松奈何得没了些气力。武松把左手紧紧地揪住顶花皮，偷出右手来，提起铁锤般大小拳头，尽平生之力，只顾打。打到五七十拳，那大虫眼里、口里、鼻子里、耳朵里，都迸出鲜血来。……

当下景阳冈上那只猛虎，被武松没顿饭之间，一顿拳脚，打得那大虫动弹不得，使得口里兀自气喘。武松放了手，来松树边寻那打折的棒橛，拿在手里，只怕大虫不死，把棒橛又打了一回。那大虫气都没了。武松再寻思道："我就地拖得这死大虫下冈子去。"就血泊里双手来提时，那里提得动？原来使尽了气力，手脚都苏软了，动弹不得。

武松再来青石坐了半歇，寻思道："天色看看黑了，倘或又跳出一只大虫来时，我却怎地斗得他过？且挣扎下冈子去，明早却来理会。"就石头边寻了毡笠儿，转过乱树林边，一步步捱下冈子来。

（7）第 25 回　王婆计啜西门庆　淫妇药鸩武大郎

武大一病五日，不能够起。更兼要汤不见，要水不见，每日叫那妇人不应。又见他浓妆艳抹了出去，归来时便面颜红色。武大几遍气得发昏，又没人来睬着。武大叫老婆来分付道："你做的勾当，我亲手来捉着你奸，你倒挑拨奸夫，踢了我心，至今求生不生，求死不死，你们却自去快活！我死自不妨，和你们争不得了！我的兄弟武二，你须得知他性格。倘或早晚归来，他肯干休？你若肯可怜我，早早伏侍我好了，他归来时，我都不提。你若不看觑我时，待他归来，却和你们说话！"

这妇人听了这话，也不回言，却踅过来一五一十都对王婆和西门庆说了。那西门庆听了这话，却似提在冰窖子里，说道："苦也！我须知景阳冈上打虎的武都头，他是清河县第一个好汉！我如今却和你眷恋日久，情孚意合，却不恁地理会。如今这等说时，正是怎地好？却是苦也！"王婆冷笑道："我倒不曾见，你是个把舵的，我是乘船的，我倒不慌，你倒慌了手脚。"西门庆道："我枉自做了男子汉，到这般去处，却摆布不开。你有甚么主见？遮藏我们则个。"王婆道："你们却要长做夫妻，短做夫妻？"西门庆道："干娘，你且说如何是长做夫妻，短做夫妻？"王婆道："若是短做夫妻，你们只就今日便分散，等武大将息好了起来，与他陪了话。武二归来，都没言语。待他再差使出去，却再来相约。这是短做夫妻。你们若要长做夫妻，每日同一处，不担惊受怕，我却有一条妙计，只是难教你。"

西门庆道："干娘周全了我们则个，只要长做夫妻。"王婆道："这条计用着件东西，别人家里都没，天生天化，大官人家里却有。"西门庆道："便是要我的眼睛，也剜来与你。却是甚么东西？"王婆道："如今这捣子病得重，趁他狼狈里，便好下手。大官人家里取些砒霜来，却教大娘子自去赎一帖心疼的药来，把这砒霜下在里面，把这矮子结果了。一把火烧得干干净净的，没了踪迹，便是武二回来，待敢怎地？自古道：'嫂叔不通问；初嫁从亲，再嫁由身。'阿叔如何管得？暗地里来往半年一载，等待夫孝满日，大官人娶了家去，这个不是长远夫妻，谐老同欢？此计如何？"西门庆道："干娘此计甚妙。自古道：'欲求生快活，须下死工夫。'罢，罢，罢！一不做，二不休！"王婆道："可知好哩！这是斩草除根，萌芽不发；若是斩草不除根，春来萌芽再发。官人便去取些砒霜来，我自教娘子下手。事了时，却要重重谢我。”西门庆道：“这个自然，不消你说。”有诗为证：

恋色迷花不肯休，机谋只望永绸缪。谁知武二刀头毒，更比砒霜狠一筹。

且说西门庆去不多时，包了一包砒霜来，把与王婆收了。这婆子却看着那妇人道：“大娘子，我教你下药的法度。如今武大不对你说道，教你看活他。你便把些小意儿贴恋他。他若问你讨药吃时，便把这砒霜调在心疼药里。待他一觉身动，你便把药灌将下去，却便走了起身。他若毒药转时，必然肠胃迸裂，大叫一声，你却把被只一盖，都不要人听得。预先烧下一锅汤，煮着一条抹布。他若毒药发时，必然七窍内流血，口唇上有牙齿咬的痕迹。他若放了命，便揭起被来，却将煮的抹布一揩，都没了血迹，便入在棺材里，扛出去烧了，有甚么鸟事？”那妇人道：“好却是好，只是奴手软了，临时安排不得尸首。”王婆道：“这个容易。你只敲壁子，我自过来相帮你。”西门庆道：“你们用心整理，明日五更来讨回报。”西门庆说罢，自去了。王婆把这砒霜用手捻为细末，把与那妇人将去藏了。

那妇人却踅将归来，到楼上看武大时，一丝没两气，看看待死，那妇人坐在床边假哭。武大道：“你做甚么来哭？”那妇人拭着眼泪说道：“我的一时间不是了，吃那厮局骗了。谁想却踢了你这脚！我问得一处好药，我要去赎来医你，又怕你疑忌了，不敢去取。”武大道：“你救得我活，无事了，一笔都勾，并不记怀，武二家来，亦不提起。快去赎药来救我则个！”那妇人拿了些铜钱，径来王婆家里坐地，却叫王婆去赎了药来。把到楼上，教武大看了，说道：“这帖心疼药，太医叫你半夜里吃。吃了倒头把一两床被发些汗，明日便起得来。”武大道：“却是好也。生受大嫂，今夜醒睡些个，半夜里调来我吃。”那妇人道：“你自放心睡，我自伏侍你。”

看看天色黑了，那妇人在房里点上碗灯，下面先烧了一大锅汤，拿了一片抹布，煮在汤里。听那更鼓时，却好正打三更。那妇人先把毒药倾在盏子里，却舀一碗白汤，把到楼上，叫声：“大哥，药在那里？”武大道：“在我席子底下枕头边，你快调来与我吃。”那妇人揭起席子，将那药抖在盏子里；把那药贴安了，将白汤冲在盏内；把头上银牌儿只一搅，调得匀了，左手扶起武大，右手把药便灌。武大呷了一口，说道：“大嫂，这药好难吃！”那妇人道：“只要他医治得病，管甚么难吃！”武大再呷第二口时，被这婆娘就势只一灌，一盏药都灌下喉咙去了。那妇人便放倒武大，慌忙跳下床来。武大“哎”了一声，说道：“大嫂，吃下这药去，肚里倒疼起来。苦呀！苦呀！倒当不得了！”这妇人便去脚后扯过两床被来，没头没脸只顾盖。武大叫道：“我也气闷。”那妇人道：“太医分付，教我与你发些汗，便好得快。”武大再要说时，这妇人怕他挣扎，便跳上床来，骑在武大身上，把手紧紧地按住被角，那里肯放些松宽。

（8）第40回　梁山泊好汉劫法场　白龙庙英雄小聚义

没多时，法场中间人分开处，一个报，报道一声：“午时三刻！”监斩官便道：“斩讫报来。”两势下刀棒刽子便去开枷，行刑之人，执定法刀在手。说时迟，一个个要见分明；那时快，闹攘攘一齐发作。只见那伙客人在车子上听得“斩”字，数内一个客人便向怀中取出一面小锣儿，立在车子上当当地敲得两三声，四下里一齐动手。……

又见十字路口茶坊楼上，一个虎形黑大汉脱得赤条条的，两只手握两把板斧，大吼一声，却似半天起个霹雳，从半空中跳将下来。手起斧落，早砍翻了两个行刑的刽子，便望监斩官马前砍将来。众士兵急待把枪去搠时，那里拦当得住？众人且簇拥蔡九知府逃命去了。

只见东边那伙弄蛇的丐者，身边都掣出尖刀，看着士兵便杀；西边那伙使枪棒的，大发喊声，只顾乱杀将来，一派杀倒士兵狱卒；南边那伙挑担的脚夫，抡起扁担，横七竖八，都打翻了士兵和那看的人；北边那伙客人，都跳下车来，推过车子，拦住了人。两个客商钻将入来，一个背了宋江，一个背了戴宗。其余的人，也有取出弓箭来射的，也有取出石子来打的，也有取出标枪来标的。原来扮客商的这伙，便是晁盖、花荣、黄信、吕方、郭盛；那伙扮使枪棒的，便是燕顺、刘唐、杜迁、宋万；扮挑担的，便是朱贵、王矮虎、郑天寿、石勇；那伙扮丐者的，便是阮小二、阮小五、阮小七、白胜。这一行梁山泊共是十七个头领到来，带领小喽罗一百余人，四下里杀将起来。只见那人丛里那个黑大汉，抡两把板斧，一味地砍将来，晁盖等却不认得，只见他第一个出力，杀人最多。晁盖猛省起来：戴宗曾说一个黑旋风李逵，和宋三郎最好，是个莽撞之人。晁盖便叫道："前面那好汉，莫不是黑旋风？"那汉那里肯应，火杂杂地抡着大斧，只顾砍人。晁盖便叫背宋江、戴宗的两个小喽罗，只顾跟着那黑大汉走。当下去十字街口，不问军官百姓，杀得尸横遍野，血流成渠，推倒倾翻的，不计其数。众头领撇了车轮担仗，一行人尽跟了黑大汉，直杀出城来。背后花荣、黄信、吕方、郭盛，四张弓箭，飞蝗般望后射来。那江州军民百姓，谁敢近前。这黑大汉直杀到江边来，身上血溅满身，兀自在江边杀人。百姓撞着的，都被他翻筋斗砍下江里去。晁盖便挺朴刀叫道："不干百姓事，休只管伤人！"那汉那里来听叫唤，一斧一个，排头儿砍将去。

约莫离城沿江上也走了五七里路，前面望见尽是淘淘一派大江，却无了旱路。晁盖看见，只叫得苦，那黑大汉方才叫道："不要慌，且把哥哥背来庙里。"众人都来看时，靠江一所大庙，两扇门紧紧闭着。黑大汉两斧砍开，便抢入来。晁盖众人看时，两边都是老桧苍松，林木遮映，前面牌额上四个金书大字，写道："白龙神庙。"小喽罗把宋江、戴宗背到庙里歇下，宋江方才敢开眼，见了晁盖等众人，哭道："哥哥，莫不是梦中相会？"晁盖便劝道："恩兄不肯在山，致有今日之苦。这个出力杀人的黑大汉是谁？"宋江道："这个便是叫做黑旋风李逵。他几番就要大牢里放了我，却是我怕走不脱，不肯依他。"晁盖道："却是难得这个人！出力最多，又不怕刀斧箭矢。"花荣便叫："且将衣服与俺二位兄长穿了。"

正相聚间，只见李逵提着双斧，从廊下走出来。宋江便叫住道："兄弟那里去？"李逵应道："寻那庙祝，一发杀了，叵耐那厮不来接我们，倒把鸟庙门闭上了。我指望拿他来祭门，却寻那厮不见。"宋江道："你且来，先和我哥哥头领相见。"李逵听了，丢了双斧，望着晁盖跪了一跪，说道："大哥休怪铁牛粗卤。"与众人都相见了，却认得朱贵是同乡人，两个大家欢喜。花荣便道："哥哥，你教众人只顾跟着李大哥走，如今来到这里，前面又是大江拦截住，断头路了，却又没一只船接应。倘或城中官军赶杀出来，却怎生迎敌？将何接济？"李逵便道："不要慌，我与你们再杀入城去，和那个鸟蔡九知府一发都砍了便走。"戴宗此时方才苏醒，便叫道："兄弟，使不得莽性！城里有五七千军马，若杀入去，必然有失。"阮小七便道："远望隔江，那里有数只船在岸边，我兄弟三个赴水过去，夺那几只船过来载众人如何？”晁盖道：“此计是最上着。”

（9）第72回 柴进簪花入禁院 李逵元夜闹东京

写毕，递与李师师反覆看了，不晓其意。宋江只要等他问其备细，却把心腹衷曲之事告诉。只见奶子来报：“官家从地道中来至后门。”李师师忙道：“不能远送，切乞恕罪。”自来后门接驾，奶子、丫鬟连忙收拾过了杯盘什物，扛过台桌，洒扫亭轩。宋江等都未出来，却闪在黑暗处，张见李师师拜在面前，奏道：“起居，圣上龙体劳困。”只见天子头戴软纱唐巾，身穿滚龙袍，说道：“寡人今日幸上清宫方回，教太子在宣德楼赐万民御酒，令御弟在千步廊买市。约下杨太尉，久等不至，寡人自来，爱卿近前与朕攀话。”……

宋江在黑地里说道：“今番挫过，后次难逢。俺三个就此告一道招安赦书，有何不好？”柴进道：“如何使得？便是应允了，后来也有翻变。”三个正在黑影里商量。却说李逵见了宋江、柴进和那美色妇人吃酒，却教他和戴宗看门，头上毛发倒竖起来，一肚子怒气正没发付处。只见杨太尉揭起帘幕，推开扇门，迳走入来，见了李逵，喝问道：“你这厮是谁？敢在这里？”李逵也不回应，提起把交椅，望杨太尉脸打来。杨太尉倒吃了一惊，措手不及，两交椅打翻地下。戴宗便来救时，那里拦挡得住。李逵扯下书画来，就蜡烛上点着，东焠西焠，一面放火，香桌椅凳，打得粉碎。宋江等三个听得，赶出来看时，见“黑旋风”褪下半截衣裳，正在那里行凶。四个扯出门外去时，李逵就街上夺条棒，直打出小御街来。宋江见他性起，只得和柴进、戴宗先赶出城，恐关了禁门，脱身不得，只留燕青看守着他。李师师家火起，惊得赵官家一道烟走了。邻佑人等一面救火，一面救起杨太尉，这话都不必说。

城中喊起杀声，震天动地。高太尉在北门上巡警，听了这话，带领军马，便来追赶。燕青伴着李逵，正打之间，撞着穆弘、史进，四人各执枪棒，一齐助力，直打到城边。把门军士急待要关门，外面鲁智深抡铁禅杖，武行者使起双戒刀，朱仝、刘唐手拈着朴刀，早杀入城来，救出里面四个。方才出得城门，高太尉军马恰好赶到城外来。八个头领不见宋江、柴进、戴宗，正在那里心慌。原来军师吴用已知此事，定教大闹东京。克时定日，差下五员虎将，引领带甲马军一千骑，是夜恰好到东京城外等接，正逢着宋江、柴进、戴宗三人。带来的空马，就教上马。随后众人也到。正都上马时，于内不见了李逵，高太尉军马冲将出来。宋江手下的五虎将：关胜、林冲、秦明、呼延灼、董平，突到城边，立马于濠堑上，大喝道："梁山泊好汉全伙在此！早早献城，免汝一死。"高太尉听得，那里敢出城来，慌忙教放下吊桥，众军上城堤防。宋江便唤燕青吩咐道："你和黑厮最好，你可略等他一等，随后与他同来。我和军马众将先回，星夜还寨，恐怕路上别有枝节。"

不说宋江等军马去了，且说燕青立在人家房檐下看时，只见李逵从店里取了行李，拿着双斧，大吼一声，跳出店门，独自一个，要去打这东京城池。

（10）第82回　梁山泊分金大买市　宋公明全伙受招安

且说宿太尉奉诏来梁山泊招安，一干人马，迤逦都到济州。太守张叔夜出郭，迎接入城，馆驿中安下。太守起居宿太尉已毕，把过接风酒。张叔夜禀道："朝廷颁诏来招安，已是二次。

盖因不得其人，误了国家大事。今者太尉此行，必与国家立大功也！”宿太尉乃言：“天子近闻梁山泊一伙，以义为主，不侵州郡，不害良民，口称替天行道。今差下官赍到天子御笔亲书丹诏，并赐金牌三十六面，银牌七十二面，红锦三十六匹，绿锦七十二匹，黄封御酒一百八瓶，表里二十四匹，来此招安。礼物轻否？”张叔夜道：“这一班人，非在礼物轻重，要图忠义报国，扬名后代。若得太尉早来如此，也不教国家损兵折将，虚耗了钱粮。此一伙义士归降之后，必与朝廷建功立业。”宿太尉道：“下官在此专待，有烦太守亲往山寨报知，着令准备迎接。”张叔夜答道：“小官愿往。”随即上马出城，带了十数个从人，径投梁山泊来。

到得山下，早有小头目接着，报上寨里来。宋江听罢，慌忙下山迎接。张太守上山，到忠义堂上。相见罢，张叔夜道：“义士恭喜！朝廷特遣殿前宿太尉。赍擎丹诏，御笔亲书，前来招安，并赐金牌、表里、御酒、缎匹，见在济州城内。义士可以准备迎接诏旨。”宋江大喜，以手加额道：“宋江等再生之幸！”当时留请张太守茶饭。张叔夜道：“非是下官拒意，惟恐太尉见怪回迟。敢为礼。”张叔夜坚执便行。宋江忙教托出一盘金银相送。张太守见了，便道：“决不敢受！”道：“些少微物，聊表寸心。若事毕之后，尚容图报。”张叔夜道：“深感义士厚意，且留于大寨，却来请领，亦未为晚。”……

宋江便差大小军师吴用、朱武并萧让、乐和四个，跟随张太守下山，直往济州来，参见宿太尉。约至后日，众多大小头目离寨三十里外，伏道相迎。当时吴用等跟随太守张叔夜连夜下山，直到济州。次日，来馆驿中，参见宿太尉。拜罢，跪在面前。宿太尉教平身起来，俱各命坐。四个谦让，那里敢坐。太尉问其姓氏，吴用答道："小生吴用，在下朱武、萧让、乐和，奉兄长宋公明命，特来迎接恩相。兄长与弟兄，后日离寨三十里外，伏道迎接。"宿太尉大喜，便道："加亮先生，自从华州一别之后，已经数载，谁想今日得与重会！下官知汝弟兄之心，素怀忠义，只被奸臣闭塞，谗佞专权，使汝众人下情不能上达。目今天子悉已知之，特命下官赍到天子御笔亲书丹诏、金银牌面、红绿锦缎、御酒、表里，前来招安。汝等勿疑，尽心受领。"吴用等再拜称谢道："山野狂夫，有劳恩相降临。感蒙天恩，皆出太尉之赐。众弟兄刻骨铭心，难以补报。"张叔夜一面设宴管待。

Chapter VII Outlaws of The Marsh

1. Introduction of the Work

Outlaws of The Marsh is a long chapter-novel written by Shi Nai'an in the late Yuan and early Ming Dynasty (in most existing books, some mention the author as Shi Nai'an, some mention the author as Luo Guanzhong, and some mention both). *Outlaws of The Marsh*, also known as "*Loyalty and Water Margin*", is one of the four great classics in China. After it came into being, it had a great influence on society and became a model for Chinese novel writing. The book describes a story in the Song Dynasty. Led by Song Jiang, one hundred and eight men of Liang Shanbo begin an uprising, and after gathering, they accept consignment and fight for the imperial court.

Outlaws of The Marsh is a long heroic saga, and it is one of the representative works of the ancient Chinese novel. It was based on the story of the uprising of Song Jiang which took place in the Northern Song Dynasty during the period of Emperor Huizong. This event was recorded in the history of the Song Dynasty, *The Biography of Huizong*, *The Biography of Hou Meng*, and *The Biography of Zhang Shuye*. Since the Southern Song Dynasty, the story of Song Jiang's uprising had spread among the people. *The Pact is Talking* About records some independent legends about the heroes in *Outlaws of The Marsh. Incidents of the Age of Xuanhe* links many stories of Outlaws of The Marsh, which is quite similar to the novel. The Yuan Dynasty saw the emergence of many plays about *The Outlaws of The Marsh* and a number of Liangshan heroes on the stage.

Outlaws of The Marsh is based on the story of the Song Jiang's uprising which was spread through folk tales, and was inspired by folk literature. *Outlaws of The Marsh* is one of the most beloved classical novels in the vernacular for Chinese. It was produced in the Ming Dynasty, and was processed, sorted and created by the author on the basis of the story, script and opera, referring to the stories of *Water Margin* since the song and Yuan Dynasties. The main theme of the book is the Peasant Uprising led by Song Jiang, which is an artistic representation of the tragic and heroic struggle of the ancient Chinese people against oppression. The work fully exposes the decadence and brutality of the feudal ruling class, the sharp social contradictions in the society at that time and the cruel reality of an oppressive government which drives the people to rebellion. It successfully shapes heroic characters like Lu Zhishen, Li Kui, Wu Song, Lin Chong, Ruan Xiaoqi and so on, with tortuous plots, vivid language and distinct characters, resulting in high artistic achievement. But his works glorify and beautify Song Jiang, advocate "Loyalty and righteousness" and "Doing justice for Heaven", and show serious ideological limitations.

2. Introduction of the Author

Shi Nai'an, a writer of the late Yuan and early Ming Dynasty, whose real name is Yanduan, is a native of the Han nationality in Xinghua, Jiangsu Province. He is erudite and informed, talented and well learned in poems and songs, astronomy, geography, medicine and divination, astrology, and other fields. Shi Nai'an was smart and studious from an early age, with outstanding talent, filial piety and a strong sense of justice. He passed the imperial examination at the county level at the age of nineteen, the examination at the provincial level at twenty-eight and finally the examination at the highest level at thirty-six with Liu Bowen. Not long after he passed the highest examination, in the second year of Zhishun (1331A.D.), he was appointed to be the county official in Qiantang, Zhejiang Province. Later he left the officialdom for his hometown, he wrote books behind closed doors. He studied books like The Romance of the Three Kingdoms and Sansui Ping Yao Zhuan with his disciple Luo Guanzhong, then collected and sorted stories about the heroes such as Song Jiang of Liangshan, and finally finished The Outlaws of The Marsh—one of the four great classics in China.

There is little information about Shi Nai'an's life, and some of the records collected are contradictory. It is said that he was born in Suzhou, later moved to Huai'an, and passed the highest imperial examination in the year of Zhishun Xinwei. He had been the official in Qiantang for two years, but did not agree with the way of the people in power there, so he left the officialdom for his hometown, writing behind closed doors.

Since the 1920s, some documents about Shi Nai'an have been found in Xinghua, Dafeng, Yandu District and other places of Jiangsu Province, such as The Genealogy of Shi Family, and The Genealogy of the Oldest Branch of Shi Family. In addition, there is an addendum of an article named Biography of Shi Nai'an in the 13th volume of Sequels of Chronicles of Xinhua County, and an addendum of an article of Epitaph of Shi Nai'an written by Wang Daosheng in the early Ming Dynasty in the 14th volume of the same book.

3. Appreciation

(1)Chapter 1

Zhang the Divine Teacher Prays to Dispel a Plague

Marshal Hong Releases Demons by Mistake

That day, the third day of the third month of the third year of the Jia You period, at the third interval of the fifth watch Emperor Ren Zong mounted his throne in the imperial palace. …

After the officials had made their obeisance, the chief of ceremonies cried: "If anyone has a petition, let him come forward. If there are none, this court will adjourn." Zhao Zhe, the Premier, and Wen Yanbo, his deputy, advanced and said: "The plague is raging unabated in the capital. Victims among the soldiers and the people are many. We hope Your Majesty, in a forgiving and benevolent spirit, will reduce prison sentences and cut taxes, and pray to Heaven that the people be relived of this affliction."

The emperor at once ordered the Hanlin Academy to draw an

edict proclaiming a general amnesty for all prisoners and canceling all taxes. He also directed that every temple and monastery in the capital offer prayers for a termination of the disaster. But the plague only became worse. The emperor was very disturbed and summoned his officials for a conference. A prominent minister stepped forth and asked to be heard ahead of turn. The emperor saw that it was Fan Zhongyan, his Deputy Premier. Fan kowtowed, then rose and said: "The plague is decimating our soldiers and citizenry. No one is safe. In my humble opinion if this pestilence is to be ended Your Majesty should summon the Divine Teacher of the Taoists, who comes from a papal line dating back to Han times. Let him travel day and night and rush here to the capital and conduct a great prayer service in the imperial park. In this way the people will be saved." Emperor Ren Zong approved Fan's proposal. He directed the scholars of the Hanlin Academy to draw up an edict, which he signed personally, and issued a bunch of royal incense sticks. He ordered that Marshal Hong Xin go as his emissary to the Dragon and Tiger Mountain in Xinzhou Prefecture of Jiangxi Province and fetch Zhang the Divine Teacher. While incense burned in the imperial hall, the emperor himself placed the edict in Marshal Hong's hands and told him to set out immediately. Hong accepted the royal edict and took leave of the emperor. With the edict in a bag on his back and the incense sticks in a golden box, he mounted his horse and left the Eastern Capital, leading a column of several score men. They headed directly for Guixi, a county town in Xinzhou Prefecture.

(2)Chapter 3

Master Shi Leaves Huayin County at Night

Major Lu Pummels the Lord of the West

There Zheng had a two-room butcher shop with two chopping blocks. Four or five sides of pork were hanging on display. Zheng sat behind a counter by the door, keeping an eye on his ten or so assistants as they cut and sold meat. Lu Da came to the door. "Butcher Zheng," he shouted. Zheng recognized him. He came out rapidly from behind the counter and greeted him with respect. "Major, a pleasure." He directed an assistant to bring a bench. "Please be seated, sir." Lu Da sat down. "The garrison commander has ordered me to buy ten catties of lean meat, chopped fine, to be used for filling. There mustn't be a speck of fat in it." "Right," said Zheng. He turned to his assistants. "Pick out a good cut and chop up ten catties." "I don't want those dirty oafs touching it," said Lu Da. "You do it yourself." "Certainly," said Zheng. "Glad to." He selected a cut of ten catties of lean meat and started mincing. The attendant from the inn, his head bound in a white handkerchief, arrived to tell Zheng about Old Jin. But when he saw Lu Da seated at the door, he was afraid to come any closer. He stood under the eaves of a house, observing the proceedings cautiously from a distance. After chopping for an hour, Zheng wrapped the minced meat in a lotus leaf. "Shall I have it delivered, sir?" he asked. "Delivered, nothing. What's your hurry? Now cut up ten catties of fat meat. There mustn't be a speck of lean in it. This is also for filling." "The lean can be put in dumplings, but what good is the fat?" Lu Da glared. "When the commander gives an order, who dares question him?" "As long as you can use it I'll chop it for you." Zheng selected a cut of ten catties of fat meat and began mincing. By the time he wrapped it in a lotus leaf the morning had gone and it was the hour for lunch. The inn attendant dared not approach. Even other customers were afraid to draw near. "Shall I have this delivered to the garrison command for you, sir?" asked Zheng. "Now I want ten catties of gristle, chopped fine, also to be used for filling, and I don't want to see any meat in it." Zheng laughed awkwardly. "Are you making fun of me?" Lu Da leaped up, one package of chopped meat in each hand, and scowled at the butcher. "That's exactly what I'm doing—making fun of you." He flung the contents of the packages full in Zheng's face. The shower of meat stung the butcher into a rage. From the soles of his feet, fury surged into his forehead. An irrepressible flame blazed in his heart. He grabbed a paring knife from the butcher's block and jumped down from the shop steps. Lu Da was waiting for him in the middle of the street. None of the dozen or so clerks from the neighboring shops dared to mediate. Passers-by stood frozen in their tracks on both sides of the street. The attendant from the inn was struck dumb. The knife in his right hand, Zheng reached for Lu Da with his left. Lu Da seized the outstretched hand, closed in and sent the butcher sprawling with a swift kick in the groin. Another step forward and he put his foot on Zheng's chest. Raising a fist like a vinegar keg, Lu Da thundered: "I was roving inspector of five western military districts under Old General Zhong. People might very well call me Lord of the West. But you're just a meat slicing butcher, a low cur. Where do you come off giving yourself such a title? And who gave you the right to force and cheat Jin's daughter Jade Lotus?" He landed a punch on Zheng's nose that flattened it to one side and brought the blood flowing like the sauces in a condiments shop- salty, sour and spicy. Zheng struggled vainly to rise. The knife fell from his hand. "A good blow," he cried. "Mother-raping thief," said the major. "How dare you talk back?" He punched the butcher on the eyebrow, splitting the lid so that the eyeball protruded. Red, black and purple gore flowed like swatches of cloth in a draper's shop.

The spectators were all afraid of Lu Da. None of them ventured to intervene. Vanquished, Zheng begged to be spared. "You scurvy knave," the major exclaimed scornfully. "If you had shown any guts I might have let you off. But since you're so lily-livered, I won't." He struck the butcher a heavy blow on the temple. Zheng's head rang like the clanging of gongs, bells and cymbals in a big memorial service. The butcher lay stretched on the ground. Breath was coming out of his mouth, but none was going in. He didn't move. Lu Da pretended to be incensed. "Playing dead, eh? I'll hit you a few more!" He had observed that Zheng's face was changing color. "I only wanted to give the varlet a beating," he said to himself. "Who would have thought that three blows would kill him? They're sure to hold me for trial, and I've nobody to bring me food in prison. I'd better get out of here." He rose and strode away, pausing briefly to look back, shake his finger at Zheng's corpse and shout: "Go on playing dead. I'll settle with you later." Neither the butcher's assistants nor the clerks in the neighboring shops had the courage to stop him. Lu Da returned to his quarters and hastily packed. He took only some travelling clothes and a bit of silver.

His old garments and heavier things he left behind. Carrying a staff as a weapon, he sped out of the South Gate like a wisp of smoke.

(3)Chapter 9

Chai Jin Keeps Open House for All Bold Men

Lin Chong Defeats Instructor Hong in a Bout with Staves

By the time they had consumed another six or seven rounds, the moon had risen and was shining in with such brilliance that the hall was as bright as day. Chai Jin stood up and said: "Arms Instructors, please give us a bout." Lin Chong thought to himself: "This Instructor Hong must be Chai Jin's arms teacher. If I beat him, His Lordship will lost face." Observing Lin Chong's hesitation, Chai Jin said: "Instructor Hong has not been here long either. No one has taken him on. Please don't refuse, Master Lin. I am most eager to see the skill of you two instructors." Chai Jin said this to indicate that Lin need have no fears of offending him, and that he should not hold back. Lin Chong at last felt reassured. "Come on, come on," cried Hong, rising. "I'll give you a bout with staves!" Everyone surged out of the hall into the courtyard. Vassals brought a bundle of wooden staves and laid them on the ground. Hong removed his outer robe and tied up his skirts. Selecting a staff, he struck a fighting pose. "Come on, come on," he urged. "Instructor Lin," said Chai Jin, "please start the bout." "Don't laugh at my clumsiness, Your Lordship," Lin Chong begged. He chose a staff and said to Hong: "Master, please teach me." Hong glared as if wanting to swallow him down in one gulp. Lin Chong advanced holding the staff extended in both hands. Hong rapped his staff sharply on the ground and rushed at Lin. After the two arms instructors had fought four or five rounds in the bright moonlight, Lin Chong leaped out of the combat circle. "Halt the bout," he cried. "Why won't you show us your skill, Instructor?" queried Chai Jin. "I've lost," said Lin. "But you haven't fought to a conclusion. How can you say you've lost?" "If I have to fight with this rack around my neck, I may just as well consider myself defeated." "How thoughtless of me," Chai Jin laughed. "That can be remedied easily enough." He directed his vassals to fetch ten ounces of silver. When the money was brought he said to the two guards: "May I trouble you to take Lin Chong's rack off temporarily? If there's any question raised about this when you arrive at the Cangzhou Prison, I will bear all responsibility. Divide these ten ounces between you." Chai Jin looked so lofty and dignified that the guards didn't dare refuse. They wanted to stay in Chai's good graces and wanted the silver as well. Since there was no danger of Lin Chong running away, Xue Ba removed the wooden collar from his neck. "Now the two masters can continue their match," said Chai Jin joyfully. Because Lin's tactics had been cautious, Hong regarded him with scorn. Raising his staff, he prepared to resume combat. "Just a moment," Chai Jin exclaimed. He ordered his vassals to bring an ingot of silver weighing twenty-five ounces. In no time at all, the ingot was produced. "A match between you two instructors is no ordinary contest," said Chai Jin. "Whoever wins gets this silver as a prize." He was hoping in this way to encourage Lin Chong to display his skill. Deliberately, he tossed the ingot on the ground. Hong was very annoyed that Lin Chong had come, and he coveted the big piece of silver. What's more, he was worried that a defeat would lower his prestige. Vigorously, he struck a fighting pose, then executed an opening flourish called "lifting the torch to sear the heavens." "His Lordship wants me to defeat him," thought Lin Chong. First holding his staff level, he performed a move called "separating the grass to find the snake." "Come on, come on," yelled Hong. He swung his staff downwards. Lin dodged back. Hong pressed forward another pace. Raising his staff, he again chopped down. Lin Chong saw that he was off balance and brought his staff sweeping upwards from the ground. Hong had no time to recover. He tried to twist out of the way, but Lin's staff cracked him hard on the shin bones. Hong dropped his staff and fell heavily. Delighted, Chai Jin called for wine and presented Lin Chong with a congratulatory goblet. The watchers all laughed. Hong struggled but was unable to rise to his feet. Grinning vassals helped him up. Hong, shamefaced, limped away and left the manor.

(4)Chapter 12

Lin Chong Joins the Bandits in Liangshan Marsh

Yang Zhi Sells His Sword in the Eastern Capital

Now he lumbered up to Yang and took the sword from his hand. "How much do you want for this?" "Three thousand strings of cash for a precious ancestral blade." "All that money for this shitty thing! For thirty coppers I can buy a knife that will slice meat and cut bean-curd. What's so good about your sword? What's precious about if?" "This isn't one of those iron blades they sell in the shops. This is a rare weapon." "How so?" "First," it can cut copper and pierce iron without curling the edge. Second, it can slice a tuft of hair blown against it. Third, it can kill a man and come away clean." "Would you really dare cut copper coins?" "Bring them out and I'll show you." Niu Er went to a pepper shop near the bridge and returned with twenty three-cent pieces. He piled these on the bridge railing and said to Yang: "If you can cut through these, man, I'll give you three thousand strings of cash." Though people were afraid to come close, many of them watched from a distance. "Nothing to it," said Yang. He rolled up his sleeves, grasped the sword fi and took aim. With one downward chop he cleaved the pile of coins neatly in two. The watchers set up a cheer. "Quit that bloody racket!" growled Niu Er. "What did you say the second thing was?" he asked Yang. "Take a tuft of hair and just blow it against the blade. It will cut right through it." "I don't believe you!" The bully pulled a few hairs from his head and handed them to Yang. "Go on, blow, I want to see." Yang held the hairs in his left hand and blew them with one hard puff against the sword edge. Two halves of the tuft floated to the ground. A loud cheer broke from the crowd. More and more people were gathering. "What was the third thing?" Niu Er asked. "Kill a man without staining the blade." "How can you do that?" "When you hack a man with this sword there's not a drop of blood on it. That's how sharp it is." "I don't believe it! Kill a man and show me." "Here, in the imperial city? Who would dare? I'll kill a dog for you instead." "You said a man, not a dog!" "If you don't want the sword, forget it. Quit pestering me." "Let me see it!" "Haven't you anything better to do? Don't provoke me." "Kill me, if you dare!" "You're never wronged me, we're not enemies. I've proven my claim twice. Why should I kill you?" Niu Er grasped Yang Zhi's arm. "You must sell me that sword!" "If you want to buy it, where's your money?" "I don't have any!" "What are you holding me for, then?" "I want that sword!" "You can't have it!" "Stab me, if you're so brave!" Yang angrily pushed him away. Niu Er fell to the ground. He clambered to his feet and butted Yang in the chest. "Neighbors, you're my witness," Yang shouted. "I'm selling my sword because I need money. This knave is trying to snatch it away, and now he's struck me!" But the watchers were all afraid of Niu Er. No one dared come forward to make peace. "So I struck you," cried Niu Er. "Suppose I beat you to death? What of if!" He swung his right fist in a wild punch. Yang dodged and chopped a furious blow at Niu Er's forehead. The scoundrel collapsed. Yang closed in and finished him with two thrusts in the chest. Blood gushed copiously, and Niu Er lay dead. "I've killed the wretch," Yang exclaimed. "I don't want to implicate you, but the man is dead. Please come with me to the authorities and be my witness." The neighbors quickly rallied round and accompanied Yang to the Kaifeng prefectural office. They all presented themselves and knelt where the prefect was holding court. Yang laid the sword before him. "I was formerly an aide in the palace, but because I lost a cargo of grotesque and colored stones, I was dismissed. Now, I have no money, and I took my sword on the street to sell it. The rascal Niu Er grabbed for it and started to punch me. I killed him in a moment of rage. These neighbors all saw what happened." Many spoke on his behalf. "Since he has come forward voluntarily," said the prefect, "let him be spared the preliminary beating." He ordered that a long wooden rack be fitted around Yang Zhi's neck, and that two inspectors and a forensic expert take Yang and his witnesses back to the Tianhanzhou

Bridge for an examination at the scene of the crime. The prefect drew the appropriate documents. After the witnesses submitted formal statements in writing they were released under guarantees to produce themselves whenever the court summoned. Yang Zhi was locked up in the jail for condemned prisoners.

(5)Chapter 16

Yang Zhi Escorts a Convoy of Precious Goods

Wu Yong by a Ruse Captures the Birthday Gifts

Standing on the edge of the pine grove, the seven date merchants pointed at the fifteen men of the convoy and said: "Down you go! Down you go!" The fifteen, weak in the knees and heavy in the head, stared at each other as, one by one, they sank to the ground. Then the seven merchants pushed the seven wheel-barrows out of the grove and dumped the dates. Placing the eleven loads of jewels and art objects into the barrows, they covered them over. "Sorry to trouble you," they called, and trundled off down the ridge. Yang Zhi, too weak to move, could only groan inwardly. The fifteen couldn't get up. They had only been able to goggle helplessly while the seven had loaded the barrows with the precious cargo. They were paralyzed, bereft of speech. Now I ask you—who were those seven men? None other than Chao Gai, Wu Yong, Gongsun Sheng, Liu Tang and the three Ruan brothers. And the wine vendor was Bai Sheng, nicknamed Daylight Rat. And how was the wine drugged? When the buckets were carried up the ridge, they contained pure wine. After the seven finished the first bucket, Liu Tang removed the cover from the second and deliberately drank half a ladleful so as to dull the others'suspicions. Next, inside the grove,

Wu Yong poured the drug into the other ladle. Then he came out and spilled it into the wine while taking a "free scoop." As he pretended to drink, Bai Sheng grabbed the ladle and dumped the wine back in the bucket. That was the ruse. Planned entirely by Wu Yong, it can be called "Capturing the Birthday Gifts by a Ruse." Yang Zhi had not drunk much, and he recovered first. Crawling to his feet, he could hardly stand. He looked at the other fourteen. Saliva was running from the corners of their mouths. None of them could move. "You've made me lose the birthday gifts," Yang Zhi muttered in angry despair. "How can I ever face Governor Liang again? These convoy documents are worthless now!" He tore them up. "I've become a man without a home or country. Where can I go? Better that I should die right here on this ridge!" Clutching his tunic, he staggered to the edge of the ridge and prepared to jump.

(6)Chapter 23

Lord Chai Accommodates Guests in Henghai County

Wu Song Kills a Tiger on Jingyang Ridge

Suddenly a wild gale blew, and when it passed a roar come from behind the thicket and out bounded a huge tiger. Its malevolent upward-slanting eyes gleamed beneath a broad white forehead. "Aiya!" cried Wu Song. He jumped down, seized his staff, and slipped behind the rock. Both hungry and thirsty, the big animal clawed the ground with its front paws a couple of times, sprang high and came hurtling forward. The wine poured out of Wu Song in a cold sweat. Quicker than it takes to say, he dodged, and the huge beast landed beyond him. Tigers can't see behind them, so as its front paws touched the ground it tried to side-swipe Wu Song with its body. Again he dodged, and the tiger missed. With a thunderous roar that shook the ridge, the animal slashed at Wu Song with its iron tail. Once more he swiveled out of the way. Now this tiger had three methods for getting its victim-spring, swipe and slash. But none of them had worked, and the beast's spirit diminished by half. Again it roared, and whirled around. Wu Song raised his staff high in a two-handed grip and swung with all his might. There was a loud crackling, and a large branch, leaves and all, tumbled past his face. In his haste, he had struck an old tree instead of the tiger, snapping the staff in two and leaving him holding only the remaining half. Lashing itself into a roaring fury, the beast charged. Wu Song leaped back ten paces, and the tiger landed in front of him. He threw away the stump of his staff, seized the animal by the ruff and bore down. The tiger struggled frantically, but Wu Song was exerting all his strength, and wouldn't give an inch. He kicked the beast in the face and eyes, again and again. The tiger roared, its wildly scrabbling claws pushing back two piles of yellow earth and digging a pit before it. Wu Song pressed the animal's muzzle into the pit, weakening it further. Still relentlessly clutching the beast by the ruff with his left hand, Wu Song freed his right, big as an iron mallet, and with all his might began to pound. After sixty or seventy blows the tiger, blood streaming from eyes, mouth, nose and ears, lay motionless, panting weakly. Wu Song got up and searched around under the pine tree until he found the stump of his broken staff. With this he beat the animal till it breathed no more. Then he tossed the staff aside. "I'd better drag this dead tiger down the mountain," he thought. He tried to lift the beast, lying in a pool of blood, but couldn't move it. He was exhausted, the strength gone out of his hands and feet. Wu Song sat down on the rock and rested. "It's nearly dark," he thought. "If another tiger comes I won't be able to fight it. I'd better get off this ridge first, somehow. Then, tomorrow morning, I can decide what to do." He collected his broad-brimmed felt hat from beside the rock, skirted the thicket, and slowly descended the ridge.

(7)Chapter 25

Mistress Wang Instigates Ximen Qing

The Adulterous Wife Poisons Wu the Elder

Wu was ill for five days and couldn't leave his bed. When he wanted soup or water she wouldn't give it to him. When he called her she didn't answer. Each day she made herself up alluringly and went out, returning always with a rosy face. Wu several times nearly fainted from sheer rage, but she paid him no heed. He called her to him and said: "I know what you're up to. I caught the two of you together. You got your lover to kick me in the chest, and I'm more dead than alive, yet you two are still going on with your games! I may die—I'm no match for you. But don't forget my brother Wu Song! You know what he's like! Sooner or later he's coming back. Do you think he's going to let you get away with it? Have pity on me. Help me recover quickly, and when he comes home I won't say anything. If you don't treat me right, he'll have something to say to the both of you!" Golden Lotus did not reply, but went next door and told Mistress Wang and Ximen what her husband had said. Ximen felt his blood run cold. He groaned. "Constable Wu is the man who killed the tiger on Jingyang Ridge.

He was the boldest fighter in Qinghe County! We've been having this affair for some time now, and we've been marvelous together in body and in mind. I forgot all about your husband's brother! What are we going to do? This is a terrible situation!" Mistress Wang laughed coldly. "I've never seen the like. You're the helmsman and I'm only a passenger, but I'm not worried and you're in a flap!" "Though it shames me to say it, I don't know how to deal with this sort of thing. Have you any idea how to cover for us?" "Do you want to be long-term lover, or short?" "What do you mean?" "If you're satisfied with being short-term lovers, separate after today and when Wu recovers, apologize to him. Nothing will be said when Wu Song comes home. When he's sent out on another mission, you can get together again. If you want to be long-term lovers, and not have to be frightened and alarmed every day, I have a clever scheme. Of course, you may not be able to do it." "Save us, godmother! We want to be long-term lovers!" "The thing we need for this scheme other households don't have. But yours, thank Heaven, does." "If you ask for my eyes, I'll gouge them out! What is this thing?" "The wretch is very ill. Take advantage of his misery to do him in. Get some arsenic from your drug shop, let this lady buy medicine for heart pains, mix the two together and finish the dwarf off. She can have him cremated, so there won't be any traces. When Wu Song comes back, what will he be able to do? You know the old sayings: 'Brother and sister-in-law must keep their distance.' 'Parents pick the first husband, widows choose the second.' A brother-in-law can't interfere. You continue to meet secretly for half a year or so till the mourning period is over, then marry her. You'll be long-term lovers, and merry till the end of your days. What do you think of my plan?" "It's a frightening crime, godmother! Never mind. We'll do it! All or nothing!" "Good. Pull it out by the roots and it won't grow again. Leave any roots and it sprouts once more, come spring. Get the arsenic, Right Honorable. I'll tell the lady how to use it. When it's over, you'll have to reward me well." "Naturally! That goes without saying!" Not long after, Ximen arrived with the arsenic and gave it to Mistress Wang. The old woman looked at Golden Lotus. "I'll teach you how to mix this in the medicine. Didn't Wu ask you to treat him better? Soften him up with a little kindness. He'll ask you to buy some medicine for his heart. Put this arsenic in it. When he wakes up at night, pour the mixture down his throat, then get out of the way. Once it starts working in him, it will split his guts, and he'll shout and scream. Muffle his cries with a quilt. Don't let anyone hear. Have a pot of hot water boiling, and soak a rag. He'll bleed from every opening, he'll bite his lips. When he dies, remove the quilt and clean away all the blood with the rag. Then into the coffin, off to the cremation, and not a frigging thing will happen!" "It sounds all right," said Golden Lotus. "Only I'm afraid I'll go soft! I won't be able to handle the corpse!" "That's easy. Just knock on the wall, and I'll come up and help you." "Do the job carefully you two," said Ximen. "I'll be back at dawn tomorrow to hear your report." He stood up and departed. Mistress Wang crushed the arsenic granules with her fingers into powder and gave it to Golden Lotus to hide. The girl crossed over to her own house and went upstairs. Wu was barely breathing. He seemed to be at death's door. She sat down on the edge of the bed and pretended to weep. “Why are you crying?” asked Wu. Golden Lotus dabbed at her eyes. “I made a mistake and let that scoundrel beguile me. I never thought he’d kick you! I’ve heard about a very good medicine. I’d like to buy it for you, but I’m afraid you don’t trust me, so I haven’t dared!” “Save my life and we’ll forget about the whole thing. I won’t hold it against you, and I’ll say nothing to Wu Song. Go buy the medicine quickly! Save me!” The girl took some coppers, hurried to Mistress Wang’s house and sent her out for the medicinal powders. Then she brought the packet upstairs and showed it to Wu. “This is heart balm,” she said. “The doctor in the drug shop says you should take it in the middle of the night and cover your head with two quilts to make you perspire. Tomorrow, you’ll be able to get up.” “That’s fine! I know it’s a lot of trouble, but stay awake till midnight and give me the potion.” “Don’t worry about a thing. Just sleep. I’ll look after you.” The day drew to a close and darkness gathered. Golden Lotus lit a lamp. Then she went down to the kitchen, set a pot of water on the stove and put a rag in to boil. When she heard the watchman’s drum thump three times, she spilled the arsenic powder into a cup, filled a bowl with hot water, and took them both up the stairs. She called to her husband. “Where did you put the medicine?” “Here under the sleeping mat, beside my pillow. Mix it quickly and give it to me.” Golden Louts took the packet of medicinal powders, sprinkled them into the cup so that they covered the arsenic, then added hot water and stirred with a silver pin which she drew from her hair. Raising Wu with her left hand, she held the cup to his lips with her right. “It’s very bitter,” he said after the first sip. “As long as it cures you, what do you care how bitter it is." He opened his mouth for another sip, and the girl tilted the cup and forced its entire contents down his throat. She let him fall back on his pillow and swiftly got off the bed. Wu gasped. "My stomach hurts! The pain, the pain! I can't stand it!" The girl grabbed two quilts from the foot of the bed and flung them over his face. "I can't breathe!" he cried. "The doctor says I should make you sweat! You'll get well quicker!" Before Wu could reply, the girl, afraid he would struggle, leaped onto the bed and knelt astride his body, pressing down on the sides of the quilts with both hands.

(8)Chapter 40

Mount Liangshan Gallants Raid the Execution Grounds

Bold Heroes Meet at White Dragon Temple

Not long after, the group of officers on the execution grounds parted and a man stepped forward and announced: "Three quarters past noon." "Cut off their heads," ordered the prefect. Soldiers opened the prisoners'racks. Two executioners stood with swords at the ready. Quicker than it takes to say, rioting broke out. One of the merchants pulled a small gong from his tunic. Standing on the cart he struck it sharply three times. On all sides, men went into action. A hulking dark tiger of a fellow, stark naked, appeared in the upper story of a tea-house beside the crossroads. Brandishing a battle-ax in each hand, he uttered a heaven-splitting roar, leaped down, hacked the executioners to death, and began carving his way towards the mounted prefect. Soldiers thrust at him with their spears, but nothing could stop his headlong advance. They crowded around Cai and rushed him off to safety. Daggers suddenly appeared in the hands of the snake charmers on the east side, and they began killing soldiers. The medicine men on the west side, holding spears and staves, let out a yell and charged into the soldiers and guards, slaughtering left and right. On the south, the porters swung their carrying-poles, felling soldiers and spectators indiscriminately. The merchants on the north jumped down from the carts and tipped them over, blocking the road. Two of the merchants darted through the melee and got Song Jiang and Dai Zong on their backs. Some of the remainder produced bows and arrows and started shooting. Others threw stones they had concealed in their clothes. A few waved pennant signal spears. The merchants were in fact Chao Gai, Hua Rong, Huang Xin, Lu Fang and Guo Sheng. The medicine men were Yan Shun, Liu Tang, Du Qian and Song Wan. Disguised as porters were Zhu Gui, Stumpy Tiger Wang, Zheng Tianshou and Shi Yong. The snake charmers were actually the three Ruan brothers and Bai Sheng. These leaders from Liangshan Marsh had brought with them more than a hundred men, and all were locked in furious battle. They saw the big dark fellow lying about him vigorously with his battle-axes. Chao Gai didn't recognize him, but he knew that he had been the first to go into action, and that he was killing more of the foe than anyone. "Dai Zong mentioned a Black Whirlwind Li Kui, a wild rash fellow who was good friend of Song Jiang," Chao Gai recalled, and he shouted: "Hey, bold fighter, aren't you the Black Whirlwind?" But Li Kui paid no attention, and continued consuming lives with his big axes like a blazing inferno. Chao Gai ordered the men carrying Song Jiang and Dai Zong to follow in the big dark fellow's wake.

By now bodies of soldiers and civilians were sprawled all over the crossroads, and blood flowed in rivulets. Countless more had been felled and wounded. The Liangshan leaders abandoned their carts and merchandise and continued behind the big fellow, fighting their way out of the city. Hua Rong, Huang Xin, Lu Fang and Guo Sheng, covering the rear, sent swarms of arrows in their pursuers. Neither the soldiers nor the people of Jiangzhou dared come too near. Li Kui slaughtered down to the stream's edge, his whole body spattered with blood. He went on killing along the bank. Halberd in hand, Chao Gai shouted: "Don't hurt the ordinary people. This has nothing to do with them!" But the big man wouldn't listen. He cut down victims one after another. They walked six or seven li along the stream outside the city until they saw before them a broad river. Here, all paths came to an end. Chao Gai was very distressed. Only then did Black Whirlwind speak: "Don't worry. Carry our brothers into that temple." Ahead, near the river, was a large temple, its double gates tightly locked. Li Kui smashed them open with his battle-axes, and they all went into the courtyard. Ancient junipers and pines blocked out the sunlight. A plaque upon the building was inscribed in letters of gold: Temple of the White Dragon Spirit. Song Jiang and Dai Zong were carried inside and set down. Song Jiang opened his eyes and saw Chao Gai and the others. "Brothers," he exclaimed, weeping, "This must be a dream." "You wouldn't stay with us on the mountain, brother. That's why you're in such a predicament today," Chao Gai expostulated. "Who is that big swarthy fellow who fights so powerfully?" "Li Kui the Black Whirlwind. He was ready to spring me out of prison all by himself. But I didn't think we could get away with it, so I didn't agree." "A remarkable man. He fought harder than any of us, and was absolutely fearless in the face of every enemy weapon." "Bring fresh clothing for our brothers," Hua Rong called. While they were changing, Li Kui started down the porch, battle-axes in hand. Song Jiang shouted after him: "Where are you going, brother?" "Looking for those monks. I'll kill them all. Not only didn't the louts come out to welcome us, they even barred their frigging gates. If I find them, I'll slay them before those gates as a sacrifice!" "Come over here, first. I want to introduce you to my brother, the chieftain." Li Kui cast aside his axes and dropped to his knees before Chao Gai. "Forgive Iron Ox's crassness, brother," he entreated. He was also introduced to the others and discovered he and Zhu Gui came from the same township. Both men were exceedingly pleased. "Brother," Hua Rong said to Chao Gai, "you told us to follow brother Li, and now here we are, with a big river cutting us off, and no boat to take us across. When the soldiers from the city catch up how will we be able to repel them and escape?" "Never mind," said Li Kui. "I'll fight my way back into the city and chop them into mincemeat, frigging prefect and all!" Dai Zong had just revived by then, and he cried: "Don't be rash, brother. There are six or seven thousand troops in the city. If you go charging in you'll be throwing your life away." Ruan the Seventh said: "I see some boats along the opposite bank. My brothers and I will swim over and haul a few back. How will that be?" "The best possible idea," said Chao Gai.

(9)Chapter 72

Chai Jin Wears a Cockade and Enters the Forbidden Courtyard

Li Kui on Festival Night Disturbs the Eastern Capital

When he had finished, he handed the poem to Li Shishi. She read it a few times, but didn't understand. He was about to explain when the courtesan's personal maid entered. "His Majesty has arrived at the rear door through the tunnel," she announced. "I won't be able to see you off," Shishi said hastily to her guests. "Please forgive me." She hurried to receive the emperor. The young maid quickly gathered the cups and utensils, carried away the small table, and swept the floor. Song Jiang and the others concealed themselves in a dark corner of the side room. From it they could see Shishi in the parlor kneeling before the sovereign. "Your Majesty must be weary from affairs of state." The emperor's head was covered by a silk gauze kerchief in the Tang style. He wore an imperial dragon robe. "I've just returned from the Upper Purity Temple," he said. "I directed my son the prince to dispense wine to the populace at Xuande House and my younger brother to attend the fair at the Thousand Paces Esplanade. I had arranged to meet Marshal Yang, but he never showed up, though I waited a long time. So I came here. Approach, beloved, let us talk together." "If we miss this chance, we may never get another," Song Jiang whispered to his cohorts in the darkness. "Why don't we three go forward and beseech an amnesty? What would be wrong with that?" "Impossible!" said Chai Jin. "Even if he agreed, he could always reverse himself later." Meanwhile, Li Kui's wrath was growing. Song Jiang and Chai Jin had sat drinking with the beauty, but he and Dai Zong had been sent to watch the door! Li Kui's hackles rose. His fury reached a boiling point. Just then, Marshal Yang raised the hanging screen and pushed open the double doors. He was about to Step in when his eyes Ml on Li Kui, Standing inside the entry. "Who are you, knave? How dare you come here?" he barked. Without a word, Li Kui picked up an armchair and flung it at Yang's head. The startled marshal tumbled backwards, knocking over another two chairs. Dai Zong rushed to intervene, but he was too late. Li Kui ripped pictures off the wall and set fire to them with a candle. Smashing left and right, he spread the blaze. Incense table, chairs, benches—he pulverized them all. Song Jiang and his companions hurried out when they heard the tumult. They found the Black Whirlwind, stripped to the waist, going on a rampage. By the time they got outside the door, Li Kui was tearing down the street with a cudgel he had grabbed somewhere. Song Jiang decided to leave the city immediately with Chai Jin and Dai Zong, lest the gates be closed before they could escape. He directed Yan Qing to remain behind and look after Li Kui. The moment the fire broke out in Li Shishi's home, the emperor was off like a streak of smoke. Neighbors who hurried to fight the blaze also rescued Marshal Yang. Of that no more need be said. The sounds of the yelling and shouting reached Marshal Gao, who was patrolling above the North Gate. He hastened down with his soldiers to give chase. Li Kui, battling madly, ran into Mu Hong and Shi Jin. They were joined by Yan Qing, and the four fought their way to the inner side of the city wall. Soldiers rushed to close the gate. But from the outside up charged Sagacious Lu with his iron staff, Wu Song with his double swords, and Zhu Tong and Liu Tang, swinging halberds. They hacked a path into the city and saved their four mates. They got through the gate just about the time Gao and his mounted force were reaching it. Song Jiang, Chai Jin and Dai Zong had vanished. The eight chieftains grew alarmed. Now it so happened that Wu Yong, the outlaws'military advisor, suspecting Song Jiang would have difficulty, had decided to raid the Eastern Capital. He fixed a time and dispatched a thousand armored cavalry under the five Tiger Chieftains. In the outskirts they met Song Jiang, Chai Jin and Dai Zong, and provided them with horses they had brought for that purpose. Then the other eight arrived and were also given mounts. But there was no sign of Li Kui. Marshal Gao and men were preparing to charge forth. Five of Song Jiang's commanders—Guan Sheng, Lin Chong, Qin Ming, Huyan Zhuo and Dong Ping, galloped up to the edge of the moat. "All the gallants of Mount Liangshan are here," they shouted. "Surrender the city and save yourselves from death!" Gao dared not come out. He hurriedly pulled up the drawbridge and retreated with his soldiers to defensive positions atop the city wall. "You're Li Kui's best friend," Song Jiang said to Yan Qing. "Wait for the swarthy oaf and bring him back. I want to return to the stronghold with our men tonight before the foe can intercept us." Song Jiang and the outlaws departed. Yan Qing, watching beneath the eaves of a house, saw Li Kui emerging from the inn with his luggage on his back. An ax in either hand, he leaped forth from the inn gate with a yell and headed, alone, to attack the Eastern Capital. Truly, he left the inn roaring like thunder, flourishing axes to split the city gate.

(10)Chapter 82

The Mount Liangshan Fortress Distributes Its Wealth

Song Jiang and All of His Men Are Amnestied

Marshal Su and his entourage, winding their way towards Mount Liangshan with the amnesty, reached Jizhou. Prefect Zhang Shuye came out to welcome them, and settled them in the hostel for officials. Politely, he raised his cup of greeting. "Twice before the royal court sent amnesties. It was a serious loss to the country that they were not effectuated because their delivery was entrusted to the wrong persons. This mission of yours, Marshal, will surely be of great benefit." "His Majesty has recently learned that the band on Mount Liangshan are interested primarily in righteousness. They neither raid the prefectures nor harm good people. They stress acting in Heaven's behalf. And so His Majesty has dispatched me with his hand-written decree, plus gifts of thirty-six slabs of gold, seventy-two slabs of silver, thirty-six bolts of red satin, seventy-two bolts of green satin, a hundred and eight bottles of yellow-sealed imperial wine, and twenty-four bolts of cloth for coats and linings, to deliver an amnesty. Do you think the gifts too trifling?" "It's not a question of gifts with these people. They want to serve the nation faithfully so as to earn fame for their posterity. If only you'd been able to come earlier, Marshal, our country wouldn't have had to suffer such heavy losses in officers and soldiers, money and grain. Once these warriors return to the fold they certainly will perform meritorious deeds for the emperor." "Can I trouble you to go to the fortress, Prefect, and tell them to prepare to receive my mission? I will wait here." "Of course." The governor mounted his horse and left the city with a dozen men. At the foot of the mountain he was met by lesser chieftains, who at once reported the news to the stronghold Song Jiang hastened down and escorted Prefect Zhang to Loyalty Hall. "Congratulations," Zhang exclaimed. "The emperor has dispatched Marshal Su with his personally hand-written amnesty, together with valuable gifts. The marshal is already at Jizhou. Prepare, warrior, to welcome the imperial decree." Pressing his fingers to his brow in a gesture of delight, Song Jiang said: "He is bringing us new life!" He begged Zhang to dine with him. "I'd love to," said the prefect, "but the marshal would be annoyed if I were slow in getting back." "At least have a drink, and accept these paltry things—I can hardly call them gifts." Song Jiang presented gold and silver on a platter. "I wouldn't dare." "A mere trifle, why refuse? Not nearly enough to express our thanks, but do take them as a small token of appreciation. Once the mission is completed, we shall offer something more substantial." "I'm deeply grateful for your good intentions. But please keep them here, for now. I can always call for them later." Prefect Zhang was absolutely incorruptible. He made strict demands upon himself. Song Jiang directed his generals Wu Yong and Zhu Wu, plus Xiao Rang and Yue Ho, to escort Prefect Zhang to Jizhou, and there see Marshal Su. On the day after the morrow all chieftains, big and small, would wait to greet the emissary thirty li from the fortress. Wu Yong and the others travelled through the night to return the prefect to Jizhou, and called on the marshal the next morning at the hostel for officials. They kowtowed and remained kneeling before him. Su directed them to rise and be seated. Deferentially, the four replied they wouldn't dare. The marshal asked their names. "I am called Wu Yong," said the brigand military advisor, "and these are Zhu Wu, Xiao Rang and Yue Ho. We have been sent by brother Song Jiang to welcome Your Excellency." "Why, Master Wu, how nice to see you again! It's been years since last we parted in Huazhou. Who would have thought that we'd meet again today. I am fully aware of the fidelity and righteousness in your hearts. Corrupt ministers have used their authority to conceal the true facts from the emperor. But now he knows, and has dispatched me with his personal amnesty, imperial wine and various gifts. You need have no hesitation about accepting them." The four kowtowed their thanks and said: "It is entirely due to the marshal's kindness that we crude rustics living in a mountain wilderness have the good fortune to meet Your Excellency and receive His Majesty's benevolence! It shall be engraved always on our hearts and bones! We don't know how we can ever repay!"

第八章 《三国演义》

1. 作品介绍

《三国演义》是中国古典四大名著之一，是中国第一部长篇章回体历史演义小说，全名为《三国志通俗演义》（又称《三国志演义》），作者是元末明初的著名小说家罗贯中。《三国志通俗演义》成书后有嘉靖壬午本等多个版本传于世，到了明末清初，毛宗岗对《三国演义》整顿回目、修正文辞、改换诗文。

《三国演义》描写了从东汉末年到西晋初年之间近百年的历史风云，以描写战争为主，诉说了东汉末年的群雄割据混战和魏、蜀、吴三国之间的政治和军事斗争，最终司马炎一统三国，建立晋朝的故事，反映了三国时代各类社会斗争与矛盾的转化，并概括了这一时代的历史巨变，塑造了一群叱咤风云的三国英雄人物形象。

全书可大致分为黄巾起义、董卓之乱、群雄逐鹿、三国鼎立、三国归晋五大部分。在广阔的历史舞台上，上演了一幕幕气势磅礴的战争场面。作者罗贯中将兵法三十六计融于字里行间，既有情节，也有兵法韬略。

《三国演义》反映了丰富的历史内容，人物名称、地理名称、主要事件与《三国志》基本相同。人物性格也是在《三国志》留下的固定形象基础上，进行夸张、美化、丑化等等，这也是历史演义小说的套路。《三国演义》一方面反映了较为真实的三国历史，照顾到读者希望了解真实历史的需要；另一方面，根据明朝社会的实际情况对三国人物进行了夸张、美化、丑化等等。

故事起自汉灵帝年间刘、关、张桃园结义，描述了东汉末年和三国时期近百年发生的重大历史事件和众多叱咤风云的英雄人物。作者通过真实动人的故事，揭示了封建统治阶级内部的黑暗和腐朽，控诉了统治者的暴虐和丑恶。东汉末年，军阀混战，所谓十八路诸侯联军征讨董卓，打的是扶持王室、拯救黎民的旗号，干的是钩心斗角、尔虞我诈的勾当，都企图称王称霸。《三国演义》以没落的汉室宗亲刘备和以宗族起兵的曹操作为两条主线展开了中前期的故事，而中后期以大汉丞相诸葛亮率领汉军北伐，与魏国重臣司马懿的斗智斗勇为主线，以三国归晋而告终。

2. 作者介绍

罗贯中（约 1330 ～约 1400），名本，字贯中，号湖海散人，山西并州太原人，汉族，元末明初著名小说家、戏曲家，中国章回小说的鼻祖，代表作《三国演义》。其他主要作品有小说《隋唐两朝志传》《残唐五代史演义》《三遂平妖传》。《三国志通俗演义》（简称《三国演义》）是罗贯中的力作，这部长篇小说对后世文学创作影响深远。除小说创作外，尚存杂剧《赵太祖龙虎风云会》。

14 岁时母亲病故，于是辍学随父亲去苏州、杭州一带做生意。元朝末年，天下大乱，群雄并起，罗贯中也曾参与其中。“有志图王”的罗贯中在苏州结识施耐庵，两人以师徒相称，一同参加位于平江（即苏州）的张士诚反元起义政权，做过一段时间幕僚后离开。曾与另一位吴王朱元璋为敌，在明朝成立之后，罗贯中放弃读书人步入官场的机会，创作《残唐五代史演义传》《隋唐志传》等著作。

3. 经典赏析

（1）第1回 宴桃园豪杰三结义 斩黄巾英雄首立功

正饮间，见一大汉，推着一辆车子，到店门首歇了；入店坐下，便唤酒保："快斟酒来吃，我待赶入城去投军。"玄德看其人：身长九尺，髯长二尺；面如重枣，唇若涂脂；丹凤眼，卧蚕眉，相貌堂堂，威风凛凛。玄德就邀他同坐，叩其姓名。其人曰："吾姓关，名羽，字长生，后改云长，河东解良人也。因本处势豪倚势凌人，被吾杀了，逃难江湖，五六年矣。今闻此处招军破贼，特来应募。"玄德遂以己志告之，云长大喜。同到张飞庄上，共议大事。

飞曰："吾庄后有一桃园，花开正盛；明日当于园中祭告天地，我三人结为兄弟，协力同心，然后可图大事。"玄德、云长齐声应曰："如此甚好。"

次日，于桃园中，备下乌牛白马祭礼等项，三人焚香再拜而说誓曰："念刘备、关羽、张飞，虽然异姓，既结为兄弟，则同心协力，救困扶危；上报国家，下安黎庶。不求同年同月同日生，只愿同年同月同日死。皇天后土，实鉴此心。背义忘恩，天人共戮！"誓毕，拜玄德为兄，关羽次之，张飞为弟。祭罢天地，复宰牛设酒，聚乡中勇士，得三百余人，就桃园中痛饮一醉。来日收拾军器，但恨无马匹可乘。正思虑间，人报有两个客人，引一伙伴当，赶一群马，投庄上来。玄德曰："此天佑我也！"三人出庄迎接。原来二客乃中山大商：一名张世平，一名苏双，每年往北贩马，近因寇发而回。玄德请二人到庄，置酒管待，诉说欲讨贼安民之意。二客大喜，愿将良马五十匹相送；又赠金银五百两，镔铁一千斤，以资器用。

（2）第5回　发矫诏诸镇应曹公　破关兵三英战吕布

古人曾有篇言语，单道着玄德、关、张三战吕布：

汉朝天数当桓灵，炎炎红日将西倾。
奸臣董卓废少帝，刘协懦弱魂梦惊。
曹操传檄告天下，诸侯奋怒皆兴兵。
议立袁绍作盟主，誓扶王室定太平。
温侯吕布世无比，雄才四海夸英伟。
护躯银铠砌龙鳞，束发金冠簪雉尾。
参差宝带兽平吞，错落锦袍飞凤起。
龙驹跳踏起天风，画戟荧煌射秋水。
出关搦战谁敢当？诸侯胆裂心惶惶。
踊出燕人张翼德，手持蛇矛丈八枪。
虎须倒竖翻金线，环眼圆睁起电光。
酣战未能分胜败，阵前恼起关云长。
青龙宝刀灿霜雪，鹦鹉战袍飞蛱蝶。
马蹄到处鬼神嚎，目前一怒应流血。
枭雄玄德掣双锋，抖擞天威施勇烈。
三人围绕战多时，遮拦架隔无休歇。
喊声震动天地翻，杀气迷漫牛斗寒。
吕布力穷寻走路，遥望家山拍马还。
倒拖画杆方天戟，乱散销金五彩幡。
顿断绒绦走赤兔，翻身飞上虎牢关。

三人直赶吕布到关下，看见关上西风飘动青罗伞盖。张飞大叫："此必董卓！追吕布有甚强处？不如先拿董贼，便是斩草除根！"拍马上关，来擒董卓。正是：擒贼定须擒贼首，奇功端的待奇人。

（3）第8回 王司徒巧使连环计 董太师大闹凤仪亭

董卓自纳貂蝉后，为色所迷，月余不出理事。卓偶染小疾，貂蝉衣不解带，曲意逢迎，卓心意喜。吕布入内问安，正值卓睡。貂蝉于床后探半身望布，以手指心，又以手指董卓，挥泪不止。布心如碎。卓朦胧双目，见布注视床后，目不转睛；回身一看，见貂蝉立于床后。卓大怒，叱布曰："汝敢戏吾爱姬耶！"唤左右逐出，今后不许入堂。吕布怒恨而归，路遇李儒，告知其故。儒急入见卓曰："太师欲取天下，何故以小过见责温侯？倘彼心变，大事去矣。"卓曰："奈何？"儒曰："来朝唤入，赐以金帛，好言慰之，自然无事。"卓依言。次日，使人唤布入堂，慰之曰："吾前日病中，心神恍惚，误言伤汝，汝勿记心。"随赐金十斤，锦二十匹。布谢归，然身虽在卓左右，心实系念貂蝉。

卓疾既愈，入朝议事。布执戟相随，见卓与献帝共谈，便乘间提戟出内门，上马径投相府来；系马府前，提戟入后堂，寻见貂蝉。蝉曰："汝可去后园中凤仪亭边等我。"布提戟径往，立于亭下曲栏之傍。良久，见貂蝉分花拂柳而来，果然如月宫仙子，——泣谓布曰："我虽非王司徒亲女，然待之如已出。自见将军，许侍箕帚。妾已生平愿足。谁想太师起不良之心，将妾淫污，妾恨不即死；止因未与将军一诀，故且忍辱偷生。今幸得见，妾愿毕矣！此身已污，不得复事英雄；愿死于君前，以明妾志！"言讫，手攀曲栏，望荷花池便跳。吕布慌忙抱住，泣曰："我知汝心久矣！只恨不能共语！”貂蝉手扯布曰：“妾今生不能与君为妻，愿相期于来世。”布曰：“我今生不能以汝为妻，非英雄也！”蝉曰：“妾度日如年，愿君怜而救之。”布曰：“我今偷空而来，恐老贼见疑，必当速去。”蝉牵其衣曰：“君如此惧怕老贼，妾身无见天日之期矣！”布立住曰：“容我徐图良策。”语罢，提戟欲去。貂蝉曰：“妾在深闺，闻将军之名，如雷灌耳，以为当世一人而已；谁想反受他人之制乎！”言讫，泪下如雨。布羞惭满面，重复倚戟，回身搂抱貂蝉，用好言安慰。两个偎偎倚倚，不忍相离。

却说董卓在殿上，回头不见吕布，心中怀疑，连忙辞了献帝，登车回府；见布马系于府前；问门吏，吏答曰：“温侯入后堂去了。”卓叱退左右，径入后堂中，寻觅不见；唤貂蝉，蝉亦不见。急问侍妾，侍妾曰：“貂蝉在后园看花。”卓寻入后园，正见吕布和貂蝉在凤仪亭下共语，画戟倚在一边。卓怒，大喝一声。布见卓至，大惊，回身便走。卓抢了画戟，挺着赶来。吕布走得快，卓肥胖赶不上，掷戟刺布。布打戟落地。卓拾戟再赶，布已走远。卓赶出园门，一人飞奔前来，与卓胸膛相撞，卓倒于地。正是：冲天怒气高千丈，仆地肥躯做一堆。

（4）第21回　曹操煮酒论英雄　关公赚城斩车胄

酒至半酣，忽阴云漠漠，骤雨将至。从人遥指天外龙挂，操与玄德凭栏观之。操曰：“使君知龙之变化否？”玄德曰：“未知其详。”操曰：“龙能大能小，能升能隐；大则兴云吐雾，小则隐介藏形；升则飞腾于宇宙之间，隐则潜伏于波涛之内。方今春深，龙乘时变化，犹人得志而纵横四海。龙之为物，可比世之英雄。玄德久历四方，必知当世英雄。请试指言之。”玄德曰：“备肉眼安识英雄？”操曰：“休得过谦。”玄德曰：“备叨恩庇，得仕于朝。天下英雄，实有未知。”操曰：“既不识其面，亦闻其名。”玄德曰：“淮南袁术，兵粮足备，可为英雄?”操笑曰：“冢中枯骨，吾早晚必擒之！”玄德曰：“河北袁绍，四世三公，门多故吏；今虎踞冀州之地，部下能事者极多，可为英雄?“操笑曰：“袁绍色厉胆薄，好谋无断，干大事而惜身，见小利而忘命，非英雄也。”玄德曰：“有一人名称八俊，威镇九州——刘景升可为英雄?”操曰：“刘表虚名无实，非英雄也。”玄德曰：“有一人血气方刚，江东领袖——孙伯符乃英雄也?”操曰：“孙策借父之名，非英雄也。”玄德曰：“益州刘季玉，可为英雄乎?”操曰：“刘璋虽系宗室，乃守户之犬耳，何足为英雄！”玄德曰：“如张绣、张鲁、韩遂等辈皆何如?”操鼓掌大笑曰：“此等碌碌小人，何足挂齿！”玄德曰：“舍此之外，备实不知。”操曰：“夫英雄者，胸怀大志，腹有良谋，有包藏宇宙之机，吞吐天地之志者也。”玄德曰：“谁能当之?”操以手指玄德，后自指，曰：“今天下英雄，惟使君与操耳！”玄德闻言，吃了一惊，手中所执匙箸，不觉落于地下。时正值天雨将至，雷声大作。玄德乃从容俯首拾箸曰：“一震之威，乃至于此。”操笑曰：“丈夫亦畏雷乎?”玄德曰：“圣人迅雷风烈必变，安得不畏?”将闻言失箸缘故，轻轻掩饰过了。操遂不疑玄德。后人有诗赞曰：

勉从虎穴暂趋身，说破英雄惊杀人。巧借闻雷来掩饰，随机应变信如神。

天雨方住，见两个人撞入后园，手提宝剑，突至亭前，左右拦挡不住。操视之，乃关、张二人也。原来二人从城外射箭方回，听得玄德被许褚、张辽请将去了，慌忙来相府打听；闻说在后园，只恐有失，故冲突而入。却见玄德与操对坐饮酒。二人按剑而立。操问二人何来。云长曰："听知丞相和兄饮酒，特来舞剑，以助一笑。"操笑曰："此非鸿门会，安用项庄、项伯乎？"玄德亦笑。操命："取酒与二樊哙压惊。"关、张拜谢。须臾席散，玄德辞操而归。云长曰："险些惊杀我两个！"玄德以落箸事说与关、张。关、张问是何意。玄德曰："吾之学圃，正欲使操知我无大志；不意操竟指我为英雄，我故失惊落箸。又恐操生疑，故借惧雷以掩饰之耳。"关、张曰："兄真高见！"

（5）第37回　司马徽再荐名士　刘玄德三顾草庐

玄德乃辞二人，上马投卧龙冈来。到庄前下马，扣门问童子曰："先生今日在庄否？"童子曰："现在堂上读书。"玄德大喜，遂跟童子而入。至中门，只见门上大书一联云："淡泊以明志，宁静而致远。"玄德正看间，忽闻吟咏之声，乃立于门侧窥之，见草堂之上，一少年拥炉抱膝，歌曰：

凤翱翔于千仞兮，非梧不栖；士伏处于一方兮，非主不依。

乐躬耕于陇亩兮，吾爱吾庐；聊寄傲于琴书兮，以待天时。

玄德待其歌罢，上草堂施礼曰："备久慕先生，无缘拜会。昨因徐元直称荐，敬至仙庄，不遇空回。今特冒风雪而来。得瞻道貌，实为万幸！"那少年慌忙答礼曰："将军莫非刘豫州，欲见家兄否？"玄德惊讶曰："先生又非卧龙耶？"少年曰："某乃卧龙之弟诸葛均也。愚兄弟三人：长兄诸葛瑾，现在江东孙仲谋处为幕宾；孔明乃二家兄。”玄德曰：“卧龙今在家否？”均曰：“昨为崔州平相约，出外闲游去矣。”玄德曰：“何处闲游？”均曰：“或驾小舟游于江湖之中，或访僧道于山岭之上，或寻朋友于村落之间，或乐琴棋于洞府之内：往来莫测，不知去所。”玄德曰：“刘备直如此缘分浅薄，两番不遇大贤！”均曰：“少坐献茶。”张飞曰：“那先生既不在，请哥哥上马。”玄德曰：“我既到此间，如何无一语而回？”因问诸葛均曰：“闻令兄卧龙先生熟谙韬略，日看兵书，可得闻乎？”均曰：“不知。”张飞曰：“问他则甚！风雪甚紧，不如早归。”玄德叱止之。均曰：“家兄不在，不敢久留车骑；容日却来回礼。”玄德曰：“岂敢望先生枉驾。数日之后，备当再至。愿借纸笔作一书，留达令兄，以表刘备殷勤之意。”均遂进文房四宝。玄德呵开冻笔，拂展云笺，写书曰：

> 备久慕高名，两次晋谒，不遇空回，惆怅何似！窃念备汉朝苗裔，滥叨名爵，伏睹朝廷陵替，纲纪崩摧，群雄乱国，恶党欺君，备心胆俱裂。虽有匡济之诚，实乏经纶之策。仰望先生仁慈忠义，慨然展吕望之大才，施子房之鸿略，天下幸甚！社稷幸甚！先此布达，再容斋戒薰沐，特拜尊颜，面倾鄙悃。统希鉴原。

玄德写罢，递与诸葛均收了，拜辞出门。均送出，玄德再三殷勤致意而别。方上马欲行，忽见童子招手篱外，叫曰：“老先生来也。”玄德视之，见小桥之西，一人暖帽遮头，狐裘蔽体，骑着一驴，后随一青衣小童，携一葫芦酒，踏雪而来；转过小桥，口吟诗一首。诗曰：

一夜北风寒，万里彤云厚。
长空雪乱飘，改尽江山旧。
仰面观火虚，疑是玉龙斗。
纷纷鳞甲飞，顷刻遍宇宙。
骑驴过小桥，独叹梅花瘦！

玄德闻歌曰："此真卧龙矣！"滚鞍下马，向前施礼曰："先生冒寒不易！刘备等候久矣！"那人慌忙下驴答礼。诸葛均在后曰："此非卧龙家兄，乃家兄岳父黄承彦也。"玄德曰："适间所吟之句，极其高妙。"承彦曰："老夫在小婿家观《梁父吟》，记得这一篇；适过小桥，偶见篱落间梅花，故感而诵之。不期为尊客所闻。"玄德曰："曾见令婿否？"承彦曰："便是老夫也来看他。"玄德闻言，辞别承彦，上马而归。正值风雪又大，回望卧龙冈，惆怏不已。后人有诗单道玄德风雪访孔明。诗曰：

一天风雪访贤良，不遇空回意感伤。
冻合溪桥山石滑，寒侵鞍马路途长。
当头片片梨花落，扑面纷纷柳絮狂。
回首停鞭遥望处，烂银堆满卧龙冈。

玄德回新野之后，光阴荏苒，又早新春。乃令卜者揲蓍，选择吉期，斋戒三日，薰沐更衣，再往卧龙冈谒孔明。关、张闻之不悦，遂一齐入谏玄德。正是：高贤未服英雄志，屈节偏生杰士疑。

（6）第 40 回　蔡夫人议献荆州　诸葛亮火烧新野

却说曹仁、曹洪引军十万为前队，前面已有许褚引三千铁甲军开路，浩浩荡荡，杀奔新野来。是日午牌时分，来到鹊尾坡，望见坡前一簇人马，尽打青、红旗号，许褚催军向前。刘封、糜芳分为四队，青、红旗各归左右。许褚勒马，教且休进："前面必有伏兵。我兵只在此处住下。"

许褚一骑马飞报前队曹仁。曹仁曰："此是疑兵，必无埋伏。可速进兵。我当催军继至。"许褚复回坡前，提兵杀入。至林下追寻时，不见一人。时日已坠西。许褚方欲前进，只听得山上大吹大擂。抬头看时，只见山顶上一簇旗，旗丛中两把伞盖：左玄德，右孔明，二人对坐饮酒。许褚大怒，引军寻路上山。山上擂木炮石打将下来，不能前进。又闻山后喊声大震。欲寻路厮杀，天色已晚。曹仁领兵到，教且夺新野城歇马。军士至城下时，只见四门大开。曹兵突入，并无阻当，城中亦不见一人，竟是一座空城了。曹洪曰："此是势孤计穷，故尽带百姓逃窜去了。我军权且在城安歇，来日平明进兵。"

此时各军走乏，都已饥饿，皆去夺房造饭。曹仁、曹洪就在衙内安歇。初更已后，狂风大作。守门军士飞报火起。曹仁曰："此必军士造饭不小心，遗漏之火，不可自惊。"说犹未了，接连几次飞报，西、南、北三门皆火起。曹仁急令众将上马时，满县火起，上下通红。是夜之火，更胜前日博望烧屯之火。后人有诗叹曰：

奸雄曹操守中原，九月南征到汉川。
风伯怒临新野县，祝融飞下焰摩天。

曹仁引众将突烟冒火，寻路奔走，闻说东门无火，急急奔出东门。军士自相践踏，死者无数。曹仁等方才脱得火厄，背后一声喊起，赵云引军赶来混战，败军各逃性命，谁肯回身厮杀。正奔走间，糜芳引一军至，又冲杀一阵。曹仁大败，夺路而走，刘封又引一军截杀一阵。到四更时分，人困马乏，军士大半焦头烂额；奔至白河边，喜得河水不甚深，人马都下河吃水，人相喧嚷，马尽嘶鸣。

却说云长在上流用布袋遏住河水，黄昏时分，望见新野火起；至四更，忽听得下流头人喊马嘶，急令军士一齐掣起布袋，水势滔天，望下流冲去，曹军人马俱溺于水中，死者极多。曹仁引众将望水势慢处夺路而走。行到博陵渡口，只听喊声大起，一军拦路，当先大将，乃张飞也，大叫："曹贼快来纳命！"曹军大惊。正是：城内才看红焰吐，水边又遇黑风来。

（7）第46回　用奇谋孔明借箭　献密计黄盖受刑

却说鲁肃私自拨轻快船二十只，各船三十余人，并布幔、束草等物，尽皆齐备，候孔明调用。第一日却不见孔明动静，第二日亦只不动。至第三日四更时分，孔明密请鲁肃到船中。肃问曰："公召我来何意？"孔明曰："特请子敬同往取箭。"肃曰："何处去取？"孔明曰："子敬休问，前去便见。"遂命将二十只船，用长索相连，径望北岸进发。是夜大雾漫天，长江之中，雾气更甚，对面不相见。孔明促舟前进，果然是好大雾！前人有篇《大雾垂江赋》曰：

大哉长江！西接岷峨，南控三吴，北带九河。汇百川而入海，历万古以扬波。至若龙伯、海若，江妃、水母，长鲸千丈，天蜈九首，鬼怪异类，咸集而有。盖夫鬼神之所凭依，英雄之所战守也。

时而阴阳既乱，昧爽不分。讶长空之一色，忽大雾之四屯。虽舆薪而莫睹，惟金鼓之可闻。初若溟濛，才隐南山之豹；渐而充塞，欲迷北海之鲲。然后上接高天，下垂厚地。渺乎苍茫，浩乎无际。鲸鲵出水而腾波，蛟龙潜渊而吐气。又如梅霖收溽，春阴酿寒；溟溟漠漠，浩浩漫漫。东失柴桑之岸，南无夏口之山。战船千艘，俱沉沦于岩壑；渔舟一叶，惊出没于波澜。甚则穹昊无光，朝阳失色；返白昼为昏黄，变丹山为水碧。虽大禹之智，不能测其浅深；离娄之明，焉能辨乎咫尺？

于是冯夷息浪，屏翳收功，鱼鳖遁迹，鸟兽潜踪。隔断蓬莱之岛，暗围阊阖之宫。恍惚奔腾，如骤雨之将至；纷纭杂沓，若寒云之欲同。乃能中隐毒蛇，因之而为瘴疠；内藏妖魅，凭之而为祸害。降疾厄于人间，起风尘于塞外。小民遇之夭伤，大人观之感慨。盖将返元气于洪荒，混天地为大块。

当夜五更时候，船已近曹操水寨。孔明教把船只头西尾东，一带摆开，就船上擂鼓呐喊。鲁肃惊曰："倘曹兵齐出，如之奈何？"孔明笑曰："吾料曹操于重雾中必不敢出。吾等只顾酌酒取乐，待雾散便回。

却说曹寨中听得擂鼓呐喊，毛玠、于禁二人慌忙飞报曹操。操传令曰："重雾迷江，彼军忽至，必有埋伏，切不可轻动。可拨水军弓弩手乱箭射之。"又差人往旱寨内唤张辽、徐晃各带弓弩军三千，火速到江边助射。比及号令到来，毛玠、于禁怕南军抢入水寨，已差弓弩手在寨前放箭；少顷，旱寨内弓弩手亦到，约一万余人，尽皆向江中放箭，箭如雨发。孔明教把船吊回，头东尾西，逼近水寨受箭，一面擂鼓呐喊。待至日高雾散，孔明令收船急回。二十只船两边束草上，排满箭枝。孔明令各船上军士齐声叫曰："谢丞相箭！"比及曹军寨内报知曹操时，这里船轻水急，已放回二十余里，追之不及。曹操懊悔不已。

却说孔明回船谓鲁肃曰："每船上箭约五六千矣。不费江东半分之力，已得十万余箭。明日即将来射曹军，却不甚便？"肃曰："先生真神人也！何以知今日如此大雾？"孔明曰："为将而不通天文，不识地利，不知奇门，不晓阴阳，不看阵图，不明兵势，是庸才也。亮于三日前已算定今日有大雾，因此敢任三日之限。公瑾教我十日完办，工匠料物，都不应手，将这一件风流罪过，明白要杀我。我命系于天，公瑾焉能害我哉！"鲁肃拜服。

船到岸时，周瑜已差五百军在江边等候搬箭。孔明教于船上取之，可得十余万枝，都搬入中军帐交纳。鲁肃人见周瑜，备说孔明取箭之事。瑜大惊，慨然叹曰："孔明神机妙算，吾不如也！"后人有诗赞曰：

一天浓雾满长江，远近难分水渺茫。
骤雨飞蝗来战舰，孔明今日伏周郎。

（8）第75回　关云长刮骨疗毒　吕子明白衣渡江

众将见公不肯退兵，疮又不痊，只得四方访问名医。忽一日，有人从江东驾小舟而来，直至寨前。小校引见关平。平视其人：方巾阔服，臂挽青囊；自言姓名，乃沛国谯郡人，姓华，名佗，字元化。因闻关将军乃天下英雄，今中毒箭，特来医治。平曰："莫非昔日医东吴周泰者乎？"佗曰："然。"平大喜，即与众将同引华佗入帐见关公。时关公本是臂疼，恐慢军心，无可消遗，正与马良弈棋；闻有医者至，即召入。礼毕，赐坐。茶罢，佗请臂视之。公袒下衣袍，伸臂令佗看视。佗曰："此乃弩箭所伤，其中有乌头之药，直透入骨；若不早治，此臂无用矣。"公曰："用何物治之？"佗曰："某自有治法，但恐君侯惧耳。"公笑曰："吾视死如归，有何惧哉？"佗曰："当于静处立一标柱，上钉大环，请君侯将臂穿于环中，以绳系之，然后以被蒙其首。吾用尖刀割开皮肉，直至于骨，刮去骨上箭毒，用药敷之，以线缝其口，方可无事。但恐君侯惧耳。"公笑曰："如此，容易！何用柱环？"令设酒席相待。

公饮数杯酒毕，一面仍与马良弈棋，伸臂令佗割之。佗取尖刀在手，令一小校捧一大盆于臂下接血。佗曰："某便下手，君侯勿惊。"公曰："任汝医治，吾岂比世间俗子惧痛者耶！"佗乃下刀，割开皮肉，直至于骨，骨上已青；佗用刀刮骨，悉悉有声。帐上帐下见者，皆掩面失色。公饮酒食肉，谈笑弈棋，全无痛苦之色。须臾，血流盈盆。佗刮尽其毒，敷上药，以线缝之。公大笑而起，谓众将曰："此臂伸舒如故，并无痛矣。先生真神医也！"佗曰："某为医一生，未尝见此。君侯真天神也！"后人有诗曰：

治病须分内外科，世间妙艺苦无多。
神威罕及惟关将，圣手能医说华佗。

关公箭疮既愈，设席款谢华佗。佗曰："君侯箭疮虽治，然须爱护。切勿怒气伤触。过百日后，平复如旧矣。"关公以金百两酬之。佗曰："某闻君侯高义，特来医治，岂望报乎！"坚辞不受，留药一帖，以敷疮口，辞别而去。

（9）第90回 驱巨兽六破蛮兵 烧藤甲七擒孟获

孔明笑曰："非汝二人之罪。吾未出茅庐之时，先知南蛮有驱虎豹之法。吾在蜀中已办下破此阵之物也：随军有二十辆车，俱封记在此。今日且用一半；留下一半，后有别用。"遂令左右取了十辆红油柜车到帐下，留十辆黑油柜车在后。众皆不知其意。孔明将柜打开，皆是木刻彩画巨兽，俱用五色绒线为毛衣，钢铁为牙爪，一个可骑坐十人。孔明选了精壮军士一千余人，领了一百，口内装烟火之物，藏在军中。次日，孔明驱兵大进，布于洞口。蛮兵探知，入洞报与蛮王。木鹿大王自谓无敌，即与孟获引洞兵而出。孔明纶巾羽扇，身衣道袍，端坐于车上。孟获指曰："车上坐的便是诸葛亮！若擒住此人，大事定矣！"木鹿大王口中念咒，手摇蒂钟。顷刻之间，狂风大作，猛兽突出。孔明将羽扇一摇，其风便回吹彼阵中去了，蜀阵中假兽拥出。蛮洞真兽见蜀阵巨兽口吐火焰，鼻出黑烟，身摇铜铃，张牙舞爪而来，诸恶兽不敢前进，皆奔回蛮洞，反将蛮兵冲倒无数。孔明驱兵大进，鼓角齐鸣，望前追杀。木鹿大王死于乱军之中。洞内孟获宗党，皆弃宫阙，扒山越岭而走。孔明大军占了银坑洞。

次日，孔明正要分兵缉擒孟获，忽报："蛮王孟获妻弟带来洞主，因劝孟获归降，获不从，今将孟获并祝融夫人及宗党数百余人尽皆擒来，献与丞相。"孔明听知，即唤张嶷、马忠，分付如此如此。二将受了计，引二千精壮兵，伏于两廊。孔明即令守门将，俱放进来。带来洞主引刀斧手解孟获等数百人，拜于殿下。孔明大喝曰："与吾擒下！"两廊壮兵齐出，二人捉一人，尽被执缚。孔明大笑曰："量汝些小诡计，如何瞒得过我！汝见二次俱是本洞人擒汝来降，吾不加害；汝只道吾深信，故来诈降，欲就洞中杀吾！"喝令武士搜其身畔，果然各带利刀。孔明问孟获曰："汝原说在汝家擒住，方始心服；今日如何？"获曰："此是我等自来送死，非汝之能也。吾心未服。"孔明曰："吾擒住六番，尚然不服，欲待何时耶？"获曰："汝第七次擒住，吾方倾心归服，誓不反矣。"孔明曰："巢穴已破，吾何虑哉！"令武士尽去其缚，叱之曰："这番擒住，再若支吾，必不轻恕！"孟获等抱头鼠窜而去。

（10）第95回　马谡拒谏失街亭　武侯弹琴退仲达

孔明分拨已定，先引五千兵退去西城县搬运粮草。忽然十余次飞马报到，说："司马懿引大军十五万，望西城蜂拥而来！"时孔明身边别无大将，只有一班文官，所引五千兵，已分一半先运粮草去了，只剩二千五百军在城中。众官听得这个消息，尽皆失色。孔明登城望之，果然尘土冲天，魏兵分两路望西城县杀来。孔明传令，教"将旌旗尽皆隐匿；诸军各守城铺，如有妄行出入，及高言大语者，斩之！大开四门，每一门用二十军士，扮作百姓，洒扫街道。如魏兵到时，不可擅动，吾自有计。"孔明乃披鹤氅，戴纶巾，引二小童携琴一张，于城上敌楼前，凭栏而坐，焚香操琴。

却说司马懿前军哨到城下，见了如此模样，皆不敢进，急报与司马懿。懿笑而不信，遂止住三军，自飞马远远望之。果见孔明坐于城楼之上，笑容可掬，焚香操琴。左有一童子，手捧宝剑；右有一童子，手执麈尾。城门内外，有二十余百姓，低头洒扫，傍若无人，懿看毕大疑，便到中军，教后军作前军，前军作后军，望北山路而退。次子司马昭曰："莫非诸葛亮无军，故作此态？父亲何故便退兵？"懿曰："亮平生谨慎，不曾弄险。今大开城门，必有埋伏。我兵若进，中其计也。汝辈岂知？宜速退。"

于是两路兵尽皆退去。孔明见魏军远去，抚掌而笑。众官无不骇然，乃问孔明曰："司马懿乃魏之名将，今统十五万精兵到此，见了丞相，便速退去，何也？"孔明曰："此人料吾生平谨慎，必不弄险；见如此模样，疑有伏兵，所以退去。吾非行险，盖因不得已而用之。此人必引军投山北小路去也。吾已令兴、苞二人在彼等候。"众皆惊服曰："丞相之机，神鬼莫测。若某等之见，必弃城而走矣。"孔明曰："吾兵止有二千五百，若弃城而走，必不能远遁。得不为司马懿所擒乎？"后人有诗赞曰：

瑶琴三尺胜雄师，诸葛西城退敌时。
十五万人回马处，土人指点到今疑。

言讫，拍手大笑，曰："吾若为司马懿，必不便退也。"遂下令，教西城百姓，随军入汉中；司马懿必将复来。于是孔明离西城望汉中而走。天水、安定、南安三郡官吏军民，陆续而来。

Chapter VIII The Romance of the Three Kingdoms

1. Introduction of the Work

The Romance of the Three Kingdoms is one of the four classic Chinese novels. It was the first long-chapter historical novel in ancient China, with the full title "*Popular Romance of the Three Kingdoms*" (also known as "*The Records of the Three Kingdoms*"), whose writer was Luo Guanzhong, a famous novelist in the late Yuan Dynasty and the early Ming Dynasty. After the completion of *Popular Romance of the Three Kingdoms*, several editions such as the Jiajing Renwu edition were handed down. By the end of the Ming Dynasty and the beginning of the Qing Dynasty, Mao Zonggang rectified *The Romance of the Three Kingdoms*, revised the diction and changed relative poems and proses.

The Romance of the Three Kingdoms describes the history of nearly a hundred years from the end of the Eastern Han Dynasty to the beginning of the Western Jin Dynasty. It mainly talks about the war, and the story of the Great Battles at the end of the East Han Dynasty and the political and military struggles between the States of Wei, Shu and Wu, as well as the story of how SiMa Yan eventually unified the three kingdoms and established the Jin Dynasty. It reflects the transformation of various social struggles and contradictions in the three kingdoms period, summarizes the historical changes of this era, and shapes a group of all-powerful heroes.

The book can be roughly divided into five major parts, including the Yellow Turban Uprising, Dong Zhuo's Rebellion, Struggles for the Deer, the Tripartite Confrontation of the Three Kingdoms, and Jin's Unification of the Three Kingdoms. In the broad historical stage, it shows magnificent scenes of the wars. The author, Luo Guanzhong, combines the thirty-six stratagems of war into the lines, which includes plots and tactics.

The Romance of the Three Kingdoms reflects the rich historical content, the names of characters, geographical names, and the main events are basically the same as *The Records of the Three Kingdoms*. Characters are also developed, exaggerated, beautified, uglified, etc. according to the fixed images left by The Records of the Three Kingdoms, which is a historical novel routine. On the one hand, *The Romance of the Three Kingdoms* reflects the history of the three kingdoms, catering to the needs of readers who want to know true history; on the other hand, according to the actual situation of the Ming Dynasty, the figures of the three kingdoms were exaggerated, beautified, uglified and so on.

The story goes as far as the taking of oaths in a peach garden by Liu, Guan and Zhang during the reign of Emperor Lingdi of the Han Dynasty. It describes the important historical events that took place in the last years of the Eastern Han Dynasty and the nearly one hundred years of the three kingdoms period, as well as numerous all-powerful heroes. The author reveals the darkness and decay of the feudal ruling class through a truly moving story, accusing the rulers of tyranny and ugliness. At the end of the Eastern Han Dynasty, the warlords were fighting with each other, and the so-called 18th-Route, a joint army of princes, was fighting against Dong Zhuo under the name of "supporting the royal family and saving the people". Actually the 18th Route army was engaged in political maneuvers and mind games in an attempt to claim the throne. The story of *The Romance of the Three Kingdoms* begins in the middle and early period with the declining Han clan patriarch Liu Bei and Cao Cao, who started his army from his clan, and in the latter part with the Han Prime Minister Zhuge Liang leading the Han army's northern expedition, the Battle of wits and courage with Sima Yi, an important minister in the State of Wei, and ends with the return of the three kingdoms to the Jin Dynasty.

2. Introduction of the Author

Luo Guanzhong (living around 1330—1400), whose given name was Ben, courtesy name Guanzhong, and pseudonym Hu Hai San Ren, was born in Taiyuan, Bingzhou of Shanxi Province. He was of the Han nationality. He was a famous novelist and dramatist in the late Yuan and early Ming dynasties, and was the founder of the long-chapter historical novel. His masterpiece was *The Romance of the Three Kingdoms*, though he wrote other major works such as *The Biographies of the Sui and Tang Dynasties*, *Historical Romances of the Later Tang and Five Dynasties*, and *Quelling the Demon's Revolt*,

Popular Romance of the Three Kingdoms (or *Romance of the Three Kingdoms* for short) is Luo Guanzhong's masterpiece, and exerts a profound influence on the literature for later generations. In addition to the writing novels, he also created a Zaju "Heroes'Meeting Held by Zhao Taizu". When his mother died of illness at the age of fourteen, he had to drop out of school and went to Suzhou and Hangzhou with his father to do business. At the end of the Yuan Dynasty, the world was in chaos, heroes rose one after another and Luo Guanzhong was one of them. The "Ambitious King" Luo Guanzhong met Shi Naian in Suzhou, to start up mentoring relationship. Both took part in Zhang Shicheng's Anti-Yuan uprising regime as aides and staff for a period of time, once being the enemy of another Emperor Wu, Zhu Yuanzhang. After the founding of the Ming Dynasty, Luo Guanzhong gave up the opportunity to be a scholar and go into official circles, but instead wrote *Historical Romances of the Later Tang and Five Dynasties* and *The Annals of the Sui and Tang Dynasties*.

3. Appreciation

(1)Chapter 1

Three Heroes Swear Brotherhood in the Peach Garden

One Victory Shatters the Rebels in

As they were drinking, a huge, tall fellow appeared pushing a hand-cart along the road. At the threshold he halted and entered the inn to rest awhile and he called for wine.

"And be quick!" added he. "For I am in haste to get into the town and offer myself for the army."

Liu Bei looked over the newcomer, item by item, and he noted the man had a huge frame, a long beard, a vivid face like an apple, and deep red lips. He had eyes like a phoenix's and fine bushy eyebrows like silkworms. His whole appearance was dignified and awe-inspiring. Presently, Liu Bei crossed over, sat down beside him and asked his name.

"I am Guan Yu," replied he. "I am a native of the east side of the river, but I have been a fugitive on the waters for some five years, because I slew a ruffian who, since he was wealthy and powerful, was a bully. I have come to join the army here."

Then Liu Bei told Guan Yu his own intentions, and all three went away to Zhang Fei's farm where they could talk over the grand project.

Said Zhang Fei, "The peach trees in the orchard behind the house are just in full flower. Tomorrow we will institute a sacrifice there and solemnly declare our intention before Heaven and Earth, and we three will swear brotherhood and unity of aims and sentiments: Thus will we enter upon our great task."

Both Liu Bei and Guan Yu gladly agreed.

All three being of one mind, next day they prepared the sacrifices, a black ox, a white horse, and wine for libation. Beneath the smoke of the incense burning on the altar, they bowed their heads and recited this oath:

"We three—Liu Bei, Guan Yu, and Zhang Fei—though of different families, swear brotherhood, and promise mutual help to one end. We will rescue each other in difficulty; we will aid each other in danger. We swear to serve the state and save the people. We ask not the same day of birth, but we seek to die together. May Heaven, the all-ruling, and Earth, the all-producing, read our hearts. If we turn aside from righteousness or forget kindliness, may Heaven and Human smite us!"

They rose from their knees. The two others bowed before Liu Bei as their elder brother, and Zhang Fei was to be the youngest of the trio. This solemn ceremony performed, they slew other oxen and made a feast to which they invited the villagers. Three hundred joined them, and all feasted and drank deep in the Peach Garden.

The next day weapons were mustered. But there were no horses to ride. This was a real grief. But soon they were cheered by the arrival of two horse dealers with a drove of horses.

"Thus does Heaven help us!" said Liu Bei.

And the three brothers went forth to welcome the merchants. They were Zhang Shiping and Su Shuang from Zhongshan. They went northwards every year to buy horses. They were now on their way home because of the Yellow Scarves. The brothers invited them to the farm, where wine was served before them. Then Liu Bei told them of the plan to strive for tranquillity. Zhang Shiping and Su Shuang were glad and at once gave the brothers fifty good steeds, and besides, five hundred ounces of gold and silver and one thousand five hundred pounds of steel fit for the forging of weapons.

(2)Chapter 5

Cao Cao Appeals to the Powerful Lords

The Three Brothers Fight Against Lu Bu

An ancient poet has told of this famous fight in these lines:

The fateful day of Han came in the reigns of Huan and Ling,

Their glory declined as the sun sinks at the close of day.

Dong Zhuo, infamous minister of state, pulled down the youthful Bian.

It is true the new Xian was a weakling, too timid for his times.

Then Cao Cao proclaimed abroad these wicked deeds,

And the great lords, moved with anger, assembled their forces.

In council met they and chose as their oath-chief Yuan Shao,

Pledged themselves to maintain the ruling house and tranquillity.

Of the warriors of that time matchless Lu Bu was the boldest.

His valor and prowess are sung by all within the four seas.

He clothed his body in silver armor like the scales of a dragon,

On his head was a golden headdress with pheasant tails,

About his waist a shaggy belt, the clasp, two wild beasts'heads with gripping jaws,

His flowing, embroidered robe fluttered about his form,

His swift courser bounded over the plain, a mighty wind following,

His terrible trident halberd flashed in the sunlight, bright as a placid lake.

Who dared face him as he rode forth to challenge?

The bowels of the confederate lords were torn with fear and their hearts trembled.

Then leaped forth Zhang Fei, the valiant warrior of the north,
Gripped in his mighty hand the long serpent halberd,
His mustache bristled with anger, standing stiff like wire.
His round eyes glared, lightning flashes darted from them.
Neither quailed in the fight, but the issue was undecided.
Guan Yu stood out in front, his soul vexed within him,
His green-dragon saber shone white as frost in the sunlight,
His bright colored fighting robe fluttered like butterfly wings,
Demons and angels shrieked at the thunder of his horse hoofs,
In his eyes was fierce anger, a fire to be quenched only in blood.
Next Liu Bei joined the battle, gripping his twin sword blades,
The heavens themselves trembled at the majesty of his wrath.
These three closely beset Lu Bu and long drawn out was the battle,
Always he warded their blows, never faltering a moment.
The noise of their shouting rose to the sky, and the earth reechoed it,
The heat of battle ranged to the frozen pole star.
Worn out, feeling his strength fast ebbing, Lu Bu thought to flee,
He glanced at the hills around and thither would fly for shelter,
Then, reversing his halberd and lowering its lofty point,
Hastily he fled, loosing himself from the battle;
With head low bent, he gave the rein to his courser,
Turned his face away and fled to Tiger Trap Pass.

The three brothers maintained the pursuit to the Pass. Looking up they saw an immense umbrella of black gauze fluttering in the west wind.

"Certainly there is Dong Zhuo," cried Zhang Fei. "What is the use of pursuing Lu Bu? Better far seize the chief rebel and so pluck up the evil by the roots!"

And he whipped up his steed toward the Pass.

To quell rebellion seize the leader if you can;

If you need a wondrous service then first find a wondrous man.

(3)Chapter 8

Wang Yun Prepares the Chaining Scheme

Dong Zhuo Rages at Phoenix Pavilion

Dong Zhuo now thought of nothing but his new mistress and for more than a month neglected all affairs, devoting himself entirely to pleasure. Once he was a little indisposed, and Diao Chan was constantly at his side, never even undressing to show her solicitude. She gratified his every whim. Dong Zhuo grew fonder of her.

One day Lu Bu went to inquire after his father's health. Dong Zhuo was asleep, and Diao Chan was sitting at the head of his couch. Leaning forward she gazed at the visitor, with one hand pointed to her heart, the other at Dong Zhuo asleep, and her tears fell. Lu Bu felt heartbroken. Dong Zhuo drowsily opened his eyes; and seeing his son's gaze fixed on something behind him, he turned over and saw who it was.

He angrily rebuked his son, saying, "Dare you make love to my beauty?"

He told the servants to turn Lu Bu out, shouting, "Never let him enter here again!"

Lu Bu went off home very wrath. Meeting Li Ru, he told Li Ru the cause of his anger.

The adviser hastened to see his master and said, “Sir, you aspire to be ruler of the empire. Why then for a small fault do you blame the General? If he turns against you, it is all over.”

“Then what can I do?” said Dong Zhuo.

“Recall him tomorrow; treat him well; overwhelm him with gifts and fair words; and all will be well.”

So Dong Zhuo did so. He sent for Lu Bu and was very gracious and said, “I was irritable and hasty yesterday owing to my illness and I wronged you, I know. Forgive me.”

He gave Lu Bu three hundred ounces of gold and twenty rolls of brocade. And so the quarrel was made up. But though Lu Bu’s body was with his adopted father Dong Zhuo, his heart was with his promised bride Diao Chan.

Dong Zhuo having quite recovered went to court again, and Lu Bu followed him as usual. Seeing Dong Zhuo deep in conversation with the Emperor, Lu Bu, armed as he was, went out of the Palace and rode off to his chief’s residence. He tied up his steed at the entrance and, halberd in hand, went to the private apartment to seek his love. He found Diao Chan, and she told him to go out into the garden where she would join him soon. He went, taking his halberd with him, and he leaned against the rail of the Phoenix Pavilion to wait for Diao Chan.

After a long time she appeared, swaying gracefully as she made her way under the drooping willows and parting the flowers as she passed. She was exquisite, a perfect fairy from the Palace of the Moon.

Tears were in her eyes as she came up and said, “Though I am not the Minister’s real daughter, yet he treated me as his own child. The desire of my life was fulfilled when he plighted me to you. But oh! To think of the wickedness of the Prime Minister, stealing my poor self as he did. I suffered so much. I longed to die, only that I had not told you the real truth. So I lived on, bearing my shame as best as I could but feeling it mean still to live. Now that I have seen you, I can end it all. My poor sullied body is no longer fit to serve a hero. I can die before your eyes and so prove how true I am!"

Thus speaking she seized the curving rail and started into the lily pond. Lu Bu caught her in his strong arms and wept as he held her close.

"I knew it: I always knew your heart," he sobbed. "Only we never had a chance to speak."

She threw her arms about Lu Bu.

"If I cannot be your wife in this life, I will in the ages to come," she whispered.

"If I do not marry you in this life, I am no hero," said he.

"Every day is a year long. O pity me! Rescue me! My lord!"

"I have only stolen away for a brief moment, and I am afraid that old rebel will suspect something, so I must not stay too long," said Lu Bu.

Diao Chan clung to his robe, saying, "If you fear the old thief so much, I shall never see another sunrise."

Lu Bu stopped.

"Give me a little time to think," said he.

And he picked up his halberd to go.

"In the deep seclusion of the harem, I heard the stories of your prowess. You were the one man who excelled all others. Little did I think that you of all heroes would rest content under the dominion of another."

And tears rained again!

A wave of shame flooded his face. Leaning his halberd against the railing, he turned and clasped the girl to his breast, soothing her with fond words. The lovers held each other close, swaying to and fro with emotion. They could not bring themselves to say farewell.

In the meantime Dong Zhuo missed his henchman, and doubt filled his heart. Hastily taking leave of the Emperor, he mounted his chariot and returned to his palace. There at the gate stood Lu Bu's well known steed Red Hare, riderless. Dong Zhuo questioned the doorkeepers, and they told him the General was within. He sent away his attendants and went alone to the private apartments. Lu Bu was not there. He called Diao Chan, but there was no reply. He asked where she was, and the waiting maids told him she was in the garden among the flowers.

So Dong Zhuo went into the garden, and there he saw the lovers in the pavilion in most tender talk. Lu Bu's trident halberd was leaning on the railing beside him.

A howl of rage escaped Dong Zhuo and startled the lovers. Lu Bu turned, saw who it was, and ran away. Dong Zhuo caught up the halberd and ran in pursuit. But Lu Bu was fleet of foot while his master was very stout. Seeing no hope of catching the runaway, Dong Zhuo hurled the halberd. Lu Bu fended it off and it fell to the ground. Dong Zhuo picked it up and ran on. But by this time Lu Bu was far ahead.

Just as Dong Zhuo was running out at the garden gate, he dashed full tilt against another man running in, and down he went.

Surged up his wrath within him as the billows heavenward leap.

Crashed his unwieldy body to earth in a shapeless heap.

(4)Chapter 21

In a Plum Garden, Cao Cao Discusses Heroes

Using the Host's Forces, Guan Yu Takes Xuzhou

As they drank, the weather gradually changed, clouds gathering and threatening rain. The servants pointed out a mass of cloud that looked like a dragon hung in the sky. Both host and guest leaned over the balcony looking at it.

"Do you understand the evolution of dragons?" asked Cao Cao of the guest.

"Not in detail."

"A dragon can assume any size, can rise in glory or hide from sight. Bulky, it generates clouds and evolves mist; attenuated, it can scarcely hide a mustard stalk or conceal a shadow. Mounting, it can soar to the empyrean; subsiding, it lurks in the uttermost depths of the ocean. This is the mid-spring season, and the dragon chooses this moment for its transformations like a person realizing his own desires and overrunning the world. The dragon among animals compares with the hero among people. You, General, have traveled all lakes and rivers. You must know who the heroes of the present day are, and I wish you would say who they are."

"I am just a common dullard. How can I know such things?"

"Do not be so modest," said Cao Cao.

"Thanks to your kindly protection I have a post at court. But as to heroes I really do not know who they are."

"You may not have looked upon their faces, but you must have heard their names."

"Yuan Shu of the South of River Huai, with his strong army and abundant resources: Is he one?" asked Liu Bei.

His host laughed, "A rotting skeleton in a graveyard. I shall put him out of the way shortly."

"Well, Yuan Shao then. The highest offices of state have been held in his family for four generations, and his clients are many in the empire. He is firmly posted in Jizhou, and he commands the services of many able people. Surely he is one."

"A bully, but a coward. He is fond of grandiose schemes, but is devoid of decision. He makes for great things but grudges the necessary sacrifice. He loses sight of everything else in view of a little present advantage. He is not one."

"There is Liu Biao of Jingzhou. He is renowned as a man of perfection, whose fame has spread on all sides. Surely he is a hero."

"He is a mere semblance, a man of vain reputation. No, not he."

"Sun Ce is a sturdy sort, the chief of all in the South Land. Is he a hero?"

"He has profited by the reputation of his father Sun Jian. Sun Ce is not a real hero."

"What of Liu Zhang of Yizhou?"

"Though he is of the reigning family, he is nothing more than a watch dog. How could you make a hero of him?"

"What about Zhang Xiu, Zhang Lu, Han Sui, and all those leaders?"

Cao Cao clapped his hands and laughed very loudly, saying, "Paltry people like them are not worth mentioning."

"With these exceptions I really know none."

"Now heroes are the ones who cherish lofty designs in their bosoms and have plans to achieve them. They have all-embracing schemes, and the whole world is at their mercy."

"Who is such a person?" said Liu Bei.

Cao Cao pointed his finger first at his guest and then at himself, saying, "The only heroes in the world are you and I."

Liu Bei gasped, and the spoon and chopsticks rattled to the floor. Now just at that moment the storm burst with a tremendous peal of thunder and rush of rain.

Liu Bei stooped down to recover the fallen articles, saying, "What a shock! And it was quite close."

"What! Are you afraid of thunder?" said Cao Cao.

Liu Bei replied, "The Sage One paled at a sudden peal of thunder or fierce gust of wind. Why should one not fear?"

Thus he glossed over the real fact, that it was the words he had heard that had so startled him.

Constrained to lodge in a tiger's lair,

He played a waiting part,

But when Cao Cao talked of breaking humans,

Then terror gripped his heart.

But he cleverly used the thunder peal

As excuse for turning pale;

O quick to seize occasions thus!

He surely must prevail.

The shower had passed, and there appeared two men rushing through the garden, both armed. In spite of the attendants, they forced their way to the pavilion where sat the two friends. They were Guan Yu and Zhang Fei.

The two brothers had been outside the city at archery practice when Cao Cao's invitation had come so peremptorily. On their return they heard that two officers had arrived and led away Liu Bei to the Prime Minister. They hastened to his palace and were told their brother was with his host in the grounds, and they feared something had happened. So they rushed in.

Now when they saw their brother quietly talking with Cao Cao and enjoying a cup of wine, they took up their usual places and meekly stood waiting.

"Why did you come?" said Cao Cao.

"We heard that you, Sir, had invited our brother to a wine party, and we came to amuse you with a little sword play," said they.

"This is not a Hongmen Banquet," replied Cao Cao. "What use have we for Xiang Chang and Xiang Ba of old?"

Liu Bei smiled. The host ordered wine to be served to the two "Fan Kuais" to allay their anxiety and, soon after, the three took their leave and returned homeward.

"We were nearly frightened to death," said Guan Yu.

The story of the dropped chopsticks was told. The two asked

what their brother intended by his actions.

"My learning gardening was to convince Cao Cao of my perfect simplicity and the absence of any ambition. But when he suddenly pointed to me as one of the heroes, I was startled, for I thought he had some suspicions. Happily the thunder at that moment supplied the excuse I wanted."

"Really you are very clever," said they.

(5)Chapter 37

Sima Hui Recommends a Scholar to Liu Bei

Liu Bei Pays Three Visits to the Sleeping Dragon Ridge

So he remounted and went his way. He reached the little cottage, dismounted, and tapped at the door. The same lad answered his knock, and he asked whether the Master had returned.

"He is in his room reading," said the boy.

Joyful indeed was Liu Bei as he followed the lad in. In front of the middle door he saw written this pair of scrolls:

By purity inspire the inclination;

By repose affect the distant.

As Liu Bei was looking at this couplet, he heard someone singing in a subdued voice and stopped by the door to peep in. He saw a young man close to a charcoal brazier, hugging his knees while he sang:

"The phoenix dies high, O!

And only will perch on a magnolia tree.

The scholar is hidden, O!

Till his lord appears he can patient be.

He tills his fields, O!

He is well-content and loves his home,

He awaits his day, O!

His books and his lute to leave and roam.

As the song ended Liu Bei advanced and saluted, saying, "Master, long have I yearned for you, but have found it impossible to salute you. Lately Water Mirror spoke of you and I hastened to your dwelling, only to come away disappointed. This time I have braved the elements and come again and my reward is here. I see your face, and I am indeed fortunate."

The young man hastily returned the salute and said, "General, you must be that Liu Bei of Yuzhou who wishes to see my brother."

"Then, Master, you are not Sleeping Dragon!" said Liu Bei, starting back.

"I am his younger brother, Zhuge Jun. He has another elder brother, Zhuge Jin, now with Sun Quan in the South Land as a counselor. Zhuge Liang is the second of our family."

"Is your brother at home?"

"Only yesterday he arranged to go a jaunt with Cui Zhouping."

"Whither have they gone?"

"Who can say? They may take a boat and sail away among the lakes, or go to gossip with the priests in some remote mountain temple, or wander off to visit a friend in some far away village, or be sitting in some cave with a lute or a chessboard. Their goings and comings are uncertain and nobody can guess at them."

"What very poor luck have I! Twice have I failed to meet the great sage."

"Pray sit a few moments, and let me offer you some tea."

"Brother, since the master is not here, I pray you remount and go," said Zhang Fei.

"Since I am here, why not a little talk before we go home again?" said Liu Bei.

Then turning to his host he continued, "Can you tell me if your worthy brother is skilled in strategy and studies works on war?"

"I do not know." Grumbled Zhang Fei, "The wind and snow are getting worse. We ought to go back."

Liu Bei turned on him angrily and told him to stop.

Zhuge Jun said, "Since my brother is absent, I will not presume to detain you longer. I will return your call soon."

"Please do not take that trouble. In a few days I will come again. But if I could borrow paper and ink, I would leave a note to show your worthy brother that I am zealous and earnest."

Zhuge Jun produced the "four treasures" of the scholar, and Liu Bei, thawing out the frozen brush between his lips, spread the sheet of delicate note-paper and wrote:

Liu Bei has long admired your fame. He has visited your dwelling twice, but to his great regret he has gone empty away. He humbly remembers that he is a distant relative of the Emperor, that he has undeservedly enjoyed fame and rank. When he sees the proper government wrested aside and replaced by pretense, the foundation of the state crumbling away, hordes of braves creating confusion in the country, and an evil cabal behaving unseemly toward the rightful Prince, then his heart and gall are torn to shreds. Though he has a real desire to assist, yet is he deficient in the needful skill. Wherefore he turns to the Master, trusting in his kindness, graciousness, loyalty, and righteousness. Would the Master but use his talent, equal to that of Lu Wang, and perform great deeds like Zhang Liang, then would the empire be happy and the throne would be secure.

"This is written to tell you that, after purification of mind with fasting and of body with fragrant baths, Liu Bei will come again to prostrate himself in your honored presence and receive enlightenment."

The letter written and given to Zhuge Jun, Liu Bei took his leave, exceedingly disappointed at this second failure.

As he was mounting, he saw the serving lad waving his hand outside the hedge and heard him call out, "The old Master is coming!"

Liu Bei looked and then saw a figure seated on a donkey leisurely jogging along over a bridge.

The rider of the donkey wore a cap with long flaps down to his shoulders, and his body was wrapped in a fox fur robe. A youth followed him bearing a jar of wine. As he came through the snow he hummed a song:

"This is eve, the sky is overcast,
The north wind comes with icy blast,
Light snowflakes whirl down until
A white pall covers dale and hill.
Perhaps above the topmost sky
White dragons strive for mastery,
The armor scales from their forms riven

Are scattered over the world wind-driven.

Amid the storm there jogs along

A simple wight who croons a song.

'O poor plum trees, the gale doth tear

Your blossoms off and leave you bare.'"

"Here at last is Sleeping Dragon," thought Liu Bei, hastily slipping out of the saddle.

He saluted the donkey rider as he neared and said, "Master, it is hard to make way against this cold wind. I and my companions have been waiting long."

The rider got off his donkey and returned the bow, while Zhuge Jun from behind said, "This is not my brother. It is his father-in-law Huang Chenyan."

Liu Bei said, "I chanced to hear the song you were singing. It is very beautiful."

Huang Chenyan replied, "It is a little poem I read in my son in-law's house, and I recalled it as I crossed the bridge and saw the plum trees in the hedge. And so it happened to catch your ear, Noble Sir."

"Have you seen your son-in-law lately?" asked Liu Bei.

"That is just what I have come to do now."

At this Liu Bei bade him farewell and went on his way. The storm was very grievous to bear, but worse than the storm was the grief in his heart as he looked back at Sleeping Dragon Ridge.

One winter's day through snow and wind

A prince rode forth the sage to find;

Alas! His journey was in vain,

And sadly turned he home again.
The stream stood still beneath the bridge
A sheet of ice draped rock and ridge,
His steed benumbed with biting cold
But crawled as he were stiff and old.
The snowflakes on the rider's head
Were like pear-blossoms newly shed,
Or like the willow-catkins light
They brushed his cheek in headlong flight.
He stayed his steed, he looked around,
The snow lay thick on tree and mound,
The Sleeping Dragon Ridge lay white
A hill of silver, glistening bright.

After the return to Xinye, the time slipped away till spring was near. Then Liu Bei cast lots to find the propitious day for another journey in search of Zhuge Liang. The day being selected, he fasted for three days and then changed his dress ready for the visit. His two brothers viewed the preparations with disapproval and presently made up their minds to remonstrate.

The sage and the fighting generals never agree,
A warrior despises humility.

(6)Chapter 40

Lady Cai Renounces Jingzhou

Zhuge Liang Burns Xinye

Cao Hong and Cao Ren, with their one hundred thousand troops, preceded by Xu Chu leading three thousands of mailed men, marched toward Xinye. They formed a mighty host and reached Magpie Tail Slope about noon. Looking ahead, they saw what a goodly army with many blue and red flags seemed. Xu Chu pressed forward. As he neared, the flags moved from side to side, and he hesitated.

He began to think, "It could be an ambush. It is unwise to advance."

Finally Xu Chu decided to go no farther and called a halt, and he rode back to the main body to see Cao Ren.

"Those troops are only make-believe," said Cao Ren. "Advance, there is no ambush. I will hasten up the supports."

So Xu Chu rode to his own command again and advanced. When he reached the wood where he had seen the flags, he saw no one at all. It was then late in the afternoon but he decided to move on. Then he heard from the hills the sound of musical instruments and, looking up, saw on the hill top two umbrellas surrounded by many banners. There sat Liu Bei and Zhuge Liang quietly drinking.

Angry at their coolness, Xu Chu sought for a way up, but logs of wood and great stones were thrown down, and he was driven back. Further, from the rear of the hills came a confused roar. He could find no way to attack, and the sun began to set.

Then Cao Ren and Cao Hong arrived and ordered an attack on Xinye that he might have a place to rest in. They marched to the walls and found the gates wide open. They entered and found a deserted city. No one was visible.

"This shows they are done," said Cao Hong. "They have all run away, people and all. We may as well occupy the city and rest our soldiers ready for tomorrow."

The soldiers were fatigued with marching and hungry as well, so they lost no time in scattering among the houses and setting about preparing food in the deserted kitchens. The leaders took up their quarters in the state residence to rest.

After the first watch the wind began to blow. Soon after the gate guards reported that a fire had started.

"The careless men have let sparks fly about," said Cao Ren.

He thought no more about it just then, but along came other reports of like nature, and soon he realized that fires breaking out in all quarters were not due to accident. So he gave orders to evacuate the city. Soon the whole city seemed on fire, and a red glow hung in the sky. The army was beset with fire fiercer than what Xiahou Dun had experienced at Bowang Slope.

Thrice wicked was Cao Cao, but he was bold;
Though all in the capital he controlled,
Yet with this he was not content,
So southward his ravaging army went.
But, the autumn wind aiding, the Spirit of Fire
Wrought to his army destruction dire.

Officers and troops dashing through the smoke and fire in utter confusion sought some way of escape, and hearing that the east gate was free, they made for that quarter. Out they rushed pell-mell, many being trodden down and trampled to death. Those who got through took the road to the east.

But presently there was a shouting behind them, and Zhao Yun's company came up and attacked. Then Cao Cao's troops scattered, each fleeing for his life. No stand was made. A little later Mi Fang and Liu Feng came to take another toll. The fleeing Cao Ren then had very few followers, and those left him were scorched and burned.

They directed their way to the White River, joyfully remembering that the river was shallow and fordable. And they went down into the stream and drank their fill, humans shouting and horses neighing.

Meantime Guan Yu, higher up its course, had dammed the river with sandbags so that its waters were collected in a lake. Toward evening he had seen the red glow of the burning city and began to look out for his signal. About the fourth watch, he heard down-stream the sounds of soldiers and horse and at once ordered the breaking of the dam. The water rushed down in a torrent and overwhelmed the men just then in the bed of the river. Many were swept away and drowned. Those who escaped made their way to where the stream ran gently and got away.

Presently Cao Ren and his troops reached the Boling Ferry. Here, where they thought there would be safety, they found the road barred.

"You Cao Cao brigands!" shouted Zhang Fei. "Come and receive your fate!"

Within the city the red flame leaps out;
On the river bank burning anger is met.

(7)Chapter 46

Using Strategy, Zhuge Liang Borrows Arrows

Joining a Ruse, Huang Gai Accepts Punishment

On his side Lu Su quietly prepared a score of light swift boats, each with its crew and the blue screens and bundles of grass complete and, when these were ready, he placed them at Zhuge Liang's disposal.

Zhuge Liang did nothing on the first day, nor on the second. On the third day at the middle of the fourth watch, Zhuge Liang sent a private message asking Lu Su to come to his boat.

"Why have you sent for me, Sir?" asked Lu Su.

"I want you to go with me to get those arrows."

"Whither are you going?"

"Do not ask. You will see."

Then the twenty boats were fastened together by long ropes and moved over to the north bank. The night proved very foggy and the mist was very dense along the river, so that one person could scarcely see another. In spite of the fog, Zhuge Liang urged the boats forward as if into the vast fairy kingdom.

There is a poem on these river fogs:

Mighty indeed is the Great River!

Rising far in the west, in the Emei and Min Mountains,

Plowing its way through Wu, east flowing, resistless,

Swelled by its nine tributary streams, rolling down from the far north,

Aided and helped by a hundred rivulets swirling and foaming,

Ocean receives it at last welcoming, joyful, its waters.

Therein abide sea nymphs and water gods,

Enormous whales a thousand fathoms long,

Nine-headed monstrous beasts, reptiles and octopi,

Demons and uncouth creatures wondrous strange.
In faith it is the home and safe retreat
Of devils and sprites, and wondrous growths,
And eke the battle ground of valiant humans.
At times occur strange strife of elements,
When darkness strives on light's domains that encroach,
Whereat arises in the vaulted dome of blue
White wreaths of fog that toward the center roll.
Then darkness falls, too dense for any torch
Illumine; only clanging sounds can pass.
The fog at first appears, a vaporous wreath
Scarce visible. But thickening fast, it veils
The Southern Hills, the painted leopard's home.
And spreads afar, until the northern sea
Leviathans are amazed and lose their course.
And denser yet it touches on the sky.
And spreads a heavy mantle over the earth.
Then, wide as is the high pitched arch of heaven,
Therein appears no single rift of blue.
Now mighty whales lead up their spouses to sport
Upon the waves, the sinuous dragons dive
Deep down and, breathing, swell the heaving sea,
The earth is moist as with the early rains,
And spring's creative energy is chilled.
Both far and wide and high the damp fog spreads,
Great cities on the eastern bank are hid,

Wide ports and mountains in the south are lost,
Whole fleets of battle ships, a thousand keels,
Hide in the misty depths; frail fishing boats
High riding on a wave are seen—-and lost.
The gloom increases and the domed sky
Grows dark and darker as the sun's light fails.
The daylight dies, dim twilight's reign begins,
The ruddy hills dissolve and lose their hue.
The skill of matchless King Yu would fail to sound
The depth and height; and Li Lou's eye, though keen,
Could never pierce this gloom.
Now is the time, O sea and river gods, to use your powers.
The gliding fish and creeping water folk
Are lost; there is no track for bird or beast.
Fair Penglai Isles are hidden from our sight,
The lofty gates of heaven have disappeared.
Nature is blurred and indistinct, as when
A driving rain storm hurries over the earth.
And then, perhaps, within the heavy haze,
A noisome serpent vents his venom foul
And plagues descend, or impish demons work
Their wicked wills.
Ills fall on humans but do not stay,
Heaven's cleansing breath sweeps them sway,
But while they last the mean ones cry,
The nobler suffer silently.

The greatest turmoil is a sign
Of quick return to state benign.

The little fleet reached Cao Cao's naval camp about the fifth watch, and Zhuge Liang gave orders to form line lying prows west, and then to beat the drums and shout.

"But what shall we do if they attack us?" exclaimed Lu Su.

Zhuge Liang replied with a smile, "I think their fleet will not venture out in this fog. Go on with your wine, and let us be happy. We will go back when the fog lifts."

As soon as the shouting from the river was heard by those in the camp, the two admirals, Mao Jie and Yu Jin, ran off to report to Cao Cao, who said, "Coming up in a fog like this means that they have prepared an ambush for us. Do not go out, but get all the force together and shoot at them."

He also sent orders to the ground camps to dispatch six thousand of archers and crossbowmen to aid the marines.

The naval forces were then lined up shooting on the bank to prevent a landing. Presently the soldiers arrived, and ten thousand and more soldiers were shooting down into the river, where the arrows fell like rain. By and bye Zhuge Liang ordered the boats to turn round so that their prows pointed east and to go closer in so that many arrows might hit them.

Zhuge Liang ordered the drums to be kept beating till the sun was high and the fog began to disperse, when the boats got under way and sailed down-stream. The whole twenty boats were bristling with arrows on both sides.

As they left, Zhuge Liang asked all the crews to shout derisively, "We thank you, Sir Prime Minister, for the arrows!"

They told Cao Cao, but by the time he came, the light boats helped by the swift current were seven miles long down the river and pursuit was impossible. Cao Cao saw that he had been duped and was very sorry, but there was no help for it.

On the way down Zhuge Liang said to his companion, "Every boat must have five or six thousand arrows and so, without the expenditure of an ounce of energy, we must have more than ten myriad arrows, which tomorrow can be shot back again at Cao Cao's army to his great inconvenience."

"You are really superhuman," said Lu Su. "But how did you know there would be a thick fog today?"

"One cannot be a leader without knowing the workings of heaven and the ways of earth. One must understand the secret gates and the interdependence of the elements, the mysteries of tactics and the value of forces. It is but an ordinary talent. I calculated three days ago that there would be a fog today, and so I set the limit at three days. Zhou Yu would give me ten days, but neither artificers nor materials, so that he might find occasion to put me to death as I knew. But my fate lies with the Supreme, and how could Zhou Yu harm me?"

Lu Su could not but agree. When the boats arrived, five hundred soldiers were in readiness on the bank to carry away the arrows. Zhuge Liang bade them go on board the boats, collect them and bear them to the tent of the Commander-in-Chief. Lu Su went to report that the arrows had been obtained and told Zhou Yu by what means.

Zhou Yu was amazed and sighed sadly, saying, "He is better than I. His methods are more than human."

Thick lies the fog on the river,
Nature is shrouded in white,
Distant and near are confounded,
Banks are no longer in sight.
Fast fly the pattering arrows,
Stick in the boats of the fleet.
Now can full tale be delivered,
Zhuge Liang is victor complete.

(8)Chapter 75

Guan Yu Has a Scraped-Bone Surgery

Lu Meng Crosses the River in White Robe

Seeing that their leader would not retire and the wound showed no signs of healing, the various generals inquired far and near for a good surgeon to attend their general.

One day a person arrived in a small ship and, having landed and come up to the gate of the camp, was led in to see Guan Ping. The visitor wore a square-cut cap and a loose robe. In his hand he carried a small black bag.

He said, "My name is Hua Tuo, and I belong to Qiao. I have heard of the wound sustained by the famous general and have come to heal it."

"Surely you must be the physician who treated Zhou Tai in the

South Land," said Guan Ping.

"I am."

Taking with him the other generals, Guan Ping went in to see his father. Guan Yu was engaging in a game of chess with Ma Liang, although his arm was very painful. But Guan Yu kept up appearances so as not to discourage the troops. When they told him that a physician had come, he consented to see him.

Hua Tuo was introduced, asked to take a seat and, after the tea of ceremony, was shown the injured arm.

"This was caused by an arrow," said the doctor. "There is poison in the wound, and it has penetrated to the bone. Unless the wound is soon treated, the arm will become useless."

"What do you propose to do?" asked Guan Yu.

"I know how to cure the wound, but I think you will be afraid of the remedy."

"Am I likely to be afraid of that when I am not even afraid of death? Death is only a return home after all."

Then Hua Tuo said, "This is what I shall do. In a private room I shall erect a post with a steel ring attached. I shall ask you, Sir, to insert your arm in the ring, and I shall bind it firmly to the post. Then I shall cover your head with a quilt so that you cannot see, and with a scalpel I shall open up the flesh right down to the bone. Then I shall scrape away the poison. This done, I shall dress the wound with a certain preparation, sew it up with a thread, and there will be no further trouble. But I think you may quail at the severity of the treatment."

Guan Yu smiled.

"It all sounds easy enough," said he. "But why are the post and the ring?"

Refreshments were then served, and after a few cups of wine, the warrior extended his arm for the operation. With his other hand he went on with his game of chess. Meanwhile the surgeon prepared his knife and called a lad to hold a basin beneath the limb.

"I am just going to cut. Do not start," said Hua Tuo.

"When I consented to undergo the treatment, did you think I was afraid of pain?"

The surgeon then performed the operation as he had predescribed. He found the bone much discolored, but he scraped it clean. When the knife went over the surface of the bone and made horrible sounds, all those near covered their eyes and turned pale. But Guan Yu went on with his game, only drinking a cup of wine now and again, and his face betrayed no sign of pain.

When the wound had been cleansed, sewn up and dressed, the patient stood up smiling and said, "This arm is now as good as it ever was. There is no pain. Indeed, Master, you are a marvel."

"I have spent my life in the art," said Hua Tuo, "but I have never seen such a patient as you, Sir. You are as if not from the earth but heaven."

Here as surgeons, there physicians, all boast their skill;
Bitter few are those that cure one when one's really ill.
As for superhuman valor rivals Guan Yu had none,
So for holy touch in healing Hua Tuo stood alone.

When the cure was well advanced, Guan Yu gave a fine banquet in honor of Hua Tuo and offered him a fee of a hundred ounces of gold.

But Hua Tuo declined it, saying, "I had come to treat you, O General, from admiration of your great virtue and not for money. Although your wound is cured, you must be careful of your health, and especially avoid all excitement for a hundred days, when you will be as well as ever you were."

Then Hua Tuo, having prepared dressings for the wound, took his leave, refusing fees to the very last.

(9)Chapter 90

Chasing Off Wild Beasts, the Prime Minister Defeats the Mangs for the Sixth Time

Burning Rattan Armors, Zhuge Liang Captures Meng Huo the Seventh Time

Zhuge Liang, however, was neither angry nor dejected.

"The fault is not yours," he said. "Long ago, when I was still in my rustic hut, I knew the Mangs possessed certain powers over beasts, and I provided against this adventure before we left Shu. You will find twenty big sealed carts in the baggage train. We will use half of them now."

He bade his staff bring forward ten of the red box-carts; the other ten black carts were left untouched. They all wondered what would happen. Then the carts were opened, and they turned out to be carved and colored models of huge wild beasts, with coats of worsted, teeth and claws of steel; each could accommodate ten people. Choosing one hundred beasts, he told off a thousand troops and bade them stuff the mouths of the beasts full of inflammables.

Next day the army of Shu marched out to the attack and was arrayed at the entrance to the Silver Pit Ravine. The Mang soldiers went into the ravine and told their king. Mu Lu, thinking himself perfectly invincible, did not hesitate, but marched out, taking Meng Huo with him. Zhuge Liang, dressed in the simple robe of a Taoist, went out in his light chariot. In his hand he held a feather fan. Meng Huo, who recognized his enemy, pointed him out to Mu Lu.

"That is Zhuge Liang in that small chariot. If we can only capture him, our task is done."

Then Mu Lu began to mutter his spells and to ring his bell. As before, the wind got up and blew with violence, and the wild beasts came on.

But at a wave of the simple feather fan! The wind turned and blew the other way. Then from out of the host of Shu there burst the horrible wild beasts. The real wild beasts of the Mang saw rushing down upon them huge creatures, whose mouths vomited flames and whose nostrils breathed out black smoke. They came along with jingling bells, snapping and clawing, and the real beasts turned tail and fled in among the host of their own side, trampling them down as they sped. Zhuge Liang gave the signal for a general onset, and his troops rushed forward with beating drums and blaring trumpets. Mu Lu was killed in the melee. Meng Huo's whole clan fled in panic and tore up among the hills out of the way. And thus the Silver Pit Ravine was taken.

Next day, as Zhuge Liang was telling off parties to search for and capture the King, it was announced that the brother-in-law of Meng Huo, Chief Dai Lai, having vainly tried to persuade the King to yield, had made prisoners of him and his wife and all his clan and were bringing them to Zhuge Liang.

Hearing this, Zhang Ni and Ma Zheng were called and received certain orders, upon which they hid themselves in the wings of the tent with a large body of sturdy warriors. This done, Zhuge Liang ordered the keepers to open the gates, and in came Chief Dai Lai with Meng Huo and his people in custody.

As Dai Lai bowed at the entrance of the hall, Zhuge Liang called out, "Let my strong captors appear!"

At once out came the hidden men, and every two of them laid hands upon a prisoner and bound him.

"Did you think your paltry ruse would deceive me?" said Zhuge Liang. "Here you are a second time captured by your own people and brought before me that you might surrender. The first time I did not hurt you. But now I firmly believe this surrender is part of a plot to kill me."

Then he called out to his guards to search the prisoners. They did so, and on every man they found a sharp knife.

"Did you not say that if your family were taken prisoners you would yield? How now?" said Zhuge Liang.

"We have come of our own will and at the risk of our lives. The credit is not yours. Still I refuse to yield," replied Meng Huo.

"This is the sixth time I have captured you, and yet you are obstinate. What do you expect?"

"If you take me a seventh time, then I will turn to you and never rebel again."

"Well, your stronghold is now destroyed. What have I to fear?" said Zhuge Liang.

He ordered the bonds to be loosed, saying, "If you are caught again and lie to me once more, I shall certainly not be inclined to let you off."

Meng Huo and his people put their hands over their heads and ran off like rats.

(10)Chapter 95

Ma Su's Disobedience Causes the Loss of Jieting

Zhuge Liang's Lute Repulses Sima Yi

All these arrangements made, Zhuge Liang took five thousand troops and set out for Xicheng to remove the stores. But messenger after messenger, more than ten of them, came to report, "Sima Yi is advancing rapidly on Xicheng with an army of one hundred fifty thousand troops."

No leader of rank was left to Zhuge Liang. He had only the civil officials and the five thousand soldiers, and as half this force had started to remove the stores, he had only two thousand five hundred left.

His officers were all frightened at the news of near approach of the enemy. Zhuge Liang himself went up on the rampart to look around. He saw clouds of dust rising into the sky. The Wei armies were nearing Xicheng along two roads.

Then he gave orders, "All the banners are to be removed and concealed. If any officer in command of soldiers in the city moves or makes any noise, he will be instantly put to death."

Next he threw open all the gates and set twenty soldiers dressed as ordinary people cleaning the streets at each gate. He told them not to react at the coming of the Wei army, as he had a plan ready for the city defense.

When all these preparations were complete, he donned the simple Taoist dress and, attended by a couple of lads, sat down on the wall by one of the towers with his lute before him and a stick of incense burning.

Sima Yi's scouts came near the city gate and saw all this. They did not enter the city, but went back and reported what they had seen. Sima Yi smiled incredulously. But he halted his army and rode ahead himself. It was exactly as the scouts had reported: Zhuge Liang sat there, his face with all smiles as he played the lute. A lad stood on one side of him bearing a treasured sword and on the other a boy with the ordinary symbol of authority, a yak's tail. Just inside the gates a score of persons with their heads down were sweeping as if no one was about.

Sima Yi hardly believed his eyes and thought this meant some peculiarly subtle ruse. So he went back to his armies, faced them about and moved toward the hills on the north.

"I am certain there are no soldiers behind this foolery," said Sima Zhao. "What do you retire for, Father?"

Sima Yi replied, "Zhuge Liang is always most careful and runs no risks. Those open gates undoubtedly mean an ambush. If our force enters the city, they will fall victims to his guile. How can you know? No; our course is to retire."

Thus were the two armies turned back from the city, much to the joy of Zhuge Liang, who laughed and clapped his hands as he saw them hastening away.

The officials gasped with astonishment, and they asked, "Sima Yi is a famous general of Wei, and he was leading one hundred fifty troops. By what reason did he march off at the sight of you, O Prime Minister?"

Zhuge Liang said, "He knows my reputation for carefulness and that I play not with danger. Seeing things as they were made him suspect an ambush, and so he turned away. I do not run risks, but this time there was no help for it. Now he will meet with Guan Xing and Zhang Bao, whom I sent away into the hills to wait for him."

They were still in the grip of fear, but they praised the depth of insight of their chief and his mysterious schemes and unfathomable plans.

"We should simply have run away," said they.

"What could we have done with two thousand five hundred soldiers even if we had run? We should not have gone far before being caught," said Zhuge Liang.

Quite open lay the city to the foe,
But Zhuge Liang's lute of jasper wonders wrought;
It turned aside the legions'onward march

For both the leaders guessed the other's thought.

"But if I had been in Sima Yi's place, I should not have turned away," said Zhuge Liang, smiling and clapping his hands.

He gave orders that the people of the place should follow the army into Hanzhong, for Sima Yi would assuredly return.

They abandoned Xicheng and returned into Hanzhong. In due course the officials and soldiers and people out of the three counties (Tianshui, Anding and Nanan) also came in.

第九章 《西游记》

1. 作品介绍

《西游记》是中国古代第一部浪漫主义章回体长篇神魔小说。现存明刊百回本《西游记》均无作者署名。清代学者吴玉搢等首先提出《西游记》作者是明代吴承恩。全书主要描写了孙悟空出世及大闹天宫后，遇见了唐僧、猪八戒、沙僧和白龙马，西行取经，一路上历经艰险、降妖伏魔，经历了九九八十一难，终于到达西天见到如来佛祖，最终五圣成真的故事。小说以“唐僧取经”这一历史事件为蓝本，通过作者的艺术加工，深刻地描绘了明代社会现实。《西游记》是中国神魔小说的经典之作，达到了古代长篇浪漫主义小说的巅峰，与《三国演义》《水浒传》《红楼梦》并称为中国古典四大名著。《西游记》自问世以来在民间广为流传，各式各样的版本层出不穷，明代刊本有六种，清代刊本、抄本也有七种，典籍所记已佚版本十三种。鸦片战争以后，《西游记》渐渐传入欧美，被译为英、法、德、意、西、世（世界语）、斯（斯瓦希里语）、俄、捷、罗、波、日、朝、越等语言。

贞观元年（627 年），25 岁的和尚玄奘徒步游学天竺（印度）。他从长安出发后，经阿富汗、巴基斯坦，历尽艰难险阻，最后到达了印度。在那里学习了两年多，于贞观十九年（645 年）玄奘回到了长安，带回佛经 657 部。后来玄奘口述西行见闻，由弟子辩机辑录成《大唐西域记》十二卷。但这部书主要讲述了路上所见各国的历史、地理及交通，没有什么故事。他的弟子慧立、彦琮撰写的《大唐大慈恩寺三藏法师传》，则为玄奘的经历增添了许多传奇色彩。从此，唐僧取经的故事便开始在中国民间广为流传。

2. 作者介绍

吴承恩（约 1500 ～ 1583），字汝忠，号射阳。汉族，淮安府山阳县人。祖籍安徽，以祖先聚居枞阳高甸，故称高甸吴氏。中国明代杰出的小说家，是《西游记》的作者。自幼敏慧，博览群书，尤喜爱神话故事。在科举中屡遭挫折，嘉靖中补贡生。嘉靖四十五年（1566 年）任浙江长兴县丞。由于宦途困顿，晚年绝意仕进，闭门著述。

吴承恩自幼喜欢读稗官野史，熟悉古代神话故事和民间传说。官场的失意，生活的困顿，使他加深了对封建科举制度、黑暗社会现实的认识，促使他运用志怪小说的形式来表达内心的不满和愤懑。他自言："虽然吾书名为志怪，盖不专明鬼，实记人间变异，亦微有鉴戒寓焉。"吴承恩还写过一部短篇小说集《禹鼎志》，不过已经失传，只能看到一篇自序。《西游记》的作者是不是吴承恩，学术界对此一直颇有争论，有学者认为《西游记》的作者不是吴承恩，而是明嘉靖的"青词宰相"李春芳。

吴承恩杰出的长篇神魔小说《西游记》以唐代玄奘和尚赴天竺学习佛教的经历为蓝本，在《大唐西域记》《大唐慈恩寺三藏法师传》等作品的基础上，经过整理、构思最终写定。作品借助神话故事抒发了作者对现实的不满和改变现实的愿望，折射出作者渴望建立"君贤神明"的王道治国的政治理想。小说借助唐僧师徒在取经路上经历的八十一难折射出人间现实社会的种种情况。小说想象大胆，构思新奇，在人物塑造上采用人、神、兽三位一体的塑造方法，创造出孙悟空、猪八戒等不朽的艺术形象。全书组织严密，繁而不乱，语言活泼生动且夹杂方言俗语，富于生活气息。主题上冲淡了故事原有的宗教色彩，大大丰富了作品的现实内容，具有民主倾向和时代特点。作品讽刺幽默，呈现出不同于以往取经故事的独特风格。

3. 经典赏析

（1）第 1 回 灵根育孕源流出 心性修持大道生

那座山，正当顶上，有一块仙石。其石有三丈六尺五寸高，有二丈四尺围圆。三丈六尺五寸高，按周天三百六十五度；二丈四尺围圆，按政历二十四气。上有九窍八孔，按九宫八卦。四面更无树木遮阴，左右倒有芝兰相衬。盖自开辟以来，每受天真地秀，日精月华，感之既久，遂有灵通之意。内育仙胞，一日迸裂，产一石卵，似圆球样大。因见风，化作一个石猴，五官俱备，四肢皆全。便就学爬学走，拜了四方。目运两道金光，射冲斗府。惊动高天上圣大慈仁者玉皇大天尊玄穹高上帝，驾座金阙云宫灵霄宝店，聚集仙卿，见有金光焰焰，即命千里眼、顺风耳开南天门观看。二将果奉旨出门外，看的真，听的明。须臾回报道："臣奉旨观听金光之处，乃东胜神洲海东傲来小国之界，有一座花果山，山上有一仙石，石产一卵，见风化一石猴，在那里拜四方，眼运金光，射冲斗府。如今服饵水食，金光将潜息矣。"玉帝垂赐恩慈曰："下方之物，乃天地精华所生，不足为异。"

那猴在山中，却会行走跳跃，食草木，饮涧泉，采山花，觅树果；与狼虫为伴，虎豹为群，獐鹿为友，猕猿为亲；夜宿石崖之下，朝游峰洞之中。真是“山中无甲子，寒尽不知年”。一朝天气炎热，与群猴避暑，都在松阴之下顽耍。你看他一个个：跳树攀枝，采花觅果；抛弹子，邷么儿；跑沙窝，砌宝塔；赶蜻蜓，扑八蜡；参老天，拜菩萨；扯葛藤，编草帓；捉虱子，咬又掐；理毛衣，剔指甲；挨的挨，擦的擦；推的推，压的压；扯的扯，拉的拉，青松林下任他顽，绿水涧边随洗濯。一群猴子耍了一会儿，却去那山涧中洗澡。见那股涧水奔流，真个似滚瓜涌溅。古云：“禽有禽言，兽有兽语。”众猴都道：“这股水不知是那里的水。我们今日赶闲无事，顺涧边往上溜头，寻看源流，耍子去耶！”喊一声，都拖男挈女，呼弟呼兄，一齐跑来，顺涧爬山，直至源流之处，乃是一股瀑布飞泉。但见那：

一派白虹起，千寻雪浪飞；海风吹不断，江月照还依。
冷气分青嶂，馀流润翠微；潺湲名瀑布，真似挂帘帷。

众猴拍手称扬道：“好水！好水！原来此处远通山脚之下，直接大海之波。”又道：“那一个有本事的，钻进去寻个源头出来，不伤身体者，我等即拜他为王。”连呼了三声，忽见丛杂中跳出一名石猴，应声高叫道：“我进去！我进去！”好猴！也是他：今日芳名显，时来大运通；有缘居此地，王遣入仙宫。

你看他瞑目蹲身，将身一纵，径跳入瀑布泉中，忽睁眼抬头观看，那里边却无水无波，明明朗朗的一架桥梁。他住了身，定了神，仔细再看，原来是座铁板桥。桥下之水，冲贯于石窍之间，倒挂流出去，遮闭了桥门。却又欠身上桥头，再走再看，却似有人家住处一般，真个好所在。但见那：

翠藓堆蓝，白云浮玉，光摇片片烟霞。虚窗静室，滑凳板生花。乳窟龙珠倚挂，萦回满地奇葩。锅灶傍崖存火迹，樽罍靠案见肴渣。石座石床 真可爱，石盆石碗更堪夸。又见那一竿两竿修竹，三点五点梅花。几树青松常带雨，浑然像个人家。

（2）第5回 乱蟠桃大圣偷丹 反天宫诸神捉怪

好大圣，捻着诀，念声咒语，对众仙女道："住！"这原来是个定身法，把那七衣仙女一个个——睁睁，白着眼，都站在桃树之下。大圣纵朵祥云，跳出园内，竟奔瑶池路上而去。正行时，只见那壁厢：

一天瑞霭光摇曳，五色祥云飞不绝。白鹤声鸣振九皋，紫芝色秀分千叶。中间现出一尊仙，相貌天然丰采别。神舞虹霓幌汉霄，腰悬宝录无生灭。名称赤脚大罗仙，特赴蟠桃添寿节。

那赤脚大仙觌面撞见大圣，大圣低头定计，赚哄真仙，他要暗去赴会，却问："老道何往？"大仙道："蒙王母见招，去赴蟠桃嘉会。"大圣道："老道不知。玉帝因老孙筋斗云疾，着老孙五路邀请列位，先至通明殿下演礼，后方去赴宴。"大仙是个光明正大之人，就以他的诳语作真，道："常年就在瑶池演礼谢恩，如何先去通明殿演礼，方去瑶池赴会？"无奈，只得拨转祥云，径往通明殿去了。

大圣驾着云，念声咒语，摇身一变，就变做赤脚大仙模样，前奔瑶池。不多时，直至宝阁，按住云头，轻轻移步，走入里面。只见那里：

琼香缭绕，瑞霭缤纷。瑶台铺彩结，宝阁散氤氲。凤翥鸾腾形缥缈，金花玉萼影浮沉。上排着九凤丹霞扆，八宝紫霓墩，五彩描金桌，千花碧玉盆。桌上有龙肝和凤髓，熊掌与猩唇。珍馐百味般般美，异果嘉肴色色新。

那里铺设得齐齐整整，却还未有仙来。这大圣点看不尽，忽闻得一阵酒香扑鼻。忽转头，见右壁厢长廊之下，有几个造酒的仙官，盘糟的力士，领几个运水的道人，烧火的童子，在那里洗缸刷瓮，已造成了玉液琼浆，香醪佳酿。大圣止不住口角流涎，就要去吃，奈何那些人都在这里。他就弄个神通，把毫毛拔下几根，丢入口中嚼碎，喷将出去，念声咒语，叫"变！"即变做几个瞌睡虫，奔在众人脸上。你看那伙人，手软头低，闭眉合眼，丢了执事，都去盹睡。大圣却拿了些百味八珍，佳肴异品，走入长廊里面，就着缸，挨着瓮，放开量，痛饮一番。吃勾了多时，酕醄醉了。自揣自摸道："不好！不好！再过会，请的客来，却不怪我？一时拿住，怎生是好？不如早回府中睡去也。"

好大圣，摇摇摆摆，仗着酒，任情乱撞，一会把路差了；不是齐天府，却是兜率天宫。一见了，顿然醒悟道："兜率宫是三十三天之上，乃离恨天太上老君之处，如何错到此间？——也罢！也罢！一向要来望此老，不曾得来，今趁此残步，就望他一望也好。"即整衣撞进去，那里不见老君，四无人迹。原来那老君与燃灯古佛在三层高阁朱陵丹台上讲道，众仙童、仙将、仙官、仙吏都侍立左右听讲。这大圣直至丹房里面，寻访不遇，但见丹灶之旁，炉中有火，炉左右安放着五个葫芦，葫芦里都是炼就的金丹。大圣喜道："此物乃仙家之至宝，老孙自了道以来，识破了内外相同之理，也要些金丹济入，不期到家无暇。今日有缘，却又撞着此物，趁老子不在，等我吃他几丸尝新。"他就把那葫芦都倾出来，就都吃了，如吃炒豆相似。一时间丹满酒醒，又自己揣度道："不好！不好！这场祸，比天还大；若惊动玉帝，性命难存。走！走！走！不如下界为王去也！"

他就跑出兜率宫，不行旧路，从西天门，使个隐身法逃去。即按云头，回至花果山界。但见那旌旗闪灼，戈戟光辉，原来是四健将与七十二洞妖王，在那里演习武艺。大圣高叫道："小的们！我来也！"众怪丢了器械，跪倒道："大圣好宽心！丢下我等许久，不来相顾！"大圣道："没多时！没多时！"且说且行，径入洞天深处。四健将打扫安歇，叩头礼拜毕，俱道："大圣在天这百十年，实受何职？"大圣笑道："我记得才半年光景，怎么就说百十年话？"健将道："在天一日，即在下方一年也。"大圣道："且喜这番玉帝相爱，果封做'齐天大圣'。起一座齐天府，又设安静、宁神二司，司设仙吏侍卫。向后见我无事，着我看管蟠桃园。近因王母娘娘设蟠桃大会，未曾请我，是我不待他请，先赴瑶池，把他那仙品、仙酒，都是我偷吃了。走出瑶池，踉踉跄跄误入老君宫阙，又把他五个葫芦金丹也偷吃了。但恐玉帝见罪，方才走出天门来也。"

众怪闻言大喜。即安排酒果接风，将椰酒满斟一石碗奉上，大圣喝了一口，即咨牙俫嘴道："不好吃！不好吃！"崩、巴二将道："大圣在天宫，吃了仙酒、仙肴，是以椰酒不甚美口。常言道：'美不美，乡中水。'"大圣道："你们就是'亲不亲，故乡人'。我今早在瑶池中受用时，见那长廊之下，有许多瓶罐，都是那玉液琼浆。你们都不曾尝着。待我再去偷他几瓶回来，你们各饮半杯，一个个也长生不老。”众猴欢喜不胜。大圣即出洞门，又翻一筋斗，使个隐身法，径至蟠桃会上。进瑶池宫阙，只见那几个造酒、盘糟、运水、烧火的，还鼾睡未醒。他将大的从左右胁下挟了两个，两手提了两个，即拨转云头回来，会众猴在于洞中，就做个仙酒会，各饮了几杯，快乐不题。

（3）第16回　观音院僧谋宝贝　黑风山怪窃袈裟

不期火起之时，惊动了一山兽怪。这观音院正南二十里远近，有座黑风山，山中有一个黑风洞，洞中有一个妖精，正在睡醒翻身，只见那窗门透亮，只道是天明。起来看时，却是正北下的火光晃亮，妖精大惊道：“呀！这必是观音院里失了火！这些和尚好不小心！我看时与他救一救来。”好妖精，纵起云头，即至烟火之下，果然冲天之火，前面殿宇皆空，两廊烟火方灼。他大拽步，撞将进去，正呼唤叫取水来，只见那后房无火，房脊上有一人放风。他却情知如此，急入里面看时，见那方丈中间有些霞光彩气，台案上有一个青毡包袱。他解开一看，见是一领锦襕袈裟，乃佛门之异宝。正是财动人心，他也不救火，他也不叫水，拿着那袈裟，趁哄打劫，拽回云步，径转东山而去。

那场火只烧到五更天明，方才灭息。你看那众僧们，赤赤精精，啼啼哭哭，都去那灰内寻铜铁，拨腐炭，扑金银。有的在墙筐里，苫搭窝棚；有的赤壁根头，支锅造饭。叫冤叫屈，乱嚷乱闹不题。

却说行者取了辟火罩，一筋斗送上南天门，交与广目天王道：“谢借！谢借！”天王收了道：“大圣至诚了。我正愁你不还我的宝贝，无处寻讨，且喜就送来也。”行者道：“老孙可是那当面骗物之人？这叫做好借好还，再借不难。”天王道：“许久不面，请到宫少坐一时何如？”行者道：“老孙比在前不同，烂板凳高谈阔论了；如今保唐僧，不得身闲。容叙！容叙！”急辞别坠云，又见那太阳星上，径来到禅堂前，摇身一变，变做个蜜蜂儿，飞将进去，现了本象，看时那师父还沉睡哩。行者叫道：“师父，天亮了，起来罢。”三藏才醒觉，翻身道：“正是。”穿了衣服，开门出来，忽抬头只见些倒壁红墙，不见了楼台殿宇，大惊道：“呀！怎么这殿宇俱无？都是红墙，何也？”行者道：“你还做梦哩！今夜走了火的。”三藏道：“我怎不知？”行者道：“是老孙护了禅堂，见师父浓睡，不曾惊动。”三藏道：“你有本事护了禅堂，如何就不救别房之火？”行者笑道：“好教师父得知，果然依你昨日之言，他爱上我们的袈裟，算计要烧杀我们。若不是老孙知觉，到如今皆成灰骨矣！”三藏闻言，害怕道：“是他们放的火么？”行者道：“不是他是谁？”三藏道：“莫不是怠慢了你，你干的这个勾当？”行者道：“老孙是这等惫懒之人，干这等不良之事？实实是他家放的。老孙见他心毒，果是不曾与他救火，只是与他略略助些风的。”三藏道：“天那！天那！火起时，只该助水，怎转助风？”行者道：“你可知古人云，人没伤虎心，虎没伤人意。他不弄火，我怎肯弄风？”三藏道：“袈裟何在？敢莫是烧坏了也？”行者道：“没事！没事！烧不坏！那放袈裟的方丈无火。”三藏恨道：“我不管你！但是有些儿伤损，我只把那话儿念动念动，你就是死了！”行者慌了道：“师父，莫念！莫念！管寻还你袈裟就是了。等我去拿来走路。”三藏才牵着马，行者挑了担，出了禅堂，径往后方丈去。

（4）第 18 回　观音院唐僧脱难　高老庄行者降魔

行者却弄神通，摇身一变，变得就如那女子一般，独自个坐在房里等那妖精。不多时，一阵风来，真个是走石飞砂。好风：

起初时微微荡荡，向后来渺渺茫茫。
微微荡荡乾坤大，渺渺茫茫无阻碍。
凋花折柳胜摁麻，倒树摧林如拔菜。
翻江搅海鬼神愁，裂石崩山天地怪。
衔花麋鹿失来踪，摘果猿猴迷在外。
七层铁塔侵佛头，八面幢幡伤宝盖。
金梁玉柱起根摇，房上瓦飞如燕块。
举棹梢公许愿心，开船忙把猪羊赛。
当坊土地弃祠堂，四海龙王朝上拜。
海边撞损夜叉船，长城刮倒半边塞。

那阵狂风过处，只见半空里来了一个妖精，果然生得丑陋：黑脸短毛，长喙大耳，穿一领青不青、蓝不蓝的梭布直裰，系一条花布手巾。行者暗笑道："原来是这个买卖！"好行者，却不迎他，也不问他，且睡在床上推病，口里哼哼啧啧的不绝。那怪不识真假，走进房，一把搂住，就要亲嘴。行者暗笑道："真个要来弄老孙哩！"即使个拿法，托着那怪的长嘴，叫做个小跌。漫头一料，扑的掼下床来。那怪爬起来，扶着床边道："姐姐，你怎么今日有些怪我？想是我来得迟了？"行者道："不怪！不怪！"那妖道："既不怪我，怎么就丢我这一跌？"行者道："你怎么就这等样小家子，就搂我亲嘴？我因今日有些不自在，若每常好时，便起来开门等你了。你可脱了衣服睡是。"那怪不解其意，真个就去脱衣。行者跳起来，坐在净桶上。那怪依旧复来床上摸一把，摸不着人，叫道："姐姐，你往那里去了？请脱衣服睡罢。”行者道：“你先睡，等我出个恭来。”那怪果先解衣上床。行者忽然叹口气，道声：“造化低了！”那怪道：“你恼怎的？造化怎么得低的？我得到了你家，虽是吃了些茶饭，却也不曾白吃你的：我也曾替你家扫地通沟，搬砖运瓦，筑土打墙，耕田耙地，种麦插秧，创家立业。如今你身上穿的锦，戴的金，四时有花果享用，八节有蔬菜烹煎，你还有那些儿不趁心处，这般短叹长吁，说甚么造化低了？”行者道：“不是这等说。今日我的父母，隔着墙，丢砖料瓦的，甚是打我骂我哩。”那怪道：“他打骂你怎的？”行者道：“他说我和你做了夫妻，你是他门下一个女婿，全没些儿礼体。这样个丑嘴脸的人，又会不得姨夫，又见不得亲戚，又不知你云来雾去，端的是那里人家，姓甚名谁，败坏他清德，玷辱他门风，故此这般打骂，所以烦恼。”那怪道：“我虽是有些儿丑陋，若要俊，却也不难。我一来时，曾与他讲过，他愿意方才招我，今日怎么又说起这话！我家住在福陵山云栈洞。我以相貌为姓，故姓猪，官名叫做猪刚鬣。他若再来问你，你就以此话与他说便了。”

行者暗喜道：“那怪却也老实，不用动刑，就供得这等明白。既有了地方、姓名，不管怎的也拿住他。”行者道：“他要请法师来拿你哩。”那怪笑道：“睡着！睡着！莫睬他！我有天罡数的变化，九齿的钉钯，怕甚么法师、和尚、道士？就是你老子有虔心，请下九天荡魔祖师下界，我也曾与他做过相识，他也不敢怎的我。”行者道：“他说请一个五百年前大闹天宫姓孙的齐天大圣，要来拿你哩。”那怪闻得这个名头，就有三分害怕道：“既是这等说，我去了罢，两口子做不成了。”行者道：“你怎的就去？”那怪道：“你不知道，那闹天宫的弼马温，有些本事，只恐我弄他不过，低了名头，不像模样。”他套上衣服，开了门，往外就走，被行者一把扯住，将自己脸上抹了一抹，现出原身，喝道："好妖怪，那里走！你抬头看看我是那个？"那怪转过眼来，看见行者咨牙俫嘴，火眼金睛，磕头毛脸，就是个活雷公相似，慌得他手麻脚软，划刺的一声，挣破了衣服，化狂风脱身而去。行者急上前，掣铁棒，望风打了一下。那怪化万道火光，径转本山而去。行者驾云，随后赶来，叫声："那里走！你若上天，我就赶到斗牛宫！你若入地，我就追至枉死狱！"

（5）第27回　尸魔三戏唐三藏　圣僧恨逐美猴王

却说那妖精，原来行者第二棍也不曾打杀他。那怪物在半空中，夸奖不尽道："好个猴王，着然有眼！我那般变了去，他也还认得我。这些和尚，他去得快，若过此山，西下四十里，就不伏我所管了。若是被别处妖魔捞了去，好道就笑破他人口，使碎自家心。我还下去戏他一戏。"好妖怪，按耸阴风，在山坡下摇身一变，变成一个老公公，真个是：

白发如彭祖，苍髯赛寿星。
耳中鸣玉磬，眼里幌金星。
手拄龙头拐，身穿鹤氅轻。
数珠掐在手，口诵南无经。

唐僧在马上见了，心中欢喜道："阿弥陀佛！西方真是福地！那公公路也走不上来，逼法的还念经哩。"八戒道："师父，你且莫要夸奖，那个是祸的根哩。"唐僧道："怎么是祸根？"八戒道："行者打杀他的女儿，又打杀他的婆子，这个正是他的老儿寻将来了。我们若撞在他的怀里呵，师父，你便偿命，该个死罪；把老猪为从，问个充军；沙僧喝令，问个摆站；那行者使个遁法走了，却不苦了我们三个顶缸？”

行者听见道：“这个呆根，这等胡说，可不唬了师父？等老孙再去看看。”他把棍藏在身边，走上前迎着怪物，叫声：“老官儿，往那里去？怎么又走路，又念经？”那妖精错认了定盘星，把孙大圣也当做个等闲的，遂答道：“长老啊，我老汉祖居此地，一生好善斋僧，看经念佛。命里无儿，止生得一个小女，招了个女婿。今早送饭下田，想是遭逢虎口。老妻先来找寻，也不见回去，全然不知下落，老汉特来寻看。果然是伤残他命，也没奈何，将他骸骨收拾回去，安葬茔中。”行者笑道：“我是个做吓虎的祖宗，你怎么袖子里笼了个鬼儿来哄我？你瞒了诸人，瞒不过我！我认得你是个妖精！”那妖精唬得顿口无言。行者掣出棒来，自忖思道：“若要不打他，显得他倒弄个风儿；若要打他，又怕师父念那话儿咒语。”又思量道：“不打杀他，他一时间抄空儿把师父捞了去，却不又费心劳力去救他？还打的是！就一棍子打杀他，师父念起那咒，常言道，虎毒不吃儿。凭着我巧言花语，嘴伶舌便，哄他一哄，好道也罢了。”好大圣，念动咒语，叫当坊土地、本处山神道：“这妖精三番来戏弄我师父，这一番却要打杀他。你与我在半空中作证，不许走了。”众神听令，谁敢不从？都在云端里照应。那大圣棍起处，打倒妖魔，才断绝了灵光。

那唐僧在马上，又唬得战战兢兢，口不能言。八戒在旁边又笑道：“好行者！风发了！只行了半日路，倒打死三个人！”唐僧正要念咒，行者急到马前，叫道：“师父，莫念！莫念！你且来看看他的模样。”却是一堆粉骷髅在那里。唐僧大惊道：“悟空，这个人才死了，怎么就化作一堆骷髅？”行者道：“他是个潜灵作怪的僵尸，在此迷人败本，被我打杀，他就现了本相。他那脊梁上有一行字，叫做白骨夫人。”唐僧闻说，倒也信了，怎禁那八戒旁边唆嘴道：“师父，他的手重棍凶，把人打死，只怕你念那话儿，故意变化这个模样，掩你的眼目哩！”唐僧果然耳软，又信了他，随复念起。行者禁不得疼痛，跪于路旁，只叫：“莫念！莫念！有话快说了罢！”唐僧道：“猴头！还有甚说话！出家人行善，如春园之草，不见其长，日有所增；行恶之人，如磨刀之石，不见其损，日有所亏。你在这荒郊野外，一连打死三人，还是无人检举，没有对头；倘到城市之中，人烟凑集之所，你拿了那哭丧棒，一时不知好歹，乱打起人来，撞出大祸，教我怎的脱身？你回去罢！”行者道：“师父错怪了我也。这厮分明是个妖魔，他实有心害你。我倒打死他，替你除了害，你却不认得，反信了那呆子谗言冷语，屡次逐我。常言道，事不过三。我若不去，真是个下流无耻之徒。我去！我去！去便去了，只是你手下无人。”唐僧发怒道：“这泼猴越发无礼！看起来，只你是人，那悟能、悟净就不是人？”

那大圣一闻得说他两个是人，止不住伤情凄惨，对唐僧道声：“苦啊！你那时节，出了长安，有刘伯钦送你上路；到两界山，救我出来，投拜你为师，我曾穿古洞，入深林，擒魔捉怪，收八戒，得沙僧，吃尽千辛万苦。今日昧着惺惺使糊涂，只教我回去：这才是鸟尽弓藏，兔死狗烹！罢！罢！罢！但只是多了那《紧箍儿咒》。”唐僧道：“我再不念了。”行者道：“这个难说。若到那毒魔苦难处不得脱身，八戒、沙僧救不得你，那时节，想起我来，忍不住又念诵起来，就是十万里路，我的头也是疼的；假如再来见你，不如不作此意。”

唐僧见他言言语语，越添恼怒，滚鞍下马来，叫沙僧包袱内取出纸笔，即于涧下取水，石上磨墨，写了一纸贬书，递于行者道："猴头！执此为照，再不要你做徒弟了！如再与你相见，我就堕了阿鼻地狱！"行者连忙接了贬书道："师父，不消发誓，老孙去罢。"他将书摺了，留在袖中，却又软款唐僧道："师父，我也是跟你一场，又蒙菩萨指教，今日半途而废，不曾成得功果，你请坐，受我一拜，我也去得放心。"唐僧转回身不睬，口里唧唧哝哝的道："我是个好和尚，不受你歹人的礼！"大圣见他不睬，又使个身外法，把脑后毫毛拔了三根，吹口仙气，叫"变！"即变了三个行者，连本身四个，四面围住师父下拜。那长老左右躲不脱，好道也受了一拜。

大圣跳起来，把身一抖，收上毫毛，却又吩咐沙僧道："贤弟，你是个好人，却只要留心防着八戒诂言诂语，途中更要仔细。倘一时有妖精拿住师父，你就说老孙是他大徒弟。西方毛怪，闻我的手段，不敢伤我师父。"唐僧道："我是个好和尚，不题你这歹人的名字。你回去罢。"那大圣见长老三番两复，不肯转意回心，没奈何才去。你看他：

噙泪叩头辞长老，含悲留意嘱沙僧。
一头拭迸坡前草，两脚蹬翻地上藤。
上天下地如轮转，跨海飞山第一能。
顷刻之间不见影，霎时疾返旧途程。

你看他忍气别了师父，纵筋斗云，径回花果山水帘洞去了。独自个凄凄惨惨，忽闻得水声聒耳，大圣在那半空里看时，原来是东洋大海潮发的声响。一见了，又想起唐僧，止不住腮边泪坠，停云住步，良久方去。

（6）第42回 大圣殷勤拜南海 观音慈善缚红孩

顷刻间，早见一座山头。行者道："这山就是号山了。从此处到那妖精门首，约摸有四百余里。"菩萨闻言，即命住下祥云，在那山头上念一声"唵"字咒语，只见那山左山右走出许多神鬼，却乃是本山土地众神，都到菩萨宝莲座下磕头。菩萨道："汝等俱莫惊张，我今来擒此魔王。你与我把这团围打扫干净，要三百里远近地方，不许一个生灵在地。将那窝中小兽，窟内雏虫，都送在巅峰之上安生。"众神遵依而退。须臾间，又来回复，菩萨道："既然干净，俱各回祠。"遂把净瓶扳倒，唿喇喇倾出水来，就如雷响。真个是：

漫过山头，冲开石壁。漫过山头如海势，冲开石壁似汪洋。黑雾涨天全水气，沧波影日幌寒光。遍崖冲玉浪，满海长金莲。菩萨大展降魔法，袖中取出定身禅。化做落伽仙景界，真如南海一般般。秀蒲挺出昙花嫩，香草舒开贝叶鲜。紫竹几竿鹦鹉歇，青松数簇鹧鸪喧。万迭波涛连四野，只闻风吼水漫天。

孙大圣见了，暗中赞叹道："果然是一个大慈大悲的菩萨！若老孙有此法力，将瓶儿望山一倒，管甚么禽兽蛇虫哩！"菩萨叫："悟空，伸手过来。"行者即忙敛袖，将左手伸出。菩萨拔杨柳枝，蘸甘露，把他手心里写一个"迷"字，教他："捏着拳头，快去与那妖精索战，许败不许胜。败将来我这跟前，我自有法力收他。"

行者领命，返云光，径来至洞口。一只手使拳，一只手使棒，高叫道："妖怪开门！"那些小妖，又进去报道："孙行者又来了！”妖王道：“紧关了门！莫睬他！”行者叫道：“好儿子！把老子赶在门外，还不开门！”小妖又报道：“孙行者骂出那话儿来了！”妖王只教：“莫睬他！”行者叫两次，见不开门，心中大怒，举铁棒，将门一下打了一个窟窿。慌得那小妖跌将进去道：“孙行者打破门了！”妖王见报几次，又听说打破前门，急纵身跳将出去，挺长枪，对行者骂道：“这猴子，老大不识起倒！我让你得些便宜，你还不知尽足，又来欺我！打破我门，你该个甚么罪名？”行者道：“我儿，你赶老子出门，你该个甚么罪名？”

那妖王羞怒，绰长枪劈胸便刺；这行者举铁棒，架隔相还。一番搭上手，斗经四五个回合，行者捏着拳头，拖着棒，败将下来。那妖王立在山前道：“我要刷洗唐僧去哩！”行者道：“好儿子，天看着你哩！你来！”那妖精闻言，愈加嗔怒，喝一声，赶到面前，挺枪又刺。这行者轮棒又战几合，败阵又走。那妖王骂道：“猴子，你在前有二三十合的本事，你怎么如今正斗时就要走了，何也？”行者笑道：“贤郎，老子怕你放火。”妖精道：“我不放火了，你上来。”行者道：“既不放火，走开些，好汉子莫在家门前打人。”那妖精不知是诈，真个举枪又赶。行者拖了棒，放了拳头，那妖王着了迷乱，只情追赶。前走的如流星过度，后走的如弩箭离弦。

不一时，望见那菩萨了。行者道：“妖精，我怕你了，你饶我罢。你如今赶至南海观音菩萨处，怎么还不回去？”那妖王不信，咬着牙，只管赶来。行者将身一幌，藏在那菩萨的神光影里。这妖精见没了行者，走近前，睁圆眼，对菩萨道：“你是孙行者请来的救兵么？”菩萨不答应。妖王拈转长枪，喝道：“咄！你是孙行者请来的救兵么？”菩萨也不答应。妖精望菩萨劈心刺一枪来，那菩萨化道金光，径走上九霄空内。行者跟定道：“菩萨，你好欺伏我罢了！那妖精再三问你，你怎么推聋装哑，不敢做声，被他一枪捌走了，却把那个莲台都丢下耶！”菩萨只教：“莫言语，看他再要怎的。”此时行者与木叉俱在空中，并肩同看。只见那妖呵呵冷笑道：“泼猴头，错认了我也！他不知把我圣婴当作个甚人。几番家战我不过，又去请个甚么脓包菩萨来，却被我一枪捌得无形无影去了。又把个宝莲台儿丢了，且等我上去坐坐。”

好妖精，他也学菩萨，盘手盘脚的坐在当中。行者看见道：“好！好！好！莲花台儿好送人了！”菩萨道：“悟空，你又说甚么？”行者道：“说甚？说甚？莲台送了人了！”那妖精坐放臀下，终不得你还要哩？”菩萨道：“正要他坐哩。”行者道：“他的身躯小巧，比你还坐得稳当。”菩萨叫：“莫言语，且看法力。”

他将杨柳枝往下指定，叫一声“退！”只见那莲台花彩俱无，祥光尽散，原来那妖王坐在刀尖之上。即命木叉：“使降妖杵，把刀柄儿打打去来。”那木叉按下云头，将降魔杵，如筑墙一般，筑了有千百余下。那妖精，穿通两腿刀尖出，血流成汪皮肉开。好怪物，你看他咬着牙，忍着痛，且丢了长枪，用手将刀乱拔。行者却道：“菩萨啊，那怪物不怕痛，还拔刀哩。”菩萨见了，唤上木叉，“且莫伤他生命。”却又把杨柳枝垂下，念声“唵”字咒语，那天罡刀都变做倒须钩儿，狼牙一般，莫能褪得。那妖精却才慌了，扳着刀尖，痛声苦告道：“菩萨，我弟子有眼无珠，不识你广大法力。千乞垂慈，饶我性命！再不敢恃恶，愿入法门戒行也。”

菩萨闻言，却与二行者、白鹦哥低下金光，到了妖精面前，问道：“你可受吾戒行么？”妖王点头滴泪道：“若饶性命，愿受戒行。”菩萨道：“你可入我门么？”妖王道：“果饶性命，愿入法门。”菩萨道：“既如此，我与你摩顶受戒。”就袖中取出一把金剃头刀儿，近前去，把那怪分顶剃了几刀，剃作一个太山压顶，与他留下三个顶搭，挽起三个窝角揪儿。行者在旁笑道：“这妖精大晦气！弄得不男不女，不知像个甚么东西！”菩萨道：“你今既受我戒，我却也不慢你，称你做善财童子，如何？”那妖点头受持，只望饶命。菩萨却用手一指，叫声“退！”撞的一声，天罡刀都脱落尘埃，那童子身躯不损。

菩萨叫：“惠岸，你将刀送上天宫，还你父王，莫来接我，先到普陀岩会众诸天等候。”那木叉领命，送刀上界，回海不题。

却说那童子野性不定，见那腿疼处不疼，臀破处不破，头挽了三个揪儿，他走去绰起长枪，望菩萨道：“那里有甚真法力降我！原来是个掩样术法儿！不受甚戒！看枪！”望菩萨劈脸刺来。恨得个行者轮铁棒要打。菩萨只叫：“莫打，我自有惩治。”却又袖中取出一个金箍儿来道：“这宝贝原是我佛如来赐我往东土寻取经人的‘金紧禁’三个箍儿。紧箍儿，先与你戴了；禁箍儿，收了守山大神；这个金箍儿，未曾舍得与人，今观此怪无礼，与他罢。”好菩萨，将箍儿迎风一幌，叫声“变！”即变作五个箍儿，望童子身上抛了去，喝声“着！”一个套在他头顶上，两个套在他左右手上，两个套在他左右脚上。菩萨道：“悟空，走开些，等我念念《金箍儿咒》。”行者慌了道：“菩萨呀，请你来此降妖，如何却要咒我？”菩萨道：“这篇咒，不是《紧箍儿咒》咒你的，是《金箍儿咒》咒那童子的。”行者却才放心，紧随左右，听得他念咒。菩萨捻着诀，默默的念了几遍，那妖精搓耳柔腮，攒蹄打滚。正是：一句能通遍沙界，广大无边法力深。

（7）第 54 回　法性西来逢女国　心猿定计脱烟花

不多时，大驾出城，早到迎阳馆驿。忽有人报三藏师徒道："驾到了。"三藏闻言，即与三徒整衣出厅迎驾。女王卷帘下辇道："那一位是唐朝御弟？"太师指道："那驿门外香案前穿襕衣者便是。"女王闪凤目，簇蛾眉，仔细观看，果然一表非凡，你看他：

丰姿英伟，相貌轩昂。齿白如银砌，唇红口四方。顶平额阔天仓满，目秀眉清地阁长。两耳有轮真杰士，一身不俗是才郎。好个妙龄聪俊风流子，堪配西梁窈窕娘。

女王看到那心欢意美之外，不觉淫情汲汲，爱欲恣恣，展放樱桃小口，呼道："大唐御弟，还不来占凤乘鸾也？"三藏闻言，耳红面赤，羞答答不敢抬头。猪八戒在旁，掬着嘴，饧眼观看那女王，却也袅娜，真个：

眉如翠羽，肌似羊脂。脸衬桃花瓣，鬟堆金凤丝。秋波湛湛妖娆态，春笋纤纤妖媚姿。斜红绡飘彩艳，高髻珠翠显光辉。说甚么昭君美貌，果然是赛过西施。柳腰微展鸣金珮，莲步轻移动玉肢。月里嫦娥难到此，九天仙子怎如斯。宫妆巧样非凡类，诚然王母降瑶池。

那呆子看到好处，忍不住口嘴流涎，心头撞鹿，一时间骨软筋麻，好便似雪狮子向火，不觉的都化去也。

只见那女王走近前来，一把扯住三藏，俏语娇声，叫道："御弟哥哥，请上龙车，和我同上金銮宝殿，匹配夫妇去来。"这长老战兢兢立站不住，似醉如痴。行者在侧教道："师父不必太谦，请共师娘上辇。快快倒换关文，等我们取经去罢。"长老不敢回言，把行者抹了两抹，止不住落下泪来。行者道："师父切莫烦恼，这般富贵，不受用还待怎么哩？"三藏没及奈何，只得依从，揩了眼泪，强整欢容，移步近前，与女主：

同携素手，共坐龙车。那女主喜孜孜欲配夫妻，这长老忧惶惶只思拜佛。一个要洞房花烛交鸳侣，一个要西宇灵山见世尊。女帝真情，圣僧假意。女帝真情，指望和谐同到老；圣僧假意，牢藏情意养元神。一个喜见男身，恨不得白昼并头谐伉俪；一个怕逢女色，只思量即时脱网上雷音。二人和会同登辇，岂料唐僧各有心！

那些文武官，见主公与长老同登凤辇，并肩而坐，一个个眉花眼笑，拨转仪从，复入城中。孙大圣才教沙僧挑着行李，牵着白马，随大驾后边同行。猪八戒往前乱跑，先到五凤楼前，嚷道："好自在！好现成呀！这个弄不成！这个弄不成！吃了喜酒进亲才是！"唬得些执仪从引导的女官，一个个回至驾边道："主公，那一个长嘴大耳的，在五凤楼前嚷道，要喜酒吃哩。"女主闻奏，与长老倚香肩，偎并桃腮，开檀口，俏声叫道："御弟哥哥，长嘴大耳的是你那个高徒？"三藏道："是我第二个徒弟，他生得食肠宽大，一生要图口肥。须是先安排些酒食与他吃了，方可行事。"女主急问："光禄寺安排筵宴，完否？"女官奏道："已完，设了荤素两样，在东阁上哩。"女王又问："怎么两样？"女官奏道："臣恐唐朝御弟与高徒等平素吃斋，故有荤素两样。"女王却又笑吟吟，偎着长老的香腮道："御弟哥哥，你吃荤吃素？"

三藏道："贫僧吃素，但是未曾戒酒，须得几杯素酒，与我二徒弟吃些。"

说未了，太师启奏："请赴东阁会宴，今宵吉日良辰，就可与御弟爷爷成亲。明日天开黄道，请御弟爷爷登宝殿，面南改年号即位。"女王大喜，即与长老携手相搀，下了龙车，共入端门里。但见那：

风飘仙乐下楼台，阊阖中间翠辇来。
凤阙大开光蔼蔼，皇宫不闭锦排排。
麒麟殿内炉烟袅，孔雀屏边房影回。
亭阁峥嵘如上国，玉堂金马更奇哉！

既至东阁之下，又闻得一派笙歌声韵美，又见两行红粉貌娇娆。正中堂排设两般盛宴：左边上首是素筵，右边上首是荤筵。下两路尽是单席。那女王敛袍袖，十指尖尖，奉着玉杯，便来安席。行者近前道："我师徒都是吃素。先请师父坐了左手素席，转下三席，分左右，我兄弟们好坐。"太师喜道："正是，正是。师徒即父子也，不可并肩。"众女官连忙调了席面。女王一一传杯，安了他弟兄三位。行者又与唐僧丢个眼色，教师父回礼。三藏下来，却也擎玉杯，与女王安席。那些文武官，朝上拜谢了皇恩，各依品从，分坐两边，才住了音乐请酒。

那八戒那管好歹，放开肚子，只情吃起。也不管甚么玉屑米饭、蒸饼、糖糕、蘑菇、香蕈、笋芽、木耳、黄花菜、石花菜、紫菜、蔓菁、芋头、萝菔、山药、黄精，一骨辣噇了个罄尽。喝了五七杯酒，口里嚷道："看添换来！拿大觥来！再吃几觥，各人干事去。"沙僧问道："好筵席不吃，还要干甚事？"呆子笑道：

“古人云，造弓的造弓，造箭的造箭。我们如今招的招，嫁的嫁，取经的还去取经，走路的还去走路，莫只管贪杯误事。快早儿打发关文。正是‘将军不下马，各自奔前程’。”女王闻说，即命取大杯来。近侍官连忙取几个鹦鹉杯、鸬鹚杓、金叵罗、银凿落、玻璃盏、水晶盆、蓬莱碗、琥珀锺，满斟玉液，连注琼浆，果然都各饮一巡。

三藏欠身而起，对女王合掌道：“陛下，多蒙盛设，酒已够了。请登宝殿，倒换关文，赶天早，送他三人出城罢。”女王依言，携着长老，散了筵宴，上金銮宝殿，即让长老即位。三藏道：“不可！不可！适太师言过，明日天开黄道，贫僧才敢即位称孤。今日即印关文，打发他去也。”女王依言，仍坐了龙床，即取金交椅一张，放在龙床左手，请唐僧坐了，叫徒弟们拿上通关文牒来。大圣便教沙僧解开包袱，取出关文。大圣将关文双手捧上。那女王细看一番，上有大唐皇帝宝印九颗，下有宝象国印，乌鸡国印，车迟国印。女王看罢，娇滴滴笑语道：“御弟哥哥又姓陈？”三藏道：“俗家姓陈，法名玄奘。因我唐王圣恩认为御弟，赐姓我为唐也。”女王道：“关文上如何没有高徒之名？”三藏道：“三个顽徒，不是我唐朝人物。”女王道：“既不是你唐朝人物，为何肯随你来？”三藏道：“大的个徒弟，祖贯东胜神洲傲来国人氏；第二个乃西牛贺洲乌斯庄人氏；第三个乃流沙河人氏。他三人都因罪犯天条，南海观世音菩萨解脱他苦，秉善皈依，将功折罪，情愿保护我上西天取经。皆是途中收得，故此未注法名在牒。”女王道：“我与你添注法名，好么？”三藏道：“但凭陛下尊意。”

女王即令取笔砚来，浓磨香翰，饱润香毫，牒文之后，写上孙悟空、猪悟能、沙悟净三人名讳，却才取出御印，端端正正印了，又画个手字花押，传将下去。孙大圣接了，教沙僧包裹停当。那女王又赐出碎金碎银一盘，下龙床递与行者道："你三人将此权为路费，早上西天。待汝等取经回来，寡人还有重谢。"行者道："我们出家人，不受金银，途中自有乞化之处。"女王见他不受，又取出绫锦十匹，对行者道："汝等行色匆匆，裁制不及，将此路上做件衣服遮寒。"行者道："出家人穿不得绫锦，自有护体布衣。"女王见他不受，教："取御米三升，在路权为一饭。"八戒听说个饭字，便就接了，捎在包袱之间。行者道："兄弟，行李见今沉重，且倒有气力挑米？"八戒笑道："你那里知道，米好的是个日消货，只消一顿饭，就了帐也。"遂此合掌谢恩。

（8）第 58 回　二心搅乱大乾坤　一体难修真寂灭

这行者与沙僧拜辞了菩萨，纵起两道祥光，离了南海。原来行者筋斗云快，沙和尚仙云觉迟，行者就要先行。沙僧扯住道："大哥不必这等藏头露尾，先去安根，待小弟与你一同走。"大圣本是良心，沙僧却有疑意，真个二人同驾云而去。不多时，果见花果山，按下云头，二人洞外细看，果见一个行者，高坐石台之上，与群猴饮酒作乐。模样与大圣无异：也是黄发金箍，金睛火眼；身穿也是锦布直裰，腰系虎皮裙；手中也拿一条儿金箍铁棒，足下也踏一双麂皮靴；也是这等毛脸雷公嘴，朔腮别土星，查耳额颅阔，獠牙向外生。

这大圣怒发，一撒手，撇了沙和尚，掣铁棒上前骂道："你是何等妖邪，敢变我的相貌，敢占我的儿孙，擅居吾仙洞，擅作这威福！"那行者见了，公然不答，也使铁棒来迎。二行者在一处，果是不分真假，好打呀：

两条棒，二猴精，这场相敌实非轻。都要护持唐御弟，各施功绩立英名。真猴实受沙门教，假怪虚称佛子情。盖为神通多变化，无真无假两相平。一个是混元一气齐天圣，一个是久炼千灵缩地精。这个是如意金箍棒，那个是随心铁杆兵。隔架遮拦无胜败，撑持抵敌没输赢。先前交手在洞外，少顷争持起半空。

他两个各踏云光，跳斗上九霄云内。沙僧在旁，不敢下手，见他们战此一场，诚然难认真假，欲待拔刀相助，又恐伤了真的。忍耐良久，且纵身跳下山崖，使降妖宝杖，打近水帘洞外，惊散群妖，掀翻石凳，把饮酒食肉的器皿，尽情打碎，寻他的青毡包袱，四下里全然不见。原来他水帘洞本是一股瀑布飞泉，遮挂洞门，远看似一条白布帘儿，近看乃是一股水脉，故曰水帘洞。沙僧不知进步来历，故此难寻。即便纵云，赶到九霄云里，抡着宝杖，又不好下手。大圣道："沙僧，你既助不得力，且回复师父，说我等这般这般，等老孙与此妖打上南海落伽山菩萨前辨个真假。"道罢，那行者也如此说。沙僧见两个相貌、声音，更无一毫差别，皂白难分，只得依言，拨转云头，回复唐僧不题。

你看那两个行者，且行且斗，直嚷到南海，径至落伽山，打打骂骂，喊声不绝。早惊动护法诸天，即报入潮音洞里道："菩萨，果然两个孙悟空打将来也。"那菩萨与木叉行者、善财童子、龙女降莲台出门喝道："那孽畜那里走！"这两个递相揪住道："菩萨，这厮果然象弟子模样。才自水帘洞打起，战斗多时，不分胜负。沙悟净肉眼愚蒙，不能分识，有力难助，是弟子教他回西路去回复师父，我与这厮打到宝山，借菩萨慧眼，与弟子认个真假，辨明邪正。"道罢，那行者也如此说一遍。众诸天与菩萨都看良久，莫想能认。菩萨道："且放了手，两边站下，等我再看。"果然撒手，两边站定。这边说："我是真的！"那边说："他是假的！"菩萨唤木叉与善财上前，悄悄吩咐："你一个帮住一个，等我暗念《紧箍儿咒》，看那个害疼的便是真，不疼的便是假。"他二人果各帮一个。菩萨暗念真言，两个一齐喊疼，都抱着头，地下打滚，只叫："莫念！莫念！"菩萨不念，他两个又一齐揪住，照旧嚷斗。菩萨无计奈何，即令诸天木叉，上前助力。众神恐伤真的，亦不敢下手。菩萨叫声"孙悟空"，两个一齐答应。菩萨道："你当年官拜弼马温，大闹天宫时，神将皆认得你，你且上界去分辨回话。"这大圣谢恩，那行者也谢恩。

（9）第59回　唐三藏路阻火焰山　孙行者一调芭蕉扇

这大圣拨转云头，径回东路，霎时按落云头，立在红砖壁下。八戒见了欢喜道："师父，师兄来了！来了！"三藏即与本庄老者同沙僧出门接着，同至舍内。把芭蕉扇靠在旁边道："老官儿，可是这个扇子？"老者道："正是！正是！"唐僧喜道："贤徒有莫大之功。求此宝贝，甚劳苦了。"行者道："劳苦倒也不说。那铁扇仙，你道是谁？那厮原来是牛魔王的妻，红孩儿的母，名唤罗刹女，又唤铁扇公主。我寻到洞外借扇，他就与我讲起仇隙，把我砍了几剑。是我使棒吓他，他就把扇子扇了我一下，飘飘荡荡，直刮到小须弥山。幸见灵吉菩萨，送了我一粒定风丹，指与归路，复至翠云山。又见罗刹女，罗刹女又使扇子，搧我不动，他就回洞。是老孙变作一个蟭蟟虫，飞入洞去。那厮正讨茶吃，是我又钻在茶沫之下，到他肚里，做起手脚。他疼痛难禁，不住口的叫我做叔叔饶命，情愿将扇借与我，我却饶了他，拿将扇来，待过了火焰山，仍送还他。"

三藏闻言，感谢不尽，师徒们俱拜辞老者。一路西来，约行有四十里远近，渐渐酷热蒸人。沙僧只叫："脚底烙得慌！"八戒又道："爪子烫得痛！"马比寻常又快，只因地热难停，十分难进。行者道："师父且请下马，兄弟们莫走，等我搧息了火，待风雨之后，地土冷些，再过山去。"行者果举扇，径至火边，尽力一扇，那山上火光烘烘腾起，再一扇，更着百倍，又一扇，那火足有千丈之高，渐渐烧着身体。行者急回，已将两股毫毛烧净，径跑至唐僧面前叫："快回去，快回去！火来了，火来了！"

那师父爬上马，与八戒沙僧，复东来有二十余里，方才歇下道："悟空，如何了呀！"行者丢下扇子道："不停当！不停当！被那厮哄了！"三藏听说，愁促眉尖，闷添心上，止不住两泪交流，只道："怎生是好！"八戒道："哥哥，你急急忙忙叫回去是怎么说？"行者道："我将扇子搧了一下，火光烘烘；第二扇，火气愈盛；第三扇，火头飞有千丈之高。若是跑得不快，把毫毛都烧尽矣！"八戒笑道："你常说雷打不伤，火烧不损，如今何又怕火？"行者道："你这呆子，全不知事！那时节用心防备，故此不伤；今日只为搧息火光，不曾捻避火诀，又未使护身法，所以把两股毫毛烧了。"沙僧道："似这般火盛，无路通西，怎生是好？"八戒道："只拣无火处走便罢。"三藏道："那方无火？"八戒道："东方、南方、北方，俱无火。"又问："那方有经？"八戒道："西方有经。"三藏道："我只欲往有经处去哩！"沙僧道："有经处有火，无火处无经，诚是进退两难！"

师徒们正自胡谈乱讲，只听得有人叫道："大圣不须烦恼，且来吃些斋饭再议。"四众回看时，见一老人，身披飘风氅，头顶偃月冠，手持龙头杖，只踏铁靿靴，后带着一个雕嘴鱼腮鬼，鬼头上顶着一个铜盆，盆内有些蒸饼糕糜，黄粮米饭，在于西路下躬身道："我本是火焰山土地，知大圣保护圣僧，不能前进，特献一斋。"行者道："吃斋小可，这火光几时灭得，让我师父过去？"土地道："要灭火光，须求罗刹女借芭蕉扇。"行者去路旁拾起扇子道："这不是？那火光越扇越着，何也？"土地看了，笑道："此扇不是真的，被他哄了。"行者道："如何方得真的？"那土地又控背躬身，微微笑道："若还要借真蕉扇，须是寻求大力王。"

（10）第100回　径回东土　五圣成真

当时多官齐贺，顶礼圣教御文，遍传内外。太宗道："御弟将真经演诵一番，何如？"长老道："主公，若演真经，须寻佛地，宝殿非可诵之处。"太宗甚喜，即问当驾官："长安城寺，有那座寺院洁净？"班中闪上大学士萧瑀奏道："城中有一雁塔寺洁净。"太宗即令多官："把真经各虔捧几卷，同朕到雁塔寺，请御弟谈经去来。"多官遂各各捧着，随太宗驾幸寺中，搭起高台，铺设齐整。长老仍命："八戒、沙僧牵龙马，理行囊，行者在我左右。"又向太宗道："主公欲将真经传流天下，须当誊录副本，方可布散。原本还当珍藏，不可轻亵。"太宗又笑道："御弟之言甚当！甚当！"随召翰林院及中书科各官誊写真经。又建一寺，在城之东，名曰誊黄寺。

长老捧几卷登台，方欲讽诵，忽闻得香风缭绕，半空中有八大金刚现身高叫道："诵经的，放下经卷，跟我回西去也。"这底下行者三人，连白马平地而起，长老亦将经卷丢下，也从台上起于九霄，相随腾空而去，慌得那太宗与多官望空下拜。这正是：

圣僧努力取经编，西宇周流十四年。
苦历程途遭患难，多经山水受迍邅。

功完八九还加九，行满三千及大千。

大觉妙文回上国，至今东土永留传。

太宗与多官拜毕，即选高僧，就于雁塔寺里，修建水陆大会，看诵《大藏真经》，超脱幽冥孽鬼，普施善庆，将誊录过经文，传布天下，不题。

却说八大金刚，驾香风，引着长老四众，连马五口，复转灵山，连去连来，适在八日之内。此时灵山诸神，都在佛前听讲。八金刚引他师徒进去，对如来道："弟子前奉金旨，驾送圣僧等，已到唐国，将经交 纳，今特缴旨。"遂叫唐僧等近前受职。如来道："圣僧，汝前世原是我之二徒，名唤金蝉子。因为汝不听说法，轻慢我之大教，故贬汝之真灵，转生东土。今喜皈依，秉我迦持，又乘吾教，取去真经，甚有功果，加升大职正果，汝为旃檀功德佛。孙悟空，汝因大闹天宫，吾以甚深法力，压在五行山下，幸天灾满足，归于释教，且喜汝隐恶扬善，在途中炼魔降怪有功，全终全始，加升大职正果，汝为斗战胜佛。猪悟能，汝本天河水神，天蓬元帅，为汝蟠桃会上酗酒戏了仙娥，贬汝下界投胎，身如畜类，幸汝记爱人身，在福陵山云栈洞造孽，喜归大教，入吾沙门，保圣僧在路，却又有顽心，色情未泯，因汝挑担有功，加升汝职正果，做净坛使者。"八戒口中嚷道："他们都成佛，如何把我做个净坛使者？"如来道："因汝口壮身慵，食肠宽大。盖天下四大部洲，瞻仰吾教者甚多，凡诸佛事，教汝净坛，乃是个有受用的品级，如何不好！沙悟净，汝本是卷帘大将，先因蟠桃会上打碎玻璃盏，贬汝下界，汝落于流沙河，伤生吃人造孽，幸皈吾教，诚敬迦持，保护圣僧，登山牵马有功，加升大职正果，为金身罗汉。"又叫那白马："汝本是西洋大海广晋龙王之子，因汝违逆父命，犯了不孝之罪，幸得皈身皈法，皈我沙门，每日家亏你驮负圣僧来西，又亏你驮负圣经去东，亦有功者，加升汝职正果，为八部天龙马。”长老四众，俱各叩头谢恩。马亦谢恩讫，仍命揭谛引了马下灵山后崖化龙池边，将马推入池中。须臾间，那马打个展身，即退了毛皮，换了头角，浑身上长起金鳞，腮颔下生出银须，一身瑞气，四爪祥云，飞出化龙池，盘绕在山门里擎天华表柱上，诸佛赞扬如来的大法。孙行者却又对唐僧道：“师父，此时我已成佛，与你一般，莫成还戴金箍儿，你还念甚么《紧箍儿咒》掯勒我？趁早儿念个松箍儿咒，脱下来，打得粉碎，切莫叫那甚么菩萨再去捉弄他人。”唐僧道：“当时只为你难管，故以此法制之。今已成佛，自然去矣，岂有还在你头上之理！你试摸摸看。”行者举手去摸一摸，果然无之。此时旃檀佛、斗战佛、净坛使者、金身罗汉，俱正果了本位，天龙马亦自归真。有诗为证，诗曰：

一体真如转落尘，合和四相复修身。
五行论色空还寂，百怪虚名总莫论。
正果旃檀皈大觉，完成品职脱沉沦。
经传天下恩光阔，五圣高居不二门。

Chapter IX Journey to the West

1. Introduction of the Work

Journey to the West was the first romantic chapter novel about gods and demons in ancient China. There are one hundred copies of *Journey to the West* in extant Ming publications without the author's signature. Wu Yuxuan, a scholar of the Qing Dynasty, first proposed that the author of *Journey to the West* was Wu Chengen of the Ming Dynasty. After Sun Wukong was born and brought havoc to Heaven, he meets Xuanzang, Zhu Bajie, Sha Seng and the White Dragon Horse, and travels west to get Buddhist scriptures. Along the way, he encounters difficulties, defeats monsters and demons, and experiences eighty-one difficulties. Finally, they reach the west to meet Tathagata Buddha, and become Five Saints. Based on the historical event of "Xuanzang's acquisition of scriptures", the novel depicts the social reality of the Ming Dynasty through the author's artistic process. *Journey to the West* is a classic novel about Chinese gods and demons, achieving the peak of ancient romantic novels, and is also known as one of the four classics of Chinese classics along with *Romance of the Three Kingdoms*, *The Outlaws of the Marsh* and *A Dream of Red Mansions*. Since its publication, *Journey to the West* has been widely circulated among the people. There are six editions from the Ming Dynasty, seven editions and copies from the Qing Dynasty, and thirteen recorded but lost editions in history books. After the Opium War, *Journey to the West* was gradually spread to Europe and the United States. It has been translated into English, French, German, Italian, Spanish, Esperanto, Swahili, Russian, Czech, Romanian, Polish, Japanese, Korean, Vietnamese and other languages.

In the first year of Emperor Taizong of Tang Dynasty (627), 25-year-old monk Xuanzang set out to Tianzhu (India) on foot. From Chang'an, he traveled through Afghanistan, Pakistan, and went through all kinds of hardships to reach India. He studied there for more than two years and in the 19th year of Zhenguan (645), Xuanzang returned to Chang'an with 657 Buddhist sutras, which made a great flutter at that time. Later, Xuanzang's dictation of what he saw on his journey to the West was compiled into twelve volumes of *Great Tang Records on the Western Regions* by his disciple, Bian Ji. The book is mostly about history, geography and transportation in the countries on his way to the west, without any narrative to it. His disciple Hui Li and Yan Cong's *Biography of Master Sanzang of Da Cien Temple of the Tang Dynasty* added a lot of mythology to Xuanzang's experience and from then on, the story of "Xuanzang's acquisition of scriptures" began to spread widely among the Chinese people.

2. Introduction of the Author

Wu Cheng'en (1500-1583), whose courtesy name is Ruzhong and pseudonym is Sheyang, is of the Han nationality, from Shanyang

County, Huaian City. His hometown is Anhui, and his ancestral family lives in Gaodian, Zongyang. Hence his family is known as Gaodian Wu. He was an outstanding novelist during the Ming Dynasty, and was the author of *Journey to the West*. Since his childhood, he had been intelligent and well-read, and especially fond of fairy tales. He suffered many setbacks in the imperial examinations, and finally passed the examination in the year of Jiajing. In the forty-fifth year of Jiajing (1566), he served as the county magistrate of Changxing, Zhejiang. As a result of official career difficulties, he later refused to be an official and wrote behind closed doors in his old age.

As a child, Wu Cheng'en loved to read unofficial histories and was familiar with ancient myths and legends. The frustration of officialdom and the difficulty of life made him know more about the feudal imperial examination system and the dark sides of social reality, which urged him to use the form of the mystery novel to express his inner dissatisfaction and resentment. He said to himself, "Although my book is called a mystery novel, the focus is not on ghosts. It indeed records some changes in human life, which can teach some lessons". Wu Cheng'en had also written a collection of short stories called Yu Ding Zhi, but it was lost, with only a preface remaining. Whether the author of *Journey to the West* is Wu Cheng'en or not, there has been much controversy in academic circles. Some scholars believe that the author is not Wu Cheng'en but Li Chunfang, the "Prime Minister of Qingci"of Jiajing in the Ming Dynasty.

Wu Cheng'en took inspiration from the experience of Monk Xuanzang in the Tang dynasty when Xuanzang went to Tianzhu to study Buddhism, and works like *Great Tang Records on the Western Regions*, *Biography of Master Sanzang of Da Cien Temple of the Tang Dynasty*, to organize, conceive and finish his outstanding novel, *Journey to the West*. With the help of mythological stories, the novel expresses the author's dissatisfaction with reality and his desire to change it, and reflects the author's political ideal of ruling the country as a wise king. The novel reflects the reality of human society by telling the story of the eighty-one difficulties experienced by Tangseng and his disciples. The novel is bold in imagination and novel in conception, and adopts the trinity of Man, God and Beast in characterization to create such immortal artistic images as Sun Wukong and Zhu Bajie. The book is well-organized, complex and orderly; it uses lively language with different dialects and idioms, permeating the story with lifelike energy. The theme dilutes the original religious color of the story, but enriches the materialistic content of the work greatly, and has democratic tendencies and characteristics of the time. It uses satirical humor to present a unique style which is different from the past narrative telling of the acquisition of the scriptures.

3. Appreciation

(1)Chapter 1

The Divine Root Conceives and the Spring Breaks Forth

As the Heart's Nature is Cultivated, the Great Way Arises

There was once a magic stone on the top of this mountain which was thirty-six feet five inches high and twenty-four feet round. It was thirty-six feet five inches high to correspond with the 365 degrees of the heavens, and twenty-four feet round to match the twenty-four divisions of the solar calendar. On top of it were nine apertures and eight holes, for the Nine Palaces and the Eight Trigrams. There were no trees around it to give shade, but magic fungus and orchids clung to its sides. Ever since Creation began it had been Journey to the West receiving the truth of Heaven, the beauty of Earth, the essence of the Sun and the splendor of the Moon; and as it had been influenced by them for so long it had miraculous powers. It developed a magic womb, which burst open one day to produce a stone egg about the size of a ball. When the wind blew on this egg it turned into a stone monkey, complete with the five senses and four limbs. When the stone monkey had learned to crawl and walk, he bowed to each of the four quarters. As his eyes moved, two beams of golden light shot towards the Pole Star palace and startled the Supreme Heavenly Sage, the Greatly Compassionate Jade Emperor of the Azure Vault of Heaven, who was sitting surrounded by his immortal ministers on his throne in the Hall of Miraculous Mist in the Golden-gated Cloud Palace. When he saw the dazzling golden light he ordered Thousand-mile Eye and Wind-accompanying Ear to open the Southern Gate of Heaven and take a look. The two officers went out through the gate in obedience to the imperial command, and while one observed what was going on the other listened carefully. Soon afterwards they reported back: "In obedience to the Imperial Mandate your subjects observed and listened to the source of the golden light. We found that at the edge of the country of Aolai, which is East of the ocean belonging to the Eastern Continent of Superior Body, there is an island called the Mountain of

Flowers and Fruit. A magic stone on the top of this mountain produced a magic egg, and when the wind blew on this egg it turned into a stone monkey which bowed to each of the four quarters. When he moved his eyes, golden light shot towards the Pole Star Palace; but now that he is eating and drinking, the golden light is gradually dying." In his benevolence and mercy the Jade Emperor said, "Creatures down below are born of the essence of heaven and earth: there is nothing remarkable about him." On his mountain the monkey was soon able to run and jump, feed from plants and trees, drink from brooks and springs, pick mountain flowers and look for fruit. He made friends with the wolves, went around with the tigers and leopards, was on good terms with the deer, and had the other monkeys and apes for relations. At night he slept under the rock faces, and he roamed around the peaks and caves by day. As the saying so rightly goes, "There is no calendar in the mountains, and when winter's over you don't know the time of year." On hot mornings he and all the other monkeys would play under the shade of some pines to avoid the heat. Just look at them all: Climbing trees, picking flowers, looking for fruit; Throwing pellets, playing knucklebones; Running round sandy hollows, building stone pagodas; Chasing dragonflies and catching locusts; Worshipping the sky and visiting Bodhisattvas; Tearing off creepers and weaving straw hats; Catching fleas then popping them with their teeth and fingers; Grooming their coats and sharpening their nails; Beating, scratching, pushing, squashing, tearing and tugging; Playing all over the place under the pine trees; Washing themselves beside the green stream. After playing, the monkeys would go and bathe in the stream, a mountain torrent that tumbled along like rolling melons. There is an old saying, "Birds have bird language and, animals have animal talk." All the monkeys said to each other, "I wonder where that water comes from. We've got nothing else to do today, so wouldn't it be fun to go upstream and find its source?" With a shout they all ran off, leading their children and calling to their brothers. They climbed up the mountain beside the stream until they reached its source, where a waterfall cascaded from a spring. They saw

One white rainbow arching, A thousand strands of flying snow,
Unbroken by the sea winds, Still there under the moon.
Cold air divides the green crags, Splashes moisten the mountainside;
A noble waterfall cascades, Hanging suspended like a curtain.

The monkeys clapped their hands and explained with delight, "What lovely water. It must go all the way to the bottom of the mountain and join the waves of the sea." Then one monkey made a suggestion: "If anyone is clever enough to go through the fall, find the source, and come out in one piece, let's make him our king." When this challenge had been shouted three times, the stone monkey leapt out from the crowd and answered at the top of his voice, "I'll go, I'll go." Splendid monkey! Indeed: Today he will make his name; Tomorrow his destiny shall triumph. He is fated to live here; As a King he will enter the Immortals'palace.

Watch him as he shuts his eyes, crouches, and springs, leaping straight into the waterfall. When he opened his eyes and raised his head to look round, he saw neither water nor waves. A bridge stood in front of him, as large as life. He stopped, calmed himself, took a closer look, and saw that the bridge was made of iron. The water that rushed under it poured out through a fissure in the rocks, screening the gateway to the bridge. He started walking towards the bridge, and as he looked he made out what seemed to be a house. It was a really good place. He saw:

Emerald moss piled up in heaps of blue, White clouds like drifting jade, While the light flickered among wisps of colored mist. A quiet house with peaceful windows, Flowers growing on the smooth bench; Dragon pearls hanging in niches, Exotic blooms all around. Traces of fire beside the stove, Scraps of food in the vessels by the table. Adorable stone chairs and beds, Even better stone plates and bowls. One or two tall bamboos, Three or four sprigs of plum blossom, A few pines that always attract rain, All just like a real home.

(2)Chapter 5

After Chaos Among the Peaches the Great Sage Steals the Pills

In the Revolt Against Heaven the Gods Capture the Demons

Splendid Great Sage. Making a magic with his hands as he spoke the words of the spell, he said to the fairies, "Stay where you are! Stay where you are!" As this was an immobilizing spell, the seven fairies were left standing in a daze under the peach tree with their eyes wide open as the Great Sage leapt out of the orchard on a somersault cloud and headed for the Jade Pool. As he traveled he saw that

The sky shimmered with auspicious light,
As clouds of many colors streamed across it.
The white stork's cry made the heavens shake;
A thousand leaves grew on the purple asphodel.
Amid it all an Immortal appeared,
Carrying himself with heaven-sent elegance,
As he danced on the rainbow, cloaked by the Milky Way,
With a talisman at his waist to ward off birth and death.

His name was Bare-Foot Immortal, and he was going to the feast of longevity-giving peaches. As the Bare-foot Immortal saw him, the Great Sage lowered his head and thought of a plan by which to trick the Immortal and get to the banquet himself. "Where are you going, reverend sir?" he asked; and the Immortal replied, "I'm going to the Peach Banquet by the invitation of the Queen Mother." "There is something you do not know, venerable sir," said the Great Sage. "As my somersault cloud is so fast, the Jade Emperor has sent me everywhere to tell all you gentlemen to go to the Hall of Universal Brightness for a ceremony before going on to the banquet." As the Immortal was an open and upright man, he took this lie for the truth, but wondered, "The thanksgiving ceremony is usually held by the Jade Pool, so why are we having the ceremony in the Hall of Universal Brightness before going to the Jade Pool for the banquet?" Nevertheless, he turned his propitious cloud around and went to the Hall of Universal Brightness. As the Great Sage rode his cloud he said a spell, shook himself, took the form of the Bare-foot Immortal, and hurried to the Jade Pool. He reached the pavilion there a moment later, stopped his cloud, and went quietly inside. He saw

Fabulous perfumes coiling, a confusion of auspicious clouds. The jade tower set with color, The precious pavilions scattering mists; the phoenix soars till almost lost to view, And jeweled flowers seem to rise and fall. Above a nine-phoenix screen A rainbow stool of the eight precious things, a colored golden table, Green jade bowls with a thousand flowers. On the table were dragon livers and marrow of phoenix bone, Bears'paws and apes'lips— A hundred different dishes, and all of them good; Rare fruits and fine delicacies, every one unique.

Everything was neatly set out, but no Immortals had yet arrived. The Great Sage had not finished looking when he smelt wine; and as he whirled round he saw under a portico to the right several immortal officials in charge of brewing liquor with some workmen who stirred the lees, a number of novices who carried water and some boys who looked after the fires. They were washing the vats and scrubbing the pots, having made jade liquor and a fragrant fermentation of the lees. The Great Sage could not stop himself from drooling, and he longed to drink some, but unfortunately all those people were there. So he performed a spell by pulling several hairs from his body, chewing them up, spitting them up, saying the magic words, and shouting "Change"; whereupon the hairs turned into sleep insects, which flew into the faces of all the liquor-makers. Watch them as their hands go limp, their heads droop, their eyes close, and they drop their symbols of office and all fall asleep. Whereupon the Great Sage grabbed the rare delicacies and exotic foods, then went under the portico and drank from the vats and pots until he was completely drunk. Only then did he think, "This won't do at all. When the guests come for the banquet they'll be furious with me, and I'll be for it if I'm caught. I'd better get back to the Residence as soon as I can and sleep it off." Our dear Great Sage staggered and swayed, charging about all over the place under the influence of the liquor, and going the wrong way. He arrived not at the Equaling Heaven Residence but at the Tushita Heavenly Palace. As soon as he saw this he sobered up and said to himself, "The Tushita Palace is the highest of the thirty-three heavens, where Lord Lao Zi of the Great Monad reigns. However did I get here? Never mind, I've always wanted to see that old chap, and I've never managed to come here before. I might as well go and have a look at him now that I'm passing this way." He straightened his clothes and rushed in, but did not see Lord Lao Zi. There was no sign of anyone. This was because Lao Zi and the Ancient Buddha Dipamkara were expounding the Way from a red dais in a triple-storied pavilion, and all the immortal boys, generals, officials and petty functionaries were standing to right and left listening to the lecture. The Great Sage went straight to the room in which the elixir was kept, and although he could not find Lao Zi there he saw that there was a small fire in the stove beside the range over which pills were made. On either side of the stove were five gourds, full of golden pills of refined elixir. "This is the Immortals' greatest treasure," he exclaimed in delight. "I've wanted to refine some of these golden pills to save people with ever since I understood the Way and mastered the principle of the correspondence of the Esoteric and Exoteric, but I've never had time to come here. Today I'm in luck—I've found them. As Lao Zi isn't here I'll try a few." He emptied the gourds of their contents and ate up all the pills as if he were eating fried beans. Before long he was full of pills and quite sober. "This is terrible," he thought, "this is a colossal disaster. If the Jade Emperor is shocked by this, I'm done for. I must get out of here. I'd be much better off as a king in the lower world." He rushed out of the Tushita Palace, avoiding his usual route. Using a spell to make himself invisible, he left by the West Gate of Heaven, and went straight down to the Mountain of Flowers and Fruit by cloud. When he got there he saw flags, banners, spears and halberds gleaming in the sun: the four Stalwart Generals and the seventy-two kings of the monsters were holding military exercises. "Children, I'm back," shouted the Great Sage in a loud voice, and all the fiends dropped their weapons and fell to their knees. "You don't care, do you, Great Sage?" they said. "It's been so long since you left us, and you never came back to see us." "I haven't been long, I haven't been long," protested the Great Sage, and as they talked they walked into the innermost part of the cave. When the four Stalwart General's had tidied the place up and made him sit down, they kowtowed to him and asked, "What office did you hold, Great Sage, during your century and more in Heaven?" The Great Sage laughed and said, "As far as I can remember it was only six months, so why do you say it was over a century?" "A day in Heaven is the same as a year on earth," the Stalwart Generals replied. "I was lucky this time," said the Great Sage. "The Jade Emperor took a liking to me and ennobled me as the Great Sage Equaling Heaven. He had an Equaling Heaven Residence built for me, complete with a Tranquility Office and a Calm Divinity Office with Immortal functionaries, attendants and guards. Later on, when he saw that I had nothing to do, he put me in charge of the Peach Orchard. Recently the Queen Mother Goddess gave a Peach Banquet, but she didn't invite me. Instead of waiting for an invitation, I went to the Jade Pool and stole all the immortal food and drink. I staggered away from the Jade Pool and blundered into Lord Lao Zi's palace, and there I ate up his five gourds of pills of immortality. Then I got out through the heavenly gates and came here because I was scared that the Jade Emperor was going to punish me." All the fiends were delighted with what they heard, and they laid on liquor and fruit with which to welcome him back. They filled a stone bowl with coconut toddy and handed it to him, but when he tasted it the Great Sage grimaced and said, "It's awful, it's awful." Two of his Stalwart Generals, Beng and Ba, explained, "You don't find coconut toddy very tasty because you have drunk immortal liquor and eaten immortal food in the heavenly palace, Great Sage. But as the saying goes, 'Sweet or not, it's water from home.'" To this the Great Sage replied, "And all of you, whether related to me or not, are from my home. When I was enjoying myself beside the Jade Pool today I saw jars and jars of jade liquor under a portico there. As none of you have ever tasted it I'll go and pinch you a few jars; then you can each have a little drink, and live forever." All the monkeys were beside themselves with glee. The Great Sage then went out of the cave, turned a somersault, made himself invisible, and went straight to the

Peach Banquet. As he went through the gates of the Jade Pool he saw that the men who made the wine, stirred the lees, carried the water, and looked after the fire were still snoring away. He tucked two big jars of wine under his arms, took two more in his hands, then turned his cloud round and went back to have a feast of immortal wine with the monkey masses in the cave. They all drank several cups and were very happy, but we will not go into this.

(3)Chapter 16

The Monks of the Guanyin Monastery Plot to Take the Treasure

The Monster of the Black Wind Mountain Steals the Cassock

When the fire broke out, all the animals and devils of the mountain were disturbed. Seven miles due South of the Guanyin Monastery was the Black Wind Mountain, on which there was a Black Wind Cave. In this cave a monster awoke and sat up. Seeing light streaming in through his window, he thought it must be dawn, but when he got up to take a better look he saw a fire blazing to the North. "Blimey," the monster exclaimed with astonishment, "those careless monks must have set the Guanyin Monastery on fire. I'd better go and help them." The good monster leapt off on a cloud and went down below the smoke and flames that reached up to the sky. The front halls were all empty, and the fire was burning bright in the cloisters on either side. He rushed forward with long strides and was just calling for water when he noticed that the rooms at the back were not burning as there was someone on the roof keeping the wind away. The moment he realized this and rushed in to look, he saw a magic glow and propitious vapors coming from a black felt bundle on the table. On opening it he found it contained a brocade cassock that was a rare treasure of the Buddhist religion. His mind disturbed by the sight of this valuable object, he forgot about putting out the fire or calling for water and grabbed the cassock, which he made off with in the general confusion. Then he went straight back to his cave by cloud. The fire blazed on till dawn before burning itself out. The undraped monks howled and wailed as they searched through the ashes for bronze and iron, and picked over the cinders to find gold and silver. Some of them fixed up thatched shelters in what remained of the frames of the buildings, and others were rigging up pots to cook food at the bases of the exposed walls. We will not describe the weeping, the shouting and the confused hubbub. Brother Monkey grabbed the Anti-fire Cover, took it back to the Southern Gate of Heaven with a single somersault, and returned it to the Broad-visioned Heavenly King with thanks. "Great Sage," said the Heavenly King as he accepted it. "You are as good as your word. I was so worried that if you didn't give me back my treasure, I'd never be able to find you and get it off you. Thank goodness you've returned it." "Am I the sort of bloke who'd cheat someone to his face?" asked Monkey. "After all, 'If you return a thing properly when you borrow it, it'll be easier to borrow it next time.'" "As we haven't met for so long, why don't you come into the palace for a while?" said the Heavenly King. "I'm no longer the man to 'sit on the bench till it rots, talking about the universe,'" Monkey replied. "I'm too busy now that I have to look after the Tang Monk. Please excuse me." Leaving with all speed, he went down on his cloud, and saw that the sun was rising as he went straight to the meditation hall, where he shook himself, turned into a bee, and flew in. On reverting to his true form he saw that his master was still sound asleep. "Master, get up, it's dawn," he called. Sanzang woke up, rolled over, and said, "Yes, so it is." When he had dressed he opened the doors, went outside, and saw the walls reddened and in ruins, and the halls and towers gone. "Goodness," he exclaimed in great astonishment, "why have the buildings all disappeared? Why is there nothing but reddened walls?" "You're still asleep," Monkey replied. "There was a fire last night." "Why didn't I know about it?" Sanzang asked. "I was protecting the meditation hall, and as I could see you were asleep, master, I didn't disturb you," Monkey replied. "If you were able to protect the meditation hall, why didn't you put out the fire in the other buildings?" Sanzang asked. Monkey laughed. "I'll tell you, master. What you predicted actually happened. They fancied that cassock of ours and planned to burn us to death. If I hadn't noticed, we'd be bones and ashes by now." "Did they start the fire?" asked Sanzang who was horrified to learn this. "Who else?" replied Monkey. "Are you sure that you didn't cook this up because they were rude to you?" Sanzang asked. "I'm not such a rascal as to do a thing like that," said Monkey. "Honestly and truly, they started it. Of course, when I saw how vicious they were I didn't help put the blaze out. I helped them with a slight breeze instead." "Heavens! Heavens! When a fire starts you should bring water, not wind." "You must know the old saying— 'If people didn't harm tigers, tigers wouldn't hurt people.' If they hadn't started a fire, I wouldn't have caused a wind." "Where's the cassock? Don't say that it's been burnt too." "It's all right; it hasn't been burnt. The abbots'cell where it was kept didn't catch fire." "I don't care what you say. If it's come to any harm, I'll recite that spell till it kills you." "Don't do that," pleaded Monkey desperately, "I promise to bring that cassock back to you. Wait while I fetch it for you, and then we'll be on our way." With Sanzang leading the horse, and Monkey carrying the luggage, they went out of the meditation hall and straight to the abbot's lodgings at the back.

(4)Chapter 18

The Tang Priest is Rescued in the Guanyin Temple

The Great Sage Removes a Monster from Gao Village

Monkey then used some of his magic powers to turn himself into the likeness of the girl with a shake of his body. Then he sat down in the room to wait for the evil spirit. Before long there was a marvelous wind that sent stones and dust flying:

At first it was a gentle breeze, that gradually became a tremendous gale.

When it was a gentle breeze, it filled Heaven and Earth;

When it grew, nothing could withstand it.

It stripped off flowers and snapped willows like stalks of hemp, uprooting forests as if it were picking vegetables.

It threw rivers and seas into turmoil, to the fury of gods and devils, splitting rocks and mountains as Heaven and Earth watched in horror.

The flower-eating deer lost their way, the fruit-plucking monkeys did not know where they were.

Seven-storied iron pagodas fell on the Buddha's head, the

streamers in the temple fell on the jeweled canopy.

Golden beams and pillars of jade were shaken from their roots, tiles flew from the roof like swallows.

As the boatman raised his oar he made a vow, quickly sacrificing a pig and a goat as he pushed off.

The guardian god of the city ward abandoned his shrine, the Dragon Kings of the Four Seas bowed to Heaven.

The yaksha demons'boats were wrecked on the coast, and half the length of the Great Wall was blown down.

As this gale wind passed, an evil spirit appeared in mid-air. He was certainly ugly with his dark face, stubbly hair, long nose, and big ears. He wore a cotton tunic that was somewhere between black and blue, and round his waist was a patterned cotton cloth. "So that's what he's like," thought Monkey with a secret smile, and without greeting him or asking him anything he lay down on the bed, breathing heavily and pretending to be ill. Not knowing who this really was, the monster came straight in, put his arms around him and was going to kiss him. Monkey laughed to himself again as he thought, "So he really wants to screw me." Then he thrust his hand up under the monster's long nose to throw him off balance. The monster fell off the bed. As the monster pulled himself up he leaned on the edge of the bed and said, "Darling, why are you so angry with me today? Is it because I'm late?" "I'm not angry," Monkey replied, "not angry at all." "If you're not angry with me, why did you make me fall over?" "You should have been more thoughtful and not tried hugging me and kissing me. I'm not feeling very well today. If I'd been my usual self I'd have been waiting for you at the door. Take your clothes off and come to bed." Not realizing what he was up to, the monster undressed. Monkey jumped out of bed and sat on the pot as the monster went back to bed and groped around without finding the girl. "Where've you gone, darling?" he asked. "Take your clothes off and come to bed." "Go to sleep," Monkey replied, "I'm taking a shit." The monster did as he was told. Monkey sighed and said, "What terrible luck." "What are you so fed up about?" the monster asked. "What do you mean by 'terrible luck'? I may have eaten some food and drunk some tea since marrying you, but I haven't been idle either. I've swept for your family and dug ditches, I've shifted bricks and tiles, I've built walls for you, I've ploughed and weeded your fields, I've sown your wheat, and I've transplanted your rice. I've made your family's fortune. These days you dress in brocade and have golden pins in your hair. You have fruit and flowers in all four seasons, and vegetables for the pot throughout the year. But despite this you're still not satisfied, groaning and moaning like that and complaining about your 'terrible luck.'" "I didn't mean that," Monkey replied. "Today I could hear my parents through the wall. They were smashing up bricks and tiles and pretending to curse and beat me." "Why should they want to do that?" the monster asked. "They said that since we married and you became their resident son-in-law, all respectability has gone by the board. They were complaining about having such an ugly fellow as you around, and about never meeting any brother-in-law or other relations of yours. Besides, with all that wind and cloud whenever you come in or go out, they wonder who on earth you can be and what you are called. You're ruining their reputation, and disgracing the family. That's why they were so angry that they went through the motions of beating and cursing me." "I may be a bit of an eyesore," the monster said, "but if you want me to be a good-looker I can fix that without any difficulty. When I first came I had a word with your father, and he agreed to the marriage of his own free will. Why is he talking like this now?" My home is the Cloud Pathway Cave on the Mount of Blessing. My surname, Zhu, is like my face—piggy—and my correct name is Zhu Ganglie, Iron-Haired pig. You tell them all that if they ask you again. "He's an honest monster," thought Monkey with delight. "If he came out with all this without being tortured. Now I know who he is and where he's from, I'm sure I can catch him." "He's sent for a priest to come and catch you," Monkey said aloud. "Come to bed, come to bed, and forget about him," the monster said with a laugh. "I can do as many transformations as the Plough, and I have my nine-pronged rake too, so what have I to fear from priests, monks or Taoists? Even if your old man were holy enough to summon the Demon-destroying Patriarch down from the Ninth Heaven, he's an old friend of mine and wouldn't do anything to harm me." "My father said that he'd asked that fellow by the name of Sun, the Great Sage Equaling Heaven who made such trouble up in the Heavenly Palace some five hundred years ago, to come and capture you." The monster was somewhat taken aback on hearing this name, and said, "In that case I'm off. We're through." "You can't just go like that," said Monkey. "You wouldn't know," the monster replied, "but that Protector of the Horses who made such trouble in the Heavenly Palace is quite a fighter. I might not be able to beat him, and that would spoil my good name." With these words he pulled on his clothes, opened the door, and was just going out when Monkey grabbed him, gave his own face a rub, and changed back into his real form. "Where'd you think you're going, my fine monster?" he roared, adding, "Take a look and see who I am." The monster turned round and saw Monkey's protruding teeth, pinched face, fiery eyes with golden pupil, bald head and hairy face. At the sight of this thunder god incarnate his hands were numbed and his legs paralyzed; then with a great tearing sound he broke free, ripping his clothes, and escaped in the form of a hurricane. Monkey rushed after him, grabbed his iron cudgel, and took a swipe at the wind. The monster then changed into ten thousand sparks and went straight back to his mountain. Monkey mounted his cloud and went after him shouting, "Where'd you think you're going? If you go up to Heaven, I'll chase you as far as the Dipper and Bull Palace, and if you go into the Earth, I'll pursue you as far as the Hell of the Unjustly Slain."

(5)Chapter 27

The Corpse Fiend Thrice Tricks Tang Sanzang

The Holy Monk Angrily Dismisses the Handsome Monkey King

The evil spirit, who had not been killed the second time Monkey hit it either, was full of admiration as it floated in mid-air. "What a splendid Monkey King," it thought, "and what sharp eyes. He saw who I was through both my transformations. Those monks are travelling fast, and once they're over the mountain and fifteen miles to the West they'll be out of my territory. And other fiends and monsters who catch them will be laughing till their mouths split, and I'll be heartbroken with sorrow. I'll have to have another go at tricking them." The excellent evil spirit brought its negative wind down to the mountainside and with one shake turned itself into an old man.

His hair was as white as Ancient Peng's,

His temples as hoary as the Star of Longevity.

Jade rang in his ears, And his eyes swam with golden stars.

He leant on a dragon-headed stick, And wore a cloak of crane feathers.

In his hands he fingered prayer-beads While reciting Buddhist sutras.

When Sanzang saw him from the back of his horse he said with great delight, "Amitabha Buddha! The West is indeed a blessed land. That old man is forcing himself to recite scriptures although he can hardly walk." "Master," said Pig, "don't be so nice about him. He's going to give us trouble." "What do you mean?" Sanzang asked. "My elder brother has killed the daughter and the old woman, and this is the old man coming to look for them. If we fall into his hands you'll have to pay with your life. It'll be the death penalty for you, and I'll get a long sentence for being your accomplice. Friar Sand will be exiled for giving the orders. That elder brother will disappear by magic, and we three will have to carry the can." "Don't talk such nonsense, you moron," said Monkey. "You're terrifying the master. Wait while I go and have another look." Hiding the cudgel about his person he went up to the monster and said, "Where are you going, venerable sir? And why are you reciting scriptures as you walk along?" The monster, failing to recognize his opponent, thought that the Great Sage Monkey was merely a passer-by and said, "Holy sir, my family has lived here for generations, and all my life I have done good deeds, fed monks, read the scriptures, and repeated the Buddha's name. As fate has it I have no son, only a daughter, and she lives at home with her husband. She went off to the fields with food early this morning, and I'm afraid she may have been eaten by a tiger. My wife went out to look for her, and she hasn't come back either. I've no idea what's happened to them, so I've come to search for them. If they have died, I shall just have to gather their bones and take them back for a decent burial." "I'm a master of disguise," replied Monkey with a grin, "so don't try to pull the wool over my eyes. You can't fool me. I know that you're an evil spirit." The monster was speechless with fright. Monkey brandished his cudgel and thought, "If I don't kill him he'll make a getaway; but if I do, my master will say that spell." "Yet if I don't kill him," he went on to reflect, "I'll take a lot of thought and effort to rescue the master when this monster seizes some other chance to carry him off. The best thing is to kill him. If I kill him with the cudgel the master will say the spell, but then 'even a vicious tiger doesn't eat her own cubs'. I'll be able to get round my master with my smooth tongue and some well-chosen words." The splendid Great Sage uttered a spell and called out to the local deities and the gods of the mountains, "This evil spirit has tried to trick my master three times, and I'm now going to kill it. I want you to be witnesses in the air around me. Don't leave!" Hearing this command, the gods all had to obey and watch from the clouds. The Great Sage raised his cudgel and struck down the monster. Now, at last, it was dead. The Tang Priest was shaking with terror on the back of his horse, unable to speak. Pig stood beside him and said with a laugh, "That Monkey's marvelous, isn't he! He's gone mad. He's killed three people in a few hours'journey." The Tang Priest was just going to say the spell when Monkey threw himself in front of his horse and called out, "Don't say it, master, don't say it. Come and have a look at it." It was now just a pile of dusty bones. "He's only just been killed, Wukong," Sanzang said in astonishment, "so why has he turned into a skeleton?" "It was a demon corpse with magic powers that used to deceive people and destroy them. Now that I've killed it, it's reverted to its original form. The writing on her backbone says that she's called 'Lady White Bone.'" Sanzang was convinced, but Pig had to make trouble again. "Master," he said, "he's afraid that you'll say those words because he killed him with a vicious blow from his cudgel, and so he's made him look like this to fool you." The Tang Priest, who really was gullible, now believed Pig, and he started to recite the spell. Monkey, unable to stop the pain, knelt beside the path and cried, "Stop, stop. Say whatever it is you have to say," "Baboon," said Sanzang, "I have nothing more to say to you. If a monk acts rightly he will grow daily but invisibly, like grass in a garden during the spring, whereas an evildoer will be imperceptibly worn away day by day like a stone. You have killed three people, one after the other, in this wild and desolate place, and there is nobody here to find you out or bring a case against you. But if you go to a city or some other crowded place and start laying about you with that murderous cudgel, we'll be in big trouble and there will be no escape for us. Go back!"

"You're wrong to hold it against me, master," Monkey replied, "as that wretch was obviously an evil monster set on murdering you. But so far from being grateful that I've saved you by killing it, you would have to believe that idiot's tittle-tattle and keep sending me away. As the saying goes, you should never have to do anything more than three times. I'd be a low and shameless creature if I didn't go now. I'll go, I'll go all right, but who will you have left to look after you?" "Damned ape," Sanzang replied, "you get ruder and ruder. You seem to think that you're the only one. What about Pig and Friar Sand? Aren't they people?" On hearing him say that Pig and Friar Sand were suitable people too, Monkey was very hurt. "That's a terrible thing to hear, master," he said. "When you left Chang'an, Liu Boqin helped you on your way, and when you reached the Double Boundary Mountain you saved me and I took you as my master. I've gone into ancient caves and deep forests capturing monsters and demons. I won Pig and Friar Sand over, and I've had a very hard time of it. But today you've turned stupid and you're sending me back. 'When the birds have all been shot the bow is put away, and when the rabbits are all killed the hounds are stewed.' Oh well! If only you hadn't got that Band-tightening Spell." "I won't recite it again," said Sanzang. "You shouldn't say that," replied Monkey. "If you're ever beset by evil monsters from whom you can't escape, and if Pig and Friar Sand can't save you, then think of me. If it's unbearable, say the spell. My head will ache even if I'm many tens of thousands of miles away. But if I do come back to you, never say it again." The Tang Priest grew angrier and angrier as Monkey talked on, and tumbling off his horse he told

Friar Sand to take paper and brush from the pack. Then he fetched some water from a stream, rubbed the ink-stick on a stone, wrote out a letter of dismissal, and handed it to Monkey. “Here it is in writing,” he said. “I don’t want you as my disciple a moment longer. If I ever see you again may I fall into the Avichi Hell.” Monkey quickly took the document and said, “There’s no need to swear an oath, master. I’m off.” He folded the paper up and put it in his sleeve, then tried once more to mollify Sanzang. “Master,” he said, “I’ve spent some time with you, and I’ve also been taught by the Bodhisattva. Now I’m being fired in the middle of the journey, when I’ve achieved nothing. Please sit down and accept my homage, then I won’t feel so bad about going.” The Tang Priest turned away and would not look at him, muttering, “I am a good monk, and I won’t accept the respects of bad people like you.” Seeing that Sanzang was refusing to face him, the Great Sage used magic to give himself extra bodies. He blew a magic breath on three hairs plucked from the back of his head and shouted, “Change!” They turned into three more Monkeys, making a total of four with the real one, and surrounding the master on all four sides they kowtowed to him. Unable to avoid them by dodging to left or right, Sanzang had to accept their respects. The Great Sage jumped up, shook himself, put the hairs back, and gave Friar Sand these instructions: “You are a good man, my brother, so mind you stop Pig from talking nonsense and be very careful on the journey. If at any time evil spirits capture our master, you tell them that I ‘m his senior disciple. The hairy devils of the West have heard of my powers and won’t dare to harm him.” “I am a good monk,” said the Tang Priest, "and I 'd never mention the name of a person as bad as you. Go back." As his master refused over and over again to change his mind Monkey had nothing for it but to go. Look at him:

Holding back his tears he bowed good-bye to his master, then sadly but with care he gave instructions to Friar Sand.

His head pushed the hillside grass apart, his feet kicked the creepers up in the air.

Heaven and earth spun round like a wheel; at flying over mountains and seas none could beat him.

Within an instant no sign of him could be seen; he retraced his whole journey in a flash.

Holding back his anger, Monkey left his master and went straight back to the Water Curtain Cave on the Mountain of Flowers and Fruit on his somersault cloud. He was feeling lonely and miserable when he heard the sound of water. When he looked around from where he was in midair, he realized that it was the waves of the Eastern Sea. The sight of it reminded him of the Tang Priest, and he could not stop the tears from rolling down his cheeks. He stopped his cloud and stayed there a long time before going.

(6)Chapter 42

The Great Sage Reverently Visits the Southern Sea

Guanyin in Her Mercy Binds the Red Boy

Within moments they saw a mountain-top. "That's Mount Hao," said Monkey. "It's about a hundred and fifty miles from here to the demon's place." The Bodhisattva then ordered him to lower the auspicious cloud. She said the magic word "Om" above the summit, whereupon many a god and ghost—all the local spirits of the mountain—emerged from all around the mountain and gathered to kowtow to the Bodhisattva's lotus throne. "Do not be afraid," she said. "I am here to capture this demon king. I want this whole area swept completely clean, with not a living creature left behind within a hundred miles of here. All the baby animals in their dens and fledglings in holes in the trees must be put on the top of this high crag for safety." Obediently the demons withdrew, and soon they were all back. "Now that the place is clean, you may all return to your shrines," said the Bodhisattva. She then turned her vase of purity upside-down, letting the water roar out with a noise like thunder. Indeed, it Flowed down from the peak, Smashed through the rocks.

Flowed down from the peak with the force of the sea, smashed through the rocks like a mighty ocean.

Black spray rose to the watery heavens, great waves coldly reflected the sun.

Jade waves smashed through crags, while the sea was covered with golden lotuses.

Guanyin displayed her demon-quelling magic, producing a fixing dhyana from her sleeve.

She made the mountain a Potaraka Island, just like the one in the Southern Sea Tall grew the rushes, and the epiphyllum tender, Flowers were everywhere, and the pattra looked fresh.

Parrots perched in the purple bamboos, and quails were calling amid the verdant pines.

Endless lines of waves as far as the eye could see, and all that could be heard was the wind on the waters.

The Great Sage Monkey was full of silent admiration: "What great mercy and compassion. If I had that magic power I'd just have tipped the vase over, and to hell with the birds, beasts, reptiles and insects." "Stretch your hand out, Wukong," said the Bodhisattva. Monkey at once neatened his clothes and put out his left hand. The Bodhisattva drew out her sprig of willow, moistened it in the sweet dew, and wrote "Confusion" on his palm. "Make a fist," she told him, "and go to challenge the demon to battle. Let him beat you, then draw him back here. I have a Dharma power with which to subdue him." Monkey obediently took his cloud straight back to the cave entrance. Brandishing his cudgel with one hand and clenching the other into a fist, he shouted, "Open up, evil spirits." The little devils scampered back inside to report, "Sun the Novice is here again." "Shut the doors tight and ignore him," said the demon king. "What a fine son you are," shouted Monkey, "driving your own father out of doors and refusing to open the doors to him." "Sun the Novice is being very abusive," the little devils came back in to report. "Ignore him," said the demon king. When the doors were still shut after he had called twice, Monkey grew very angry. He raised his iron cudgel and smashed a hole in them. This threw the little devils into such a panic that they ran tumbling and stumbling in to say, "Sun the Novice has broken the doors down."

Hearing that the outer doors had been broken down after all the earlier reports the demon king now leapt up and sprang outside brandishing his spear and flinging insults back at Monkey: "You ape, you have no sense at all. I let you off lightly, but you don't know when enough is enough. You're trying to bully me again. I'll make you pay for the crime of smashing down my doors." "What about your crime in driving your own father away?" retorted Monkey. In his humiliation and anger the demon king thrust his spear at Brother Monkey's chest. Monkey parried this with his cudgel and hit back. Once they started they fought four or five rounds in which Monkey, one hand holding the cudgel and the other clenched in a fist, gave ground. "I'm going back to get the Tang Priest scrubbed and cleaned," said the demon. "You be careful, my boy," said Monkey. "Heaven can see what you're doing. You come here." This stung the demon king into an even greater fury. Running after Monkey he caught him up and took another thrust at him with his spear. Monkey swung back with his cudgel, and after a few more rounds ran away in defeat again. The demon king started to taunt him once more: "Last time you were good for twenty or thirty rounds. But now you're running away each time we fight. What's wrong with you?" "My dear boy," grinned Monkey, "your father's afraid you'll start that fire again." "I won't," said the demon, "now, come here." "If you're not going to start a fire," said Monkey, "let's move away from here. A tough guy doesn't attack people in front of his own door." Not realizing that this was a trick, the evil spirit raised his spear and ran after him. Monkey trailed his cudgel and opened his other hand. The demon king then fell into confusion and chased Monkey for all he was worth. The quarry moved like a shooting star, and the pursuer like a bolt that had just been shot from a crossbow. Before long Monkey saw the Bodhisattva. "Evil spirit," he said to the demon, "I'm scared of you. Please spare me. I'm going to where the Bodhisattva Guanyin of the Southern Sea lives. You go home now." The demon king was not going to believe this, so he gritted his teeth and continued the pursuit. With a shake of his body Monkey hid himself in the Bodhisattva's divine radiance. Seeing that Monkey had disappeared, the evil spirit went up to the Bodhisattva, glared at her, and asked, "Are you reinforcements sent for by Monkey?" The Bodhisattva did not answer. The demon king then twirled his spear and roared, "Hey! Are you reinforcements sent for by Monkey?" The Bodhisattva again did not answer. The demon king then thrust his spear straight at the Bodhisattva's heart, at which she turned into a beam of golden light and rose straight up to the highest heavens. Monkey went up with her and complained, "Bodhisattva, you've tricked me again. Why did you act deaf and dumb and say nothing when that demon kept asking you? One thrust from his spear and you ran away. You've even ditched your lotus throne." "Keep quiet," the Bodhisattva said, "and see what he does next." Monkey and Moksa stood next to each other up there watching while the demon said with a derisive jeer, "Insolent ape, you didn't know who you were up against. You didn't realize what sort of person I am. You fought me and lost several times, and then you sent for that putrid Bodhisattva. One thrust from my spear and she's disappeared. She's even left her lotus throne behind. Well, I'm going to sit on it now." The evil spirit then sat cross-legged in the middle of the throne, imitating the Bodhisattva. "That's just marvelous," said Monkey. "Now you've given your lotus throne away." "What are you saying now, Wukong?" the Bodhisattva asked. "What am I saying?" Monkey replied. "I'm saying you've given your lotus throne away. That fiend has just sat himself down on it. Would you care to get it back?" "But I want him to sit on it," the Bodhisattva said. "He's so small he 'll sit on it much more safely than you did," Monkey replied. "Stop talking," said the Bodhisattva, "and watch the power of the Dharma." She pointed downwards with her sprig of willow and called. "Turn back." The colors and auspicious glow of the lotus sea all disappeared, leaving the demon king sitting on the points of swords. "Drive the swords in by hitting their handles with the demon-quelling pestle," she ordered Moksa. Moksa then took his cloud straight down and struck over a thousand times with the demon-quelling pestle as if he were ramming down earth to build a wall. The demon was now pouring with blood from his open wounds as the points of two swords both came out through his thighs. Watch the demon as he grits his teeth against the agony. Throwing his spear down， he pulled furiously at the swords. "Bodhisattva," exclaimed Monkey, "that monster's not afraid of pain. He's trying to pull the swords out." Seeing this she called to Moksa, "Don't kill him." She then pointed her sprig of willow down once more, said the magic word "Om," and turned all Pole Star swords into halberds with inverted barbs like wolf's teeth that could not be pulled out. This finally made the demon desperate. Trying to bend the sword-points he pleaded in his agony, "Bodhisattva, your disciple was blind.

I failed to recognize your great Dharma powers. I beg you in your mercy to spare my life. I shall never do evil again, and I vow to become a Buddhist and observe the rules of conduct." On hearing this, the Bodhisattva went down on her golden light with Moksa, Monkey and the white parrot till she was in front of the evil spirit. "Will you really accept my rules of conduct?" The demon king nodded and said amid tears, "I will accept the rules if you spare my life." "Will you join my faith?" the Bodhisattva asked. "If you spare my life I swear I will," said the demon king. "In that case," said the Bodhisattva, "I shall lay my hands on your head and administer the vows." From her sleeve she produced a golden razor, with a few strokes of which she shaved the demon's head into a Mount Tai tonsure, leaving him with a topknot and with three little tufts. "Poor evil spirit," laughed Monkey. "Now you can't tell whether he's a boy or a girl. Goodness knows what he's meant to be." "As you have accepted my rules of conduct," said the Bodhisattva to the demon, "I will not mistreat you. I shall call you Page Sudhana. Do you accept?" The demon bowed in assent, wanting only to have his life spared. The Bodhisattva then pointed at him and called, "Withdraw!" With a crashing sound the Pole Star swords all fell into the dust. The boy was now unharmed. "Huian," said the Bodhisattva, "will you take the swords back to the Heavenly Palace and return them to His Majesty your father? You need not come back to meet me: wait with all the devas on the Pota Crag." As instructed, Moksa took the swords back to Heaven then returned to the Southern Sea. Now the boy's savage nature had not yet been tamed. When he realized that the pain in his legs had gone, that his backside was no longer wounded, and that he had three little tufts of hair on his head he ran over to grab his spear and said to the Bodhisattva, "You don't have any real Dharma powers that can put me down. It was all just an illusion. I refuse to accept your rules. Take this!" He jabbed at her face with his spear, making Monkey so angry that he struck at the boy with his cudgel. "Don't hit him," the Bodhisattva called out. "I have a way of punishing him." From her sleeve she produced a gold band and continued, "This treasure is one of the three bands—a golden one, tightening one, and a prohibition one—that the Tathagata Buddha gave me when I went to the East to find the pilgrim who would fetch the scriptures. You are wearing the tightening band. The prohibition band was used to subdue the great god guarding the mountain. I have not been able to bring myself to give the golden one away before, but as this demon is being so outrageous he shall have it." The splendid Bodhisattva then waved the band in the wind, shouted "Change!" and turned it into five bands that she threw at the boy with the command "Fix!" One went over his head, two on his hands, and two on his feet. "Stand clear, Wukong," the Bodhisattva ordered, "while I say the Gold-band Spell." "Bodhisattva," pleaded Monkey in panic, "I asked you here to subdue the demon, so why ever are you putting a curse on me?" "But this will not be the Band-tightening Spell that affects you," the Bodhisattva explained. "It will be the Gold-band Spell that works on the boy." Monkey felt easier in his mind as he stood beside the Bodhisattva and listened to her saying the spell. She made magic with her hands and recited the words silently several times over. The evil spirit twisted and tugged at his ears and cheeks, stamped his feet and rolled around. Indeed,

One phrase unites all the words without number;

Boundless and deep is the strength of the Dharma.

(7)Chapter 54

The Buddha-Nature Traveling West Enters Womankind

The Mind-Ape Makes a Plan to Escape from the Beauties

The carriage soon left the city and reached the Male-welcoming Post Station. At once the queen's arrival was announced to Sanzang and his disciples, who straightened up their clothes and came out to meet the queen's carriage. The queen raised the curtain and came out. "Which of these gentlemen is the Tang emperor's brother?" she asked. "The gentleman in front of the post station who is wearing a long gown," the tutor replied. The queen took a very careful look at him with her phoenix eyes, her moth-eyebrows raised. He was indeed an exceptional sight. Look at him:

A noble manner, Distinguished features.

White teeth as if made of silver, A square-cut mouth with lips of red.

The top of the head flat, the forehead broad and ample, fine eyes, a clear brow, and a long jaw.

His ears had the round lobes of a great man, his body was that of one with no ordinary talent.

A handsome, intelligent and gallant gentleman, the ideal consort for the graceful queen.

As the queen was gazing at him with delight and admiration she felt a great surge of desire and passion. Opening her cherry lips she said, "Younger brother of the Great Tang emperor, won't you ride in my royal carriage?" This made Sanzang blush from ear to ear. He was too embarrassed to look up at her. Pig, who was standing beside him, put his hands to his snout and devoured the queen with his eyes. She was a slim beauty:

> Brows like green willow, Flesh like mutton fat,cheeks set off with plum blossom, hair like the plumage of a golden phoenix. The autumn waves of her eyes were full of charm,like bamboo shoot in spring was her graceful posture. Red tassels floated with elegance over her temples, pearls and kingfisher feathers adorned her high-piled hair. Why talk now of the Princess Zhaojun's beauty? This queen is lovelier than the legendary Xi Shi. as her willow waist gently bends gold pendants tinkle, her lotus feet move lightly with her limbs of jade. The Lady of the Moon could not compare with her, No heavenly fairy could be her match, Her exquisite palace clothes were not those of a mere mortal,She was the Queen Mother of the West come to the Jade Pool.

Seeing how beautiful she was the idiot could not help drooling. His heart pounded and his limbs went weak; he melted like a snow lion next to a bonfire. When the queen came closer to Sanzang she took hold of him and said in a most beguiling voice, "Dear emperor's brother, won't you come into my dragon coach, ride back with me to the throne hall and marry me?" The venerable elder trembled, feeling unsteady on his feet. It was as if he were drunk or stupefied. "Don't be so shy and modest, Master," urged monkey, who was standing beside him. "Please get into the carriage with your future wife. Have our passport returned to us as soon as possible so that we can continue on our journey to fetch the scriptures." Sanzang could not bring himself to reply as he put his hand on Monkey, unable to hold back his tears. "Don't be so upset, Master," Monkey said. "Here's your chance to enjoy wealth and honor, so make the most of it." Sanzang had no choice but to do as Monkey bade him. Wiping his tears away he forced himself to smile as he stepped forward to hold the queen's white hand Sitting in the dragon carriage.

The queen was in raptures at the prospect of a husband, the elder in his terror wanted only to worship the Buddha. One longed to embrace her man in the candle-lit bedroom, tThe other wanted to see the World-honored on Vulture Peak. The queen was sincere, The holy monk was pretending. The queen in her sincerity Hoped that they would grow old in harmony together. The holy monk pretending Controlled his tender feeling to nourish his primal spirit. One was so happy to see her husband She wished they could be man and wife in broad daylight. The other was afraid of woman's beauty, Longing to escape her clutches and climb to the Thunder Monastery. The two ascended the carriage together, But the Tang Priest's intentions were far away.

When the civil and military officers saw their mistress enter the royal coach with the venerable Sanzang sitting beside her their faces were all wreathed in smiles. The procession turned around and went back into the city. Monkey told Friar Sand to carry the luggage while he led the horse as they followed behind the coach. Pig rushed wildly ahead, and when he reached the Tower of Five Phoenixes he started shouting, "This is very fine and splendid, but it won't do, it won't do at all. We've got to have some wedding drinks to toast the groom." He so alarmed the women officials carrying ceremonial insignia who were leading the procession that they all went back to the queen's carriage to report, "Your Majesty, the one with big ears and a long snout is making a row in front of the Tower of Five Phoenixes and demanding wedding drinks." On hearing this the queen leant her fragrant shoulder against Sanzang, pressed her peach-blossom cheek against his, and opened her sandalwood-scented mouth to murmur in her seductive voice, "Dear emperor's brother, is the one with big ears and a long snout one of your distinguished disciples?" "He is my second disciple," Sanzang replied. "He has an enormous appetite, and he has spent all his life trying to get good things to eat. We must lay on some food and drink for him before we can get on with things." The queen then asked anxiously if the office dealing with foreign relation had yet prepared the banquet. "It is ready," the women officials reported. "It is set out on the Eastern hall and includes both meat and vegetarian dishes." "Why both sorts?" the queen asked. "Your subjects thought that the Tang emperor's brother and his distinguished disciples might be vegetarians," the officials replied. "That was why we had both sorts of food provided." "Dear emperor's brother," said the queen with another little laugh of pleasure as she rubbed herself against Sanzang's fragrant cheek, "do you eat meat or vegetarian food?" "I eat vegetarian food," Sanzang replied, "but I have never given up wine. We must have a few cups of light wine for my second disciple to drink." Before he had finished speaking the queen's tutor said to the queen, "If it pleases Your Majesty, will you come to the Eastern hall for the banquet? Today is an auspicious day, and at a lucky hour tonight you may marry the emperor's brother. Tomorrow a new ecliptic begins, and I beg that the emperor's younger brother will enter the throne hall tomorrow to take his throne facing South as monarch and inaugurate a new reign." The queen was delighted by this suggestion. Descending from the coach hand-in-hand with Sanzang she went in through the palace's main gate. This is what they saw and heard:

Magic music wafting down from a gallery, as the turquoise carriage came within the palace.

The phoenix gates stood wide open amid gentle light, the harem in all its splendor was not closed.

Incense smoke curled aloft in the unicorn hall, shadows were moving behind the peacock screen.

The buildings were magnificent as those of a mighty state, the jade halls and golden horses were even more splendid.

When they reached the Eastern hall the harmonious sounds of panpipes and singing could be heard and two rows of powdered beauties seen. In the middle of the hall two sumptuous banquets were set out; a vegetarian one to the left and a meat one on the right. Below were two rows of individual places. The queen folded back her sleeves, took a jade goblet with her ten delicate fingers, and led Sanzang to the feast. Monkey went up to her and said, "We are all vegetarians, so would you ask my master to sit at the vegetarian feast to the left while three places are set below him for us three disciples?" "Yes, that's right," said the queen's tutor. "Master and disciples are like father and sons. It would be wrong to seat them side by side." The women officials quickly rearranged the seating, and the queen gave goblets to each of them as she led them to their places. Monkey gave the Tang Priest a look to remind him to return her courtesies, at which he came down from his seat with a jade goblet in his hand and led the queen to her place. The civil and military officials all kowtowed to the queen in gratitude and took their seats in order of precedence on either side. Only then did the music cease and the toasts begin. Pig did not worry about anything as he relaxed his belly and ate for all he was worth. He did not care whether it was jade-flake rice, steamed buns, sweet cakes, mushrooms, gill fungus, bamboo shoots, tree-ear fungus, day lilies, agar, laver, turnips, taro, devil-pepper, yams or seal-wort: he wolfed the whole lot down together. Then he drank some six or seven goblets of wine and shouted, "Fill it up, bring me another. I want a big goblet. Give me a few more drinks, then we can all go off and do what we've got to do." "What is there so important that makes us have to leave this fine banquet?" Friar Sand asked. "There's an old saying," replied the idiot with a grin, " 'that each man should stick to his trade. Some of us are getting married now, and others of us have to be on our way to fetch the scriptures. We mustn't ruin everything for the sake of a few more drinks. We want our passport returned as soon as possible. As they say, 'The warriors stay on their horses, all of them pressing ahead.'" When the queen heard this she sent for big cups, and the officials in attendance quickly fetched some parrot-shaped goblets, cormorant ladles, golden baskets, silver beakers, glass chargers, crystal dishes, immortals'bowls and amber goblets. Ambrosial liquor was now served out and everybody drank of it. Sanzang then bowed, rose to his feet, put his hands together in front of his chest and said to the queen, "Your Majesty, I am very grateful for this sumptuous banquet. We have had enough now. Could you now go to the throne hall and return the passport so that I may see the three of them off from the city tomorrow morning?" Doing as he asked, the queen led Sanzang by the hand as they ended the banquet and climbed the steps to the throne hall, where she invited the Tang Priest to sit on the throne. "No," he said, "it would be wrong. As Your Majesty's tutor said, a new ecliptic begins tomorrow: only then will I dare to take the throne. Today the passport must be stamped so that they can be sent on their way." The queen accepted his suggestions, sat on the dragon throne again, had a gilt chair placed to the left of it for Sanzang to sit on, and told the disciples to bring the passport. The Great Sage asked Friar Sand to open the cloth wrapper and take it out, then offered it with both hands to the queen, who examined it carefully. At the top were nine stamps from the Great Tang emperor's seals, and underneath were the seals of the countries of Elephantia, Wuji and Tarrycart. When she had looked at them the queen said with a delightful, tinkling smile in her voice, "Is your surname Chen, emperor's brother?" "My lay surname was Chen," he replied, "and my religious name is Xuanzang. It was when the Tang emperor in his wisdom and mercy took me as his younger brother that he granted me the surname Tang." "Why do your illustrious disciples'names not appear on the passport?" the queen asked. "My three stupid disciples are not men of Tang." Sanzang replied. "But if they are not from Tang why have they come here with you?" the queen asked again. "My senior disciple," Sanzang answered, "was originally from the country of Aolai in the Eastern Continent of Superior Body. My second disciple is from Gao Village in Stubet in the Western Continent of Cattle-gift. My third disciple is from the Flowing Sands River. They were all punished for offences against the laws of Heaven until the Bodhisattva Guanyin delivered them from their sufferings. Since then they have been converted to the faith and have volunteered to escort me on my journey to fetch the scriptures from the Western Heaven to redeem their past crimes. I won each of them during the journey, which is why their religious names have not been entered on the passport." "Would you like me to add their names to it?" said the queen. "If that is Your Majesty's pleasure," Sanzang replied. The queen then sent for brush and ink-stone, and when she had rubbed the ink-stick on the stone to produce a thick and fragrant ink with which she filled the hairs of her writing brush she wrote the names of the three disciples—Sun Wukong, Zhu Wuneng and Sha Wujing—at the bottom of the passport. Then she stamped it fair and square with her royal seal, wrote her signature, and handed it down to Monkey, who told Friar Sand to wrap it up again carefully. The queen then presented them with a dish of small pieces of gold and silver, came down from her throne and said to Monkey, "You three must take this to help with the costs of your journey and go to the Western Heaven as quickly as you can. When you come back with the scriptures we shall richly reward you again." "We are men of religion," said Brother Monkey, "and we do not accept gold and silver. There will be places along the way for us to beg food from." Seeing that they were not going to accept it the queen had ten bolts of damask and brocade brought out that she gave to Monkey with the words, "You are in such a hurry that we do not have time for this to be made up. Please take this to have some clothes made on the journey to keep you warm." "We monks may not wear damask or brocade," Monkey said. "We are only allowed to cover ourselves with cotton cloth." Seeing that he would not accept the silk either, the queen ordered that three pints of rice be brought out to provide them with a meal on their journey. The moment Pig heard the word "rice" he took it and put it with the bundles of luggage. "Brother," Monkey said to him, "the luggage is very heavy now. Will you be able to carry the rice as well?" "You wouldn't know that rice is best eaten the same day it's cooked," Pig replied. "One meal and it'll be finished." He then put his hands together in thanks.

(8)Chapter 58

Two Minds Throw Heaven and Earth into Uproar

One Body Cannot Achieve True Nirvana

When Monkey and Friar Sand took their leave of the Bodhisattva they departed from the Southern Ocean by two beams of auspicious light. Now Monkey's somersault cloud was much faster than Friar Sand's immortal's cloud, so Monkey was drawing ahead when Friar Sand pulled him back and said, "There's no need for you to show me your heels like that, brother, rushing ahead to sort things out at home. Wait for me to come with you." Although Brother Monkey's intentions were good Friar Sand could not help being suspicious. The two of them then flew their clouds together and were soon in sight of the Mountain of Flowers and Fruit. They brought their clouds down and had a good look at the outside of the cave, where there was indeed a Monkey sitting on a high stone terrace, drinking and making merry with his monkey hosts. He looked exactly the same as the Great Sage: yellow hair held in a golden band, fiery eyes with golden pupils, a brocade tunic, a tiger-skin kilt, a gold-banded iron cudgel in his hands, and deerskin boots. He had the same: Hairy face like a thunder god, cheeks like the planet Saturn; pointed ears and a forehead broad, and long, protruding fangs.

In an explosion of fury the Great Sage left Friar Sand behind as he went up to the other, brandishing his cudgel and shouting abusively, "What sort of demon do you think you are? How dare you! You make yourself look like me, you steal my children and grandchildren, you occupy my immortal's cave, and on top of that you live it up like this." When the other Monkey heard all this he did not deign to reply but went for him with his own iron cudgel. When the two Monkeys were together there was no way of telling the true from the false. It was a splendid fight:

> Two cudgels and a pair of monkey spirits, a couple of truly formidable foes. Both want to escort the Tang emperor's brother, each longs to achieve what will make him famous. The true Monkey now accepts Sakyamuni's teachings, the false demon only pretends to be a Buddhist. In magic powers and transformations, the false and true are evenly balanced. One is the Sage Equaling Heaven of primal energy, the other an earth spirit who has long refined his powers. One wields an As-You-Will gold-banded cudgel, the other an iron bar that follows the heart's desire. As they block and parry neither comes out on top. First they fight each other outside the cave, but soon they carry on the struggle in mid-air.

Each of them rose on his clouds and light till they were fighting up in the clouds of the ninth heaven. As Friar Sand stood beside them he dared not intervene in their fight as he really could not tell the true Monkey from the false one. He longed to draw his sword and join in, but he was frightened of wounding the real Monkey. When he had endured this dilemma for a long time he shot back down to the mountain scar, where he used his demon-quelling staff to fight his way to the outside of the Water Curtain Cave. Here he sent all the demons fleeing in terror, turned the stone benches over, and smashed the tableware from which they had been eating and drinking to their hearts'content. But although he looked everywhere for the blue felt bundles he failed to find them. Now the Water Curtain Cave was so called because the waterfall screening its entrance looked from a distance like a white cloth curtain and only appeared as the waterfall it was from close to. As Friar Sand did not know that the entrance to the cave was behind it he was unable to find the way in, so he took his cloud back up to the Ninth Heaven and started swinging his staff again, still unable to strike. "Friar Sand," said the Great Sage, "you can't help much here. Go back and tell the master what's been happening to us while I drive this demon to Potaraka Island in the Southern Ocean for the Bodhisattva to identify me as the real Monkey." The other Monkey then repeated what he had said. As they looked and sounded exactly the same Friar Sand really could not tell them apart. He could only do as he was told and ride his cloud back to rejoin the Tang Priest. The two Monkeys meanwhile fought and shouted their way to the Southern Ocean, where they went straight to Potaraka Island still throwing blows and abuse at each other. Their unending shouts disturbed all the devas who protected the Law, so that they went to the Tide Cave and reported, "Bodhisattva, two Sun Wukongs really have fought their way here." The Bodhisattva came down from her lotus throne and went with Moksa, the page Sudhana and the Naga Maiden to the entrance, where she shouted, "Stay where you are, evil beast." Each Monkey grabbed hold of the other one while the real one said, "Bodhisattva, this damned fiend really does look just like me. Our fight started at the Water Curtain Cave and has been going on for a very long time without getting anywhere. Friar Sand's mortal eyes are too weak to tell us apart, so he can't help at all. I sent him back West to report to the master while I fought this bloody impostor here for you to distinguish the true from the false. Your eyes are perceptive, Bodhisattva." The other Monkey then said exactly the same. Look long and hard though they did, the devas and the Bodhisattva could not tell which was which. "Let go of each other and stand one on each side while I take another look," the Bodhisattva said. Doing as she told them, the one on her left said, "I'm the real Monkey," and the one on her right said, "He's an impostor." The Bodhisattva then called Moksa and Sudhana to her and whispered these instructions: "I want one of you to stand very close to each of them while I recite the Band-tightening Spell quietly. The one in agony will be the real one, and the one who isn't will be the impostor." One of them went up to each of the Monkeys, but as the Bodhisattva secretly said the words of the spell they both yelled out in pain, clutched their heads, and rolled on the ground shouting, "Stop! Stop!" The moment she did they grabbed each other again and went on fighting and shouting. At her wit's end, the Bodhisattva ordered the devas and Moksa to help, but none of them dared strike a blow for fear of wounding the real Monkey. "Sun Wukong," called the Bodhisattva, and both the Monkeys answered her. "As you were once appointed the Protector of the Horses," said the Bodhisattva, "When you made havoc in the Heavenly Palace, all the heavenly generals recognize you. Go to the upper world: let it distinguish between you two. Come back and tell me the result." The Great Sage thanked the Bodhisattva for her kindness and the other Monkey also thanked her.

(9)Chapter 59

Sanzang's Way is Blocked at the Fiery Mountains

Monkey First Tries to Borrow the Plantain Fan

The Great Sage then turned his cloud around and headed back

East. A moment later he had landed the cloud and was standing by the red brick wall. Pig was very pleased indeed to see him. “Master,” he said, “Monkey’s here! He’s back!” Sanzang went out with the old man of the farm and Friar Sand to greet him, and they all went back inside. Propping the fan against the wall, Monkey asked, “Tell me sir, is this the fan?” “Yes, yes,” the old man said. “This is a great achievement, disciple,” said Sanzang. “Fetching this treasure must have cost you a great deal of trouble.” “No trouble at all,” said Monkey. “Do you know who that Iron Fan Immortal is? She’s Raksasi, the wife of the Bull Demon King and the Red Boy’s mother. Her other name is Princess Iron Fan. I found her outside her cave and asked to borrow the fan, but all she could talk of were her old grudges. She took a few cuts at me with her swords, but when I gave her a bit of a scare with the cudgel she fanned me with the fan and blew me all the way to Little Mount Sumeru. I was lucky enough to be able to see the Bodhisattva Lingji who gave me a tablet that stops winds and showed me the way back to Mount Turquoise Cloud. Then I saw Raksasi again, but this time her fan did not move me an inch, so she went back into her cave and I turned into a tiny insect to fly back in after her. When the damned woman-asked for some tea I slipped in under the froth at the top, got inside her, and started giving her a few punches and kicks. She couldn’t take the pain. She kept saying, ‘Spare me, brother-in-law, spare me.’ As she agreed to lend me the fan I spared her life and took the fan. I’ll give it back to her after we’ve crossed the Fiery Mountains.” When Sanzang heard this he was extremely grateful. Master and disciples then took their leave of the old man and traveled about fifteen miles West. The heat was becoming unbearable. "The soles of my feet are being roasted," Friar Sand complained. "My trotters are getting burnt and it hurts," said Pig. The horse was going much faster than usual too. The ground was so hot that they could not stop, but every step was painful. "Please dismount, Master," said Monkey, "and brothers, stay here while I use the fan to put the fire out. When the wind and the rain come the ground will be a lot cooler and we'll be able to get across the mountains." He then raised the fan and fanned it hard once in the direction of the fire: tongues of flame rose above the mountains. He fanned again, and they were a hundred times as high. He fanned a third time, and now they were a couple of miles high and beginning to burn him. Monkey fled, but not before two patches of fur had been burnt away. He ran straight back to the Tang Priest and said, "Hurry back, hurry back, the flames are coming." The master remounted and headed back East with Pig and Friar Sand some seven miles before stopping and asking, "What happened, Wukong?" "It's the wrong one," Monkey said, flinging the fan down, "it's the wrong one. The damned woman fooled me." When Sanzang heard this he frowned and felt thoroughly depressed. "What are we to do?" he sobbed, the tears flowing freely down his cheeks. "Brother," said Pig, "why did you come back in such a mad rush and send us back here?" "The first time I fanned there were flames," Monkey replied, "the second time the fire got fiercer, and the third time the flames were a couple of miles high. If I hadn't run fast all my fur would have been burnt off." "But you're always telling us that you can't be hurt by thunder and lightning and that fire can't burn you," said Pig with a laugh. "How come you're afraid of fire now?" "Idiot," said Monkey, "you don't understand anything. The other times I was ready: that's why I wasn't hurt. Today I didn't make any flame-avoiding spells or use magic to defend myself. That's why two patches of my fur were singed." "If the fire's so fierce and there's no other way to the West what are we going to do?" Friar Sand asked. "We'll just have to find somewhere where there isn't any fire," Pig replied. "Which way will that be?" Sanzang asked. "East, North or South: there's no fire those ways," said Pig. "But which way are the scriptures?" "Only in the West," Pig replied. "I only want to go where the scriptures are," Sanzang said. "We 're well and truly struck," said Friar Sand. "Where there are scriptures there's fire, and where there's no fire there are no scriptures." While master and disciples were talking this nonsense they heard someone call, "Don't get upset, Great Sage. Come and have some vegetarian food before you take your discussions any further." The four of them looked round to see an old man wearing a cloak that floated in the wind and a hat the shape of a half moon. In his hand he held a dragon-headed stick, and on his legs were boots of iron. With him was a demon with the beak of an eagle and the cheeks of a fish carrying on his head a copper bowl full of steamed buns, millet cakes, cooked millet and rice. The old man bowed to them on the road to the West and said, "I am the local god of the Fiery Mountains. As I know that you are escorting this holy monk, Great Sage, and can't go any further I have brought this meal as an offering." "Eating doesn't matter," Monkey replied. "When are these fires going to be put out so that my master can cross the mountains?" "If you want to put the fires out you must first ask Raksasi to lend you the plantain fan," the local god said. Monkey went to the side of the path, picked the fan up, and said, "This is it, isn 't it? The more I fan the flames the more fiercely they burn. Why?" "Because it's not the real one," said the local deity with a laugh when he looked at it. "She fooled you." "Then how am I to get the real one?" Monkey said. The local god bowed again and had a slight smile on his face as he replied, "If you want to borrow the real plantain fan you will have to ask the Strong-arm King."

(10)Chapter 100

The Journey Back to the East is Made

The Five Immortals Achieve Nirvana

The officials all expressed their congratulations and kowtowed before the imperial text on the holy teaching, which was going to be published everywhere in the capital and the provinces. "Would you be willing to recite some of the true scriptures for us, Younger Brother?" Taizong asked. "Your Majesty," Sanzang replied, "if true scriptures are to be recited it must be done in the Buddha's ground. A throne hall is no place for the recital of scriptures." Taizong was most pleased to accept this. "Which is the purest monastery in the city of Chang'an?" he asked his officers it attendance, at which the Academician Xiao Yu slipped forward from his rank to memorialize, "The Monastery of the Wild Goose Stupa in the city is the purest of them all." Taizong then ordered his officials, "Each of you is reverently to bring a few rolls of the true scriptures and accompany us to the Monastery of the Wild Goose Stupa, where we shall invite our younger brother to preach on the scriptures." The officials, all carrying some rolls of the scriptures, went with Taizong to the monastery, where a high platform was erected and everything was neatly set out. "Pig, Friar Sand," the venerable elder commanded, "bring the dragon horse with you and put the luggage in order. Monkey will stay beside me." He then addressed the emperor, saying, "If Your Majesty wishes to spread the true scriptures throughout the world copies must be made before they can be published. The original texts must be stored as great treasures. They may not be shown any disrespect or be defiled." "Younger Brother," replied Taizong with a smile, "what you say is very correct, very correct." He then ordered the officials of the Hanlin Academy and the Palace Secretariat to copy out the true scriptures and had another monastery, the Copying Monastery, founded to the East of the city wall. The venerable elder mounted the platform with several scriptures in his hands. He was just about to begin reciting them when scented breezes began to waft around and the Eight Great Vajrapanis appeared in mid-air to shout aloud, "Scripture-reciter, put those scriptures down and come back to the West with us." Monkey and the other two, who were standing below Sanzang, all rose up above the ground together with the white horse. Sanzang put the scriptures down and also rose up to the ninth level of clouds, then went away with them through the air. Taizong and his officials were all so alarmed that they kowtowed to the sky.

This was indeed a case of the holy monk long strove to fetch the scriptures, for fourteen years across the West he strayed.

He journeyed hard and met with much disaster, by

mountains and by rivers long delayed.

Completing eight times nine and one nine more, his deeds filled worlds in numbers beyond measure.

He went back to his country taking sutras, that people in the East will always treasure.

When Taizong and all the officials had finished worshipping, eminent monks were selected to prepare a great Land and Sea Mass in the Monastery of the Wild Goose Stupa at which the true scriptures of the Great Store would be recited, and by which all evil-doing ghosts in the underworld would be saved, and goodness would spread all around. We will not describe how copies were made of the scriptures and published throughout the empire. The story tells instead how the Eight Vajrapanis led the venerable elder, his three disciples and the horse, all five of them back to Vulture Peak. The journey to Chang'an and back had taken eight days. Just when all the deities of Vulture Peak were listening to the Buddha preaching, the Eight Vajrapanis led master and disciples in. "In obedience to the golden command," they reported to the Tathagata, "your disciples have carried the holy monks back to the land of Tang, where they handed the scriptures over. We have now come to report our mission completed." The Tang Priest and his disciples were then told to step forward and be given their jobs. "Holy Monk," the Tathagata said, "in an earlier life you were my second disciple, and called Master Golden Cicada. But because you would not listen to my sermon on the Dharma and had no respect for my great teaching I demoted your soul to be reborn in the East.

Now, happily, you have come over to the faith and rely on our support; and in following our teaching your achievement in fetching the true scriptures has been very great. Your reward will be to be promoted to high office as the Candana-punya Buddha. Sun Wukong, when you made great havoc in the palaces of heaven I had to use powerful magic to crush you under the Five Elements Mountain until, happily, your heaven-sent punishment was completed and you were converted to the Sakyamuni's faith. It was also fortunate that you suppressed your evil side and gave play to your good side as you won glory by defeating monsters and demons along the journey. All that was begun has now been completed and you too will be rewarded with high office as the Victorious Fighting Buddha. Zhu Wuneng; you used to be a water god in the River of Heaven as Marshal Tian Peng. Because of your drunken flirtation with an immortal maiden at the Peach Banquet you were sent down to be born in the lower world as a beast. From your love of the human body you sinned in the Cloud Pathway Cave on the Mount of Blessing before your conversion to the great faith and entry into our Buddhist sect. You guarded the holy monk on his journey, but your heart is still unregenerate, and you are not yet purged of your lust. But as you won merit by carrying the luggage you will be rewarded with promotion as the Altar Cleanser." "They've both been made Buddhas," Pig shouted, "so why am I only the Altar Cleanser?" "Because you have a voracious appetite, a lazy body and a huge belly," the Tathagata replied. "Now very many people in the world's four continents believe in our teachings. I will ask you to clean up the altars after all Buddhist services: your post is of a rank that provides plenty to eat. What is wrong with that?" "Sha Wujing, you used to be the Curtain-lifting General until you were banished to the lower world for smashing a crystal bowl at a Peach Banquet. You fell into the River of Flowing Sands where you sinned by killing and eating people, until, thank goodness, you were converted to our teaching, sincerely relied on our support, and won merit by protecting the holy monk and leading the horse up the mountain. Your reward will be elevation to high office as the Golden Arhat." Then he said to the white horse. "You were originally the son of Guangjin, the Dragon King of the Western Ocean. Because you disobeyed your father you were punished for being unfilial until you too were converted to the Dharma and to our faith. Every day you carried the holy monk to the West, and after that you carried the holy scriptures back to the East. For these achievements you will be rewarded by being made a Heavenly Dragon of the Eight Classes of Being." The venerable elder and his three disciples all kowtowed to express their thanks, and the horse showed its gratitude too. A protector was then ordered to take the horse straight down to the Dragon-transforming Pool by the precipice at the back of Vulture Peak and push him into the pool. At once the horse stretched itself out, shed all its hair, and acquired horns. Golden scales grew all over its body and a silver beard sprouted on its cheeks and chin. Then, shining all over with auspicious aura and with clouds of good omen in every claw, it flew up from the Dragon-transforming Pool to coil itself around the Heaven-supporting Winged Column. All the Buddhas expressed their admiration for the Tathagata's great magic. "Master," Monkey said to the Tang Priest, "now that I've become a

Buddha just like you, surely I don't have to go on wearing this golden band. Do you plan to say any more Band-tightening Spells to tighten it round my head? Say a Band-loosening Spell as quickly as you can, take it off, and smash it to smithereens. Don't let that Bodhisattva or whatever she is make life miserable for anyone else with it." "It was because you were so uncontrollable in those days that this magic was needed to keep you in order." Sanzang replied. "Now that you are a Buddha it can of course go. There is no reason for it to stay on your head any longer. Feel there now." When Monkey raised his hands to feel he found that it had indeed gone. The Candana-punya Buddha, the Victorious Fighting Buddha, the Altar Cleanser and the Golden Arhat had all completed the true achievement and reached their proper places. The heavenly dragon horse had also come back to its true self. There is a poem to prove this that goes:

All of reality turns to dust, when the four appearances combine the body is renewed.

The substance of the Five Elements is all void, forget about the passing fame of fiends.

With Candana-punya comes the great awakening, when duties are completed they escape from suffering.

Great is the blessing of scriptures spread abroad, within the only gate five sages dwell on high.

第十章 《红楼梦》

1. 作品介绍

《红楼梦》，中国古代章回体长篇小说，中国古典四大名著之一，一般认为是清代作家曹雪芹所著。小说以贾、史、王、薛四大家族的兴衰为背景，以富贵公子贾宝玉为视角，以贾宝玉与林黛玉、薛宝钗的爱情婚姻悲剧为主线，描绘了一批举止见识出于须眉之上的闺阁佳人的人生百态，展现了真正的人性美和悲剧美，可以说是一部从各个角度展现女性美以及中国古代社会世态百相的史诗性著作。

《红楼梦》版本有120回“程本”和80回“脂本”两大系统。“程本”为程伟元排印的印刷本，“脂本”为脂砚斋在不同时期的早期手抄本。“脂本”是“程本”的底本。

《红楼梦》开篇以神话形式介绍作品的由来，说女娲补天之石剩一块未用，弃在大荒山无稽崖青埂峰下。茫茫大士、渺渺真人经过该地，施法使其有了灵性，携带下凡。不知过了几世几劫，空空道人路过，见石上刻录了一段故事，便受石之托，抄写下来传世。辗转传到曹雪芹手中，经他批阅十载、增删五次而成书。

《红楼梦》是一部具有世界影响力的人情小说，举世公认的中国古典小说巅峰之作，中国封建社会的百科全书，传统文化的集大成者。小说作者以“大旨谈情，实录其事”自勉，只按自己的事体情理，按迹循踪，摆脱旧套，新鲜别致，取得了非凡的艺术成就。“真事隐去，假语村言”的特殊笔法更是令后世读者脑洞大开，揣测之说久而遂多。20世纪以来，学术界因《红楼梦》异常出色的艺术成就和丰富深刻的思想底蕴而产生了以《红楼梦》为研究对象的专门学问——红学。

2. 作者介绍

曹雪芹（约1715年5月28日～约1763年2月12日），名霑，字梦阮，号雪芹，又号芹溪、芹圃，中国古典名著《红楼梦》作者，关外祖籍辽宁铁岭（存在争议），生于江宁（今南京），曹雪芹出身清代内务府正白旗包衣世家，他是江宁织造曹寅之孙，曹颙之子（一说曹頫之子）。

曹雪芹早年在南京江宁织造府亲历了一段锦衣纨绔、富贵风流的生活。曾祖父曹玺任江宁织造；曾祖母孙氏做过康熙帝的保姆；祖父曹寅做过康熙帝的伴读和御前侍卫，后任江宁织造，兼任两淮巡盐监察御史，极受康熙宠信。雍正六年（1728年），曹家因亏空获罪被抄家，曹雪芹随家人迁回北京老宅。后又移居北京西郊，靠卖字画和朋友救济为生。曹家从此一蹶不振，日渐衰微。经历了生活中的重大转折，曹雪芹深感世态炎凉，对封建社会有了更清醒、更深刻的认识。他蔑视权贵，远离官场，过着贫困如洗的艰难日子。曹雪芹素性放达，爱好广泛，对金石、诗书、绘画、园林、中医、织补、工艺、饮食等均有所研究。他以坚韧不拔的毅力，历经多年艰辛，终于创作出极具思想性、艺术性的伟大作品——《红楼梦》。

乾隆二十七年（1762年），幼子夭亡，他陷于过度的忧伤和悲痛，卧床不起。乾隆二十八年除夕（1763年2月12日），因贫病无医而逝。关于曹雪芹逝世的年份，另有乾隆二十九年除夕（1764年2月1日）、甲申（1764年）初春之说。

3. 经典赏析

（1）第3回 贾雨村夤缘复旧职 林黛玉抛父进京都

一语未了，只听后院中有人笑声说："我来迟了，不曾迎接远客！"黛玉纳罕道："这些人个个皆敛声屏气，恭肃严整如此，这来者系谁，这样放诞无礼？"心下想时，只见一群媳妇、丫鬟围拥着一个人，从后房门进来。这个人打扮与众姊妹不同，彩绣辉煌，恍若神妃仙子：头上戴着金丝八宝攒珠髻，绾着朝阳五凤挂珠钗；项上戴着赤金盘螭璎珞圈；裙边系着豆绿宫条、双衡比目玫瑰佩；身上穿着缕金百蝶穿花大红洋缎窄褙袄，外罩五彩刻丝石青银鼠褂，下着翡翠撒花洋绉裙。一双丹凤三角眼，两弯柳叶吊梢眉；身量苗条，体格风骚；粉面含春威不露，丹唇未启笑先闻。黛玉连忙起身接见。贾母笑道："你不认得她，她是我们这里有名的一个泼皮破落户儿，南省俗谓作'辣子'，你只叫他她'凤辣子'就是。"黛玉正不知以何称呼，只见众姊妹都忙告诉她道："这是琏嫂子。"黛玉虽不识，也曾听见母亲说过，大舅贾赦之子贾琏，娶的就是二舅母王氏之内侄女，自幼假充男儿教养的，学名叫王熙凤。黛玉忙陪笑见礼，以"嫂"呼之。这熙凤携着黛玉的手，上下细细打量了一回，仍送至贾母身边坐下，因笑道："天下真有这样标致人物，我今儿才算见了！况且这通身的气派，竟不像老祖宗的外孙女儿，竟是个嫡亲的孙女，怨不得老祖宗天天口头心头，一时不忘。只可怜我这妹妹这样命苦，怎么姑妈偏就去世了！"说着，便用帕拭泪。贾母笑道："我才好了，你倒来招我！你妹妹远路才来，身子又弱，也才劝住了，快再休提前话！”这熙凤听了，忙转悲为喜道：“正是呢！我一见了妹妹，一心都在他身上了，又是喜欢，又是伤心，竟忘记了老祖宗。该打，该打！”又忙携黛玉之手，问：“妹妹几岁了？可也上过学？现吃什么药？在这里不要想家，想要什么吃的，什么玩的，只管告诉我；丫头老婆们不好了，也只管告诉我。”一面又问婆子们：“林姑娘的行李东西可搬进来了？带了几个人来？你们赶早打扫两间下房，让她们去歇歇。”

后人有《西江月》二词，批这宝玉极恰，其词曰：

无故寻愁觅恨，有时似傻如狂。纵然生得好皮囊，腹内原来草莽。

潦倒不通世务，愚顽怕读文章。行为偏僻性乖张，那管世人诽谤！

富贵不知乐业，贫穷难耐凄凉。可怜辜负好韶光，于国于家无望。

天下无能第一，古今不肖无双。寄言纨绔与膏粱：莫效此儿形状！

宝玉早已看见多了一个姊妹，便料定是林姑妈之女，忙来作揖。厮见毕，归坐，细看形容，与众各别：两弯似蹙非蹙罥烟眉，一双似喜非喜含露目。态生两靥之愁，娇袭一身之病。泪光点点，娇喘微微。闲静时如姣花照水，行动处似弱柳扶风。心较比干多一窍，病如西子胜三分。宝玉看罢，因笑道：“这个妹妹我曾见过的。”贾母笑道：“可又是胡说！你又何曾见过他？”宝玉笑道：“虽然未曾见过他，然我看着面善，心里就算是旧相识，今日只作远别重逢，亦未为不可。”贾母笑道：“更好，更好，若如此，更相和睦了！”宝玉便走近黛玉身边坐下，又细细打量一番，因问：“妹妹可曾读书？”黛玉道：“不曾读书，只上了一年学，些须认得几个字。”宝玉又道：“妹妹尊名是那两个字？”黛玉便说了名字。宝玉又问表字。黛玉道：“无字。”宝玉笑道：“我送妹妹一妙字，莫若‘颦颦’二字极好！”

（2）第 4 回 薄命女偏逢薄命郎 葫芦僧乱判葫芦案

雨村因问方才何故有不令发签之意。这门子道：“老爷既荣任到这一省，难道就没抄一张本省‘护官符’来不成？”雨村忙问：“何为‘护官符’？我竟不知。”门子道：“这还了得！连这个不知，怎能作得长远！如今凡作地方官者，皆有一个私单，上面写的是本省最有权有势、极富极贵的大乡绅名姓，各省皆然；倘若不知，一时触犯了这样的人家，不但官爵，只怕连性命还保不成呢！所以绰号叫作‘护官符’。方才所说的这薛家，老爷如何惹得他！他这件官司并无难断之处，皆因都碍着情分脸面，所以如此。”一面说，一面从顺袋中取出一张抄写的‘护官符’来，递与雨村，看时，上面皆是本地大族名宦之家的谚俗口碑。其口碑排写得明白，下面所皆注着始祖官爵并房次。石头亦曾照样抄写了一张，今据石上所抄云：

贾不假，白玉为堂金作马。（宁国、荣国二公之后，共二十房分，除宁、荣亲派八房在都外，现原籍住者十二房。）

阿房宫，三百里，住不下金陵一个史。（保龄侯尚书令史公之后，房分共十八，都中现住者十房，原籍现居八房。）

东海缺少白玉床，龙王来请金陵王。（都太尉统制县伯王公之后，共十二房，都中二房，余在籍。）

丰年好大雪，珍珠如土金如铁。（紫薇舍人薛公之后，现领内府帑银行商，共八房分。）

（3）第 18 回　隔珠帘父女勉忠勤　搦湘管姊弟裁题咏

半日静悄悄的。忽见一对红衣太监骑马缓缓的走来，至西街门下了马，将马赶出围幕之外，便垂手面西站住。半日又是一对，亦是如此。少时便来了十来对，方闻得隐隐细乐之声。一对对龙旌凤翣，雉羽夔头，又有销金提炉焚着御香。然后一把曲柄七凤黄金伞过来，便是冠袍带履。又有值事太监捧着香珠、绣帕、漱盂、拂尘等类。一队队过完，后面方是八个太监抬着一顶金顶金黄绣凤版舆，缓缓行来。贾母等连忙路旁跪下。早飞跑过几个太监来，扶起贾母、邢夫人、王夫人来。那版舆抬进大门，入仪门往东去，到一所院落门前，有执拂太监跪请下舆更衣。于是抬舆入门，太监等散去，只有昭容、彩嫔等引领元春下舆。只见院内各色花灯烂灼，皆系纱绫扎成，精致非常。上面有一匾灯，写着“体仁沐德”四字。元春入室，更衣毕，复出，上舆进园。只见园中香烟缭绕，花彩缤纷，处处灯光相映，时时细乐声喧；说不尽这太平气象，富贵风流。

（4）第 23 回　西厢记妙词通戏语　牡丹亭艳曲警芳心

宝玉笑道：“妹妹，你说好不好？”黛玉笑道：“果然有趣。”宝玉笑道：“我就是个‘多愁多病身’，你就是那‘倾国倾城貌’。”黛玉听了，不觉带腮连耳通红，登时直竖起两道似蹙非蹙的眉，瞪了两只似睁非睁的眼，微腮带怒，薄面含嗔，指宝玉道："你这该死的胡说！好好的把这淫词艳曲弄了来，还学了这些混话来欺负我。我告诉舅舅、舅母去。"说到"欺负"两个字上，早又把眼睛圈儿红了，转身就走。宝玉着了忙，向前拦住说道："好妹妹，千万饶我这一遭！原是我说错了。若有心欺负你，明儿我掉在池子里，教个癞头鼋吞了去，变个大王八，等你明儿做了一品夫人、病老归西的时候，我往你坟上替你驮一辈子的碑去。"说得黛玉嗤的一声笑了。一面揉着眼，一面笑道："一般也唬得这个调儿，还只管胡说。'呸！原来是苗而不秀，是个银样镴枪头。'"宝玉听了，笑道："你这个呢？我也告诉去。"黛玉笑道："你说你会过目成诵，难道我就不能一目十行么？"

（5）第 27 回 滴翠亭杨妃戏彩蝶 埋香冢飞燕泣残红

花谢花飞飞满天，红消香断有谁怜？
游丝软系飘春榭，落絮轻沾扑绣帘。
闺中女儿惜春暮，愁绪满怀无释处，
手把花锄出绣闺，忍踏落花来复去。
柳丝榆荚自芳菲，不管桃飘与李飞。
桃李明年能再发，明年闺中知有谁？
三月香巢已垒成，梁间燕子太无情。
明年花发虽可啄，却不道人去梁空巢也倾！
一年三百六十日，风刀霜剑严相逼。
明媚鲜妍能几时，一朝飘泊难寻觅。
花开易见落难寻，阶前闷杀葬花人。
独倚花锄泪暗洒，洒上空枝见血痕。
杜鹃无语正黄昏，荷锄归去掩重门。

青灯照壁人初睡，冷雨敲窗被未温。
怪奴底事倍伤神，半为怜春半恼春；
怜春忽至恼忽去，至又无言去不闻。
昨宵庭外悲歌发，知是花魂与鸟魂？
花魂鸟魂总难留，鸟自无言花自羞。
愿奴胁下生双翼，随花飞到天尽头。
天尽头，何处有香丘？
未若锦囊收艳骨，一抔净土掩风流。
质本洁来还洁去，强于污淖陷渠沟。
尔今死去侬收葬，未卜侬身何日丧？
侬今葬花人笑痴，他年葬侬知是谁？
试看春残花渐落，便是红颜老死时。
一朝春尽红颜老，花落人亡两不知。

（6）第 31 回　撕扇子作千金一笑　因麒麟伏白首双星

晴雯笑道："我慌张得很，连扇子还跌折了，那里还配打发吃果子！倘或再打破了盘子，更了不得了。"宝玉笑道："你爱打就打，这些东西原不过是借人所用，你爱这样，我爱那样，各自性情不同。比如那扇子原是扇的，你要撕着玩，也可以使得，只是不可生气时拿它出气。就如杯盘，原是盛东西的，你喜听那一声响，就故意的碎了也可以使得，只是别在生气时拿他出气。这就是爱物了。"晴雯听了，笑道："既这么说，你就拿扇子来我撕。我最喜欢撕的。"宝玉听了，便笑着递与她。晴雯果然接过来，"嗤"的一声撕了两半，接着"嗤嗤"又听几声。宝玉在旁笑着说："响的好，再撕响些！"

正说着，只见麝月走过来，笑道："少作些孽罢！"宝玉赶上来，一把将她手里的扇子也夺了递与晴雯。晴雯接了，也撕作几半子，二人都大笑。麝月道："这是怎么说，拿我的东西开心？"宝玉笑道："打开扇子匣子你拣去，什么好东西！"麝月道："既这么说，就把匣子搬了出来，让她尽力地撕，岂不好？"宝玉笑道："你就搬去。"麝月道："我可不造这孽。她也没折了手，叫她自己搬去。"晴雯笑着，便倚在床上说道："我也乏了，明儿再撕罢。"宝玉笑道："古人云，'千金难买一笑'，几把扇子能值几何？"一面说着，一面叫袭人。袭人才换了衣服走出来，小丫头佳蕙过来拾去破扇，大家乘凉，不消细说。

（7）第 40 回 史太君两宴大观园 金鸳鸯三宣牙牌令

只见一个媳妇端了一个盒子站在当地，一个丫鬟上来揭去盒盖，里面盛着两碗菜。李纨端了一碗放在贾母桌上，凤姐儿偏拣了一碗鸽子蛋放在刘姥姥桌上。贾母这边说声"请"，刘姥姥便站起身来，高声说道："老刘，老刘，食量大似牛，吃一个老母猪不抬头。"自己却鼓着腮不语。

众人先是发怔，后来一听，上上下下都哈哈的大笑起来。史湘云撑不住，一口饭都喷了出来；林黛玉笑岔了气，伏着桌子叫"嗳哟"；宝玉早滚到贾母怀里，贾母笑得搂着宝玉叫"心肝"；王夫人笑得用手指着凤姐儿，只说不出话来；薛姨妈也撑不住，口里的茶喷了探春一裙子；探春手里的饭碗都合在迎春身上；惜春离了座位，拉着她奶母叫揉一揉肠子。地下的无一个不弯腰屈背，也有躲出去蹲着笑去的，也有忍着笑上来替她姊妹换衣裳的，独有凤姐、鸳鸯二人撑着，还只管让刘姥姥。

刘姥姥拿起箸来，只觉不听使，又说道："这里的鸡儿也俊，下的这蛋也小巧，怪俊的。我且肏攮一个。"众人方住了笑，听见这话，又笑起来。贾母笑得眼泪出来，琥珀在后捶着。贾母笑道："这定是凤丫头促狭鬼儿闹的，快别信她的话了。"那刘姥姥正夸鸡蛋小巧，要㑇攮一个，凤姐儿笑道："一两银子一个呢，你快尝尝罢，那冷了就不好吃了。"刘姥姥便伸箸子要夹，哪里夹得起来，满碗里闹了一阵，好容易撮起一个来，才伸着脖子要吃，偏又滑下来滚在地下，忙放下箸子要亲自去捡，早有地下的人捡了出去了。刘姥姥叹道："一两银子，也没听见响声儿就没了。"众人已没心吃饭，都看着她取笑。

（8）第62回　憨湘云醉眠芍药裀　呆香菱情解石榴裙

正说着，只见一个小丫头笑嘻嘻的走来："姑娘们快瞧云姑娘去，吃醉了图凉快，在山子后头一块青板石凳上睡着了。"众人听说，都笑道："快别吵嚷。"说着，都走来看时，果见湘云卧于山石僻处一个石凳子上，业经香梦沉酣，四面芍药花飞了一身，满头脸衣襟上皆是红香散乱，手中的扇子在地下，也半被落花埋了，一群蜂蝶闹穰穰的围着她，又用鲛帕包了一包芍药花瓣枕着。众人看了，又是爱，又是笑，忙上来推唤搀扶。湘云口内犹作睡语说酒令，唧唧嘟嘟说：泉香而酒冽，玉碗盛来琥珀光，直饮到梅梢月上，醉扶归，却为宜会亲友。

众人笑推她，说道："快醒醒儿吃饭去，这潮凳上还睡出病来呢。"湘云慢启秋波，见了众人，低头看了一看自己，方知是醉了。原是来纳凉避静的，不觉的因多罚了两杯酒，娇娜不胜，便睡着了，心中反觉自愧。连忙起身，扎挣着同人来至红香圃中，用过水，又吃了两盏酽茶。探春忙命将醒酒石拿来给他衔在口内，一时又命他喝了一些酸汤，方才觉得好了些。

（9）第 97 回 林黛玉焚稿断痴情 薛宝钗出闺成大礼

黛玉瞧瞧，又闭了眼坐着，喘了一会子，又道："笼上火盆。"紫鹃打量他冷。因说道："姑娘躺下，多盖一件罢。那炭气只怕耽不住。"黛玉又摇头儿。雪雁只得笼上，搁在地下火盆架上。黛玉点头，意思叫挪到炕上来。雪雁只得端上来，出去拿那张火盆炕桌。那黛玉却又把身子欠起，紫鹃只得两只手来扶着他。黛玉这才将方才的绢子拿在手中，瞅着那火，点点头儿，往上一撂。紫鹃唬了一跳，欲要抢时，两只手却不敢动。雪雁又出去拿火盆桌子，此时那绢子已经烧着了。紫鹃劝道："姑娘，这是怎么说呢？"黛玉只作不闻，回手又把那诗稿拿起来，瞧了瞧，又撂下了。紫鹃怕他也要烧，连忙将身倚住黛玉，腾出手来拿时，黛玉又早拾起，撂在火上。此时紫鹃却够不着，干急。雪雁正拿进桌子来，看见黛玉一撂，不知何物，赶忙抢时，那纸沾火就着，如何能够少待，早已烘烘的着了。雪雁也顾不得烧手，从火里抓起来，撂在地下乱踩，却已烧得所余无几了。那黛玉把眼一闭，往后一仰，几乎不曾把紫鹃压倒。紫鹃连忙叫雪雁上来，将黛玉扶着放倒，心里突突的乱跳。欲要叫人时，天又晚了；欲不叫人时，自己同着雪雁和鹦哥等几个小丫头，又怕一时有什么原故。好容易熬了一夜。

（10）第 120 回 甄士隐详说太虚情 贾雨村归结红楼梦

一日，行到毘陵驿地方，那天乍寒下雪，泊在一个清静去处。贾政打发众人上岸投帖，辞谢朋友，总说即刻开船，都不敢劳动。船中只留一个小厮伺候，自己在船中写家书，先要打发人起早到家。写到宝玉的事，便停笔。抬头忽见船头上微微的雪影里面一个人，光着头，赤着脚，身上披着一领大红猩猩毡的斗篷，向贾政倒身下拜。贾政尚未认清，急忙出船，欲待扶住问他是谁。那人已拜了四拜，站起来打了个问讯。贾政才要还揖，迎面一看，不是别人，却是宝玉。贾政吃一大惊，忙问道：“可是宝玉么？”那人只不言语，似喜似悲。贾政又问道：“你若是宝玉，如何这样打扮，跑到这里？”宝玉未及回言，只见舡头上来了两人，一僧一道，夹住宝玉说道：“俗缘已毕，还不快走！”说着，三个人飘然登岸而去。贾政不顾地滑，疾忙来赶。见那三人在前，那里赶得上。只听见他们三人口中不知是那个作歌曰：

我所居兮，青埂之峰。
我所游兮，鸿蒙太空。
谁与我游兮，吾谁与从？
渺渺茫茫兮，归彼大荒。

贾政一面听着，一面赶去，转过一小坡，倏然不见。贾政已赶得心虚气喘，惊疑不定，回过头来，见自己的小厮也是随后赶来。贾政问道：“你看见方才那三个人么？”小厮道：“看见的。奴才为老爷追赶，故也赶来。后来只见老爷，不见那三个人了。”贾政还欲前走，只见白茫茫一片旷野，并无一人。贾政知是古怪，只得回来。

Chapter X A Dream of Red Mansions

1. Introduction of the Work

A Dream of Red Mansions, one of the four great classics of Ancient China, is generally believed to have been written by Cao Xueqin, a Qing Dynasty writer. The background of the novel is the rise and fall of Jia, Shi, Wang and Xue, four big families, and the main plot is the love and marriage tragedy of Jia Baoyu, Lin Daiyu and Xue Baochai from the perspective of the rich child Jia Baoyu. The book depicts the life of a group of boudoir ladies whose manners and knowledge are seen as above men, displaying the true beauty of human nature and tragedy. It can be said that it is an epic work that shows the beauty of women and the various social conditions in ancient China from all angles.

There are two systems including120 chapters of the "Cheng Version" and 80 chapters of the "Zhi Version" in the edition of *A Dream of Red Mansions*. Cheng Version is a printed copy by Cheng Weiyuan, while Zhi Version is an early handwritten copy from the Red Ink-stone Studio in different periods. So the latter is the basis of the former one.

The opening chapter of *A Dream of Red Mansions* introduces the origin of the work in the form of a myth, saying that Nüwa had left an unused stone to fill the sky and abandoned it at the foot of Blue Ridge Peak, a Baseless cliff of the Great Waste Mountain. The Impervioso and the Mysterioso passed through the place, cast a spell to make it spiritual and carried it down to Earth. After countless generations or aeons, a Taoist known as Reverend Void saw that upon the stone was engraved on a story. He was commissioned by the stone, and copied it down for posterity. It was passed on to Cao Xueqin, who reviewed it for a decade, finished the book by adding and subtracting from it five times.

A Dream of Red Mansions is a world-influential novel of human life. It is universally acknowledged as the peak of Chinese classical novels, the Encyclopedia of Chinese feudal society and the collection of traditional culture. The author of the novel urges himself to "Talk about love and record its facts", according to his own situation and reason, following the track, getting rid of old customs, and with fresh and unique style. Through this he has made extraordinary artistic achievements. "The truth hidden, false language in village speech", which is the special writing style to make future generations of readers to open their minds, with more and more speculation on the theory as time went by. Since the 20th century, because of the outstanding artistic achievements and rich and profound ideological details, the academic circles have produced a special study of A Dream of Red Mansions: the Redology.

2. Introduction of the Author

Cao Xueqin (May 28, 1715~February 12, 1763), first name Zhan, courtesy name of Meng Ruan, pseudonym of Xue Qin, also known as Qin Xi or Qin Pu, is the author of the classic Chinese novel—*A Dream Of Red Mansions*. His ancestral home is Tieling, Liaoning. Cao Xueqin was born in Jiangning (nowaways Nanjing) in a white flag coating family of the Qing Dynasty Ministry of Internal Order, and was Jiangning weaving merchant Cao Yin's grandson and Cao Yong's son (Cao Fu's son, one source claimed).

In his early years, Cao Xueqin lived a rich and noble life in the Weaving Office House in Jiangning, Nanjing. His great grandfather Cao Xi was an official responsible for weaving in Jiangning, while his great grandmother Sun was the nanny of Emperor Kangxi. His grandfather Cao Yin was the companion and bodyguard of Emperor Kangxi. Later, he was the officer who was in charge of weaving industry in Jiangning, and also served as a salt supervisory censor in the north and south parts of the Huai River. In these roles he was highly favored by Emperor Kangxi. In the Sixth Year of the Yongzheng Reign (1728), the Cao family was searched after being found guilty of losing money, and Cao Xueqin moved back with his family to their old residence in Beijing. After moving to the western suburbs of Beijing, he made the living by selling calligraphy or painting, and through friends'relief. The Cao family has been in decline ever since. After a major turning point in his life, Cao Xueqin was deeply moved by the bleak state of the world and gained a more sober and profound understanding of feudal society. He scorned the rich and powerful, kept away from officialdom and lived in abject poverty. Cao Xueqin, with a wide range of hobbies, had studied many fields like stonework, poetry, painting, gardening, Chinese Medicine, weaving, technology and diet. Through years of hardship and perseverance, he finally created a great work full of thought and artistry —— *A dream of the Red Mansions*. In his later years, Cao Xueqin moved to the western suburbs of Beijing. Life was poorer and more difficult: "the paths are full of withered weeds", "often on debt and congee the family live".

When his youngest son died in the twenty-seventh year of Qianlong's reign (1762), he was bedridden with excessive distress and grief. On New Year's Eve (February 12th) of Qianlong's twenty-eight year (1763), he died of poverty and illness without receiving medical treatment. As for the year of Cao Xueqin's death, there is another saying, New Year's Eve (1764 February 1st) of Qianlong's twenty-nine year and the early spring of year of Gengshen (1764).

3. Appreciation

(1)Chapter 3

Lin Ruhai recommends a private tutor to his brother-in-law

And old Lady Jia extends a compassionate welcome to the motherless child

'Oh dear! I'm late,' said the voice. 'I've missed the arrival of our guest.'

'Everyone else around here seems to go about with bated breath,' thought Daiyu. 'Who can this new arrival be who is so brash and unmannerly?'

Even as she wondered, a beautiful young woman entered from the room behind the one they were sitting in, surrounded by a bevy of serving women and maids. She was dressed quite differently from the others present, gleaming like some fairy princess with sparkling jewels and gay embroideries.

Her chignon was enclosed in a circlet of gold filigree and clustered pearls. It was fastened with a pin embellished with flying phoenixes, from whose beaks pearls were suspended On tiny chains.

Her necklet was of red gold in the form of a coiling dragon. Her dress had a fitted bodice and was made of dark red silk damask with a pattern of flowers and butterflies in raised gold thread.

Her jacket was lined with ermine. It was of a slate-blue stuff with woven insets in coloured silks.

Her under-skirt was of a turquoise-coloured imported silk crêpe embroidered with flowers.

She had, moreover, eyes like a painted phoenix, eyebrows like willow-eaves, a slender form, seductive grace; the ever-smiling summer face of hidden thunders showed no trace; the ever-bubbling laughter started almost before the lips were parted.

'You don't know her,' said Grandmother Jia merrily. 'She's a holy terror this one. What we used to call in Nanking a "peppercorn". You just call her "Peppercorn Feng". She'll know who you mean!'

Daiyu was at a loss to know how she was to address this Peppercorn Feng until one of the cousins whispered that it was 'Cousin Lian's wife', and she remembered having heard her mother say that her elder uncle, Uncle She, had a son called Jia Lian who was married to the niece of her Uncle Zheng's wife, Lady Wang. She had been brought up from earliest childhood just like a boy, and had acquired in the schoolroom the somewhat boyish-sounding name of Wang Xifeng. Daiyu accordingly smiled and curtseyed, greeting her by her correct name as she did so.

Xifeng took Daiyu by the hand and for a few moments scrutinized her carefully from top to toe before conducting her back to her seat beside Grandmother Jia.

'She's a beauty, Grannie dear! If I hadn't set eyes on her today, I shouldn't have believed that such a beautiful creature could exist! And everything about her so *distingue*!' She doesn't take after your side of the family, Grannie. She's more like a Jia. I don't blame you for having gone on so about her during the past few days - but poor little thing! What a cruel fate to have lost Auntie like that!' and she dabbed at her eyes with a handkerchief.

'I've only just recovered,' laughed Grandmother Jia. 'Don't you go trying to start me off again! Besides, your little cousin is not very strong, and we've only just managed to get her cheered up. So let's have no more of this!'

In obedience to the command Xifeng at once exchanged her grief for merriment.

'Yes, of course. It was just that seeing my little cousin here put everything else out of my mind. It made me want to laugh and cry all at the same time. I'm afraid I quite forgot about you, Grannie dear. I deserve to be spanked, don't I?'

She grabbed Daiyu by the hand.

'How old are you dear? Have you begun school yet? You mustn't feel home sick here. If there's anything you want to eat or anything you want to play with, just come and tell me. And you must tell me if any of the maids or the old nannies are nasty to you.'

Daiyu made appropriate responses to all of these questions and injunctions.

Xifeng turned to the servants.

'Have Miss Lin's things been brought in yet? How many people did she bring with her? You'd better hurry up and get a couple of rooms swept out for them to rest in.'

A perceptive poet has supplied two sets of verses, to be sung to the tune of *Moon on West River*, which contain a more accurate appraisal of our hero than the foregoing descriptions.

> Oft-times he sought Out what would make him sad, sometimes an idiot seemed and sometimes mad.
>
> Though outwardly a handsome sausage-skin, he proved to have but sorry meat within.
>
> A harum-scarum, to all duty blind, a doltish mule, to study disinclined.
>
> His acts outlandish and his nature queer, yet not a whit cared he how folk might jeer!

> Prosperous, he could not play his part with grace, nor, poor, bear hardship with a smiling face.
>
> So shamefully the precious hours he'd waste, that both indoors and out he was disgraced.
>
> For uselessness the world's prize he might bear, his

gracelessness in history has no peer.

Let gilded youths who every dainty sample, not imitate this rascal’ s dire example!

‘Fancy changing your clothes before you have welcomed the visitor!’ Grandmother Jia chided indulgently on seeing Baoyu back again. ‘Aren’t you going to pay your respects to your cousin?’

Baoyu had already caught sight of a slender, delicate girl whom he surmised to be his Aunt Lin’s daughter and quickly went over to greet her. Then, returning to his place and taking a seat, he studied her attentively. How different she seemed from the other girls he knew!

Her mist-wreathed brows at first seemed to frown, yet were not frowning. her passionate eyes at first seemed to smile, yet were not merry. Habit had given a melancholy cast to her tender face, nature had bestowed a sickly constitution on her delicate frame. Often the eyes swam with glistening tears, often the breath came in gentle gasps. In stillness she made one think of a graceful flower reflected in the water, in motion she called to mind tender willow shoots caressed by the wind. She had more chambers in her heart than the martyred Bi Gan, and suffered a tithe more pain in it than the beautiful Xi Shi.

Having completed his survey, Baoyu gave a laugh. ‘I have seen this cousin before.’

‘Nonsense!’ said Grandmother Jia. ‘How could you Possibly have done?’

‘Well, perhaps not,’ said Baoyu, ‘but her face seems so

familiar that I have the impression of meeting her again after a long separation.'

'All the better,' said Grandmother Jia. 'That means that you should get on well together.'

Baoyu moved over again and, drawing a chair up beside Daiyu, recommenced his scrutiny.

Presently: 'Do you study books yet, cousin?'

'No,' said Daiyu. 'I have only been taking lessons for a year or so. I can barely read and write.'

'What's your name?'

Daiyu told him.

'What's your school-name?'

'I haven't got one.'

Baoyu laughed. 'I'll give you one, cousin. I think "Frowner" would suit you perfectly.'

(2)Chapter 4

The Bottle-gourd girl meets an unfortunate young man

And the Bottle-gourd monk settles a protracted lawsuit

'What is the *Mandarin's Lift-Preserver*?' Yu-cun inquired curiously.

'Nowadays every provincial official carries a private hand-list with the names of all the richest, most influential people in his area. There is one for every province. They list those families which are so powerful that if you were ever to run up against one of them unknowingly, not only your job, but perhaps even your life might be in danger. That's why they are called "life-preservers".

'Now take this Xue you were dealing with just now. Your Honour couldn't possibly try conclusions with *him*! Why do you suppose this case has remained unsettled for so long? It's a straightforward enough case. The reason is simply that none of your predecessors dared touch it because of the unpleasantness and loss of face it would have caused them.'

While he was speaking he had been fishing for a copy of the *Mandarin's Lift-Preserver* in his pocket. This he now presented *10* Yu-cun for his inspection. It contained a set of doggerel verses in which were listed the big families and most powerful magnates of the area in which he was working. It went some-thing like this:

Shout hip hurrah, for the Nanking Jia! They weigh their gold out by the jar.

The Ah-bang Palace, scrapes the sky, but it could not house the Nanking Shi.

The King of the Ocean goes along, when he's short of gold beds, to the Nanking Wang.

The Nanking Xue so rich are they, to count their money would take all day...

(3)Chapter 18

A brief family reunion is permitted by the magnanimity of a gracious Emperor

And an Imperial Concubine takes pleasure in the literary progress of a younger brother

For a long time there was total silence. Then a couple of eunuchs on horseback came riding very, very slowly up to the west gate. Dismounting, they led their horses out of sight behind the cloth screens, then returned to take up their stand at the sides of the road, half-facing towards the west. After a considerable wait, two more eunuchs arrived and went through the same motions as the first pair. Then another two, and then another, until in all some ten pairs were standing at the sides of the road, their faces turned expectantly towards the west.

Presently a faint sound of music was heard and the Imperial Concubine's procession at last came in sight.

First came several pairs of eunuchs carrying embroidered banners.

Then several more pairs with ceremonial pheasant-feather fans.

Then eunuchs swinging gold-inlaid censers in which special 'palace incense' was burning.

Next came a great gold-coloured 'seven-phoenix' umbrella of state, hanging from its curve-topped shaft like a great drooping bell-flower. In its shadow was borne the Imperial Concubine's travelling wardrobe: her head-dress, robe, sash and shoes.

Eunuch gentlemen-in-waiting followed carrying her rosary, her embroidered handkerchief, her spittoon, her fly-whisk, and various other items.

Last of all, when this army of attendants had gone by, a great gold-topped palanquin with phoenixes embroidered on its yellow curtains slowly advanced on the shoulders of eight eunuch bearers.

As Grandmother Jia and the rest dropped to their knees eunuchs rushed up and helped them to get up again. The palanquin passed through the great gate and made for the entrance of a courtyard on the east side of the forecourt. There a eunuch knelt beside it and invited the Imperial Concubine to descend and 'change her clothes'. The bearers carried it through the entrance and set it down just inside the courtyard. The other eunuchs then withdrew, leaving Yuan-chun's ladies-in-waiting to help her from the palanquin.

The courtyard she now stepped out into was brilliant with coloured lanterns of silk gauze cunningly fashioned in all sorts of curious and beautiful shapes and patterns. An illuminated sign hung over the entrance of the principal building:

PILLED WITH FAVOURS BATHED IN BLESSINGS

Yuanchun passed beneath it into the room that had been prepared for her, then, having 'changed her clothes', came out again and stepped back into the palanquin, which was now borne into the garden.

Her first impression was a confused one of curling drifts of incense smoke and gleaming colours. There were lanterns everywhere, and soft strains of music. She seemed to be entering a little world wholly dedicated to the pursuit of ease and luxury and delight.

(4)Chapter 23

Words from the 'Western Chamber' supply a joke that offends

And songs from the 'Soul's Return' move a tender heart to anguish

"Well," said Baoyu,"is it good?" Daiyu smiled and nodded.

Baoyu laughed: "How can I, full of sickness and of woe, withstand that face which kingdoms could o'erthrow?"

Daiyu reddened to the tips of her ears. The eyebrows that seemed to frown yet somehow didn't were raised now in anger and the lovely eyes flashed. There was rage in her crimson cheeks and resentment in all her looks.

"You're *hateful*!'—she pointed a finger at him in angry accusal — 'deliberately using that horrid play to take advantage of me. I'm going. straight off to tell Uncle and Aunt!"

At the words 'take advantage of me' her eyes filled with tears, and as she finished speaking she turned from him and began to go. Baoyu rushed after her and held her back: "Please, *please* forgive me! Dearest coz! If I had the slightest intention of taking advantage of you, may I fall into the water and be eaten up by an old bald-headed turtle! When you have become a great lady and gone at last to your final resting-place, I shall become the stone turtle that stands in front of your grave and spend the rest of eternity carrying your tombstone on my back as a punishment!"

His ridiculous declamation provoked a sudden explosion of mirth. She laughed and simultaneously wiped the tears away with her knuckles:"Look at you - the same as ever! Scared as anything, but you still have to go on talking nonsense. Well, I know you now for what you are:"Of silver spear the leaden counterfeit!"

"Well! *You* can talk!" said Baoyu laughing. "Listen to *you*! Now I'm going off to tell on *you*!"

"You needn't imagine you're the only one with a good memory," said Daiyu haughtily. “I suppose I’m allowed to remember lines too if I like.”

(5)CHAPTER 27

Beauty Perspiring sports with butterflies by the Raindrop Pavilion and Beauty Suspiring weeps for fallen blossoms by the Flowers’ Crave

The blossoms fade and falling fill the air, of fragrance and bright hues bereft and bare.Floss drifts and flutters round the Maiden’s bower, or softly strikes against her curtained door.

The Maid, grieved by these signs of spring’s decease, seeking some means her sorrow to express, has rake in hand into the garden gone,before the fallen flowers are trampled on.

Elm-pods and willow-floss are fragrant too, why care, Maid, where the fallen flowers blew? Next year, when peach and plum-tree bloom again, which of your sweet companions will remain?

This spring the heartless swallow built his nest, beneath the eaves of mud with flowers compressed.Next year the flowers will blossom as before, but swallow, nest, and Maid will be no more.

Three hundred and three-score the year’s full tale, from swords of frost and from the slaughtering gale. How can the lovely flowers long stay intact, or, once loosed, from their drifting fate draw back?

Blooming so steadfast, fallen so hard to find! beside the flowers’grave, with sorrowing mind, the solitary Maid sheds many a tear, which on the boughs as bloody drops appear.

At twilight, when the cuckoo sings no more, the Maiden with her rake goes in at door. And lays her down between the lamplit walls, while a chill rain against the window falls.

I know not why my heart's so strangely sad, half grieving for the spring and yet half glad. Glad that it came, grieved it so soon was spent. so soft it came, so silently it went!

Last night, outside, a mournful sound was heard: the spirits of the flowers and of the bird. But neither bird nor flowers would long delay, bird lacking speech, and flowers too shy to stay.

And then I wished that I had wings to fly, after the drifting flowers across the sky. Across the sky to the world's farthest end, the flowers'last fragrant resting-place to find.

But better their remains in silk to lay, and bury underneath the wholesome clay, pure substances the pure earth to enrich, than leave to soak and stink in some foul ditch.

Can I, that these flowers'obsequies attend, divine how soon or late my life will end? let others laugh flower-burial to see: another year who will be burying me?

As petals drop and spring begins to fail, the bloom of youth, too, sickens and turns pale.One day, when spring has gone and youth has fled. The Maiden and the flowers will both be dead.

(6)CHAPTER 31

A torn fan is the price of silver laughter

And a lost kylin is the clue to a happy marriage

Skybright smiled.

'You've already told me once today how clumsy I am. I can't even drop a fan without treading on it. So I'm much too clumsy to get your fruit for you. Suppose I were to break a plate. That would be terrible!'

'If you want to break *it*, by all means break it,' said Baoyu. 'These things are there for our use. What we use *them for* is a matter of individual taste. For example, fans are made for fanning with; but if you prefer to tear them up because it gives you pleasure, there's no reason why you shouldn't. What you *mustn't* do is to use them as objects to vent your anger on. It's the same with plates and cups. Plates and cups are made to put food and drink in. But if you want to smash them on purpose because you like the noise, it's perfectly all right to do so. As long as you don't get into a passion and start taking it out on *things*—that is the golden rule.'

'All right then,' said Skybright with a mischievous smile. 'Give me your fan to tear. I love the sound of a fan being torn.'

Baoyu held it out to her. She took it eagerly and—*chah*!—promptly tore it in half. And again —*chah*! *Chah*! *chah*!—she tore it several more times. Baoyu, an appreciative onlooker, laughed and encouraged her.

'Well torn! Well torn! Now again - a really loud one!'

Just then Musk appeared. She stared at them indignantly.

'Don't do that!' she said. 'It's *wicked* to waste things like that.'

But Baoyu leaped up to her, snatched the fan from her hand, and passed it to Skybright, who at once tore it into several pieces. The two of them, Baoyu and Skybright, then burst into uproarious laughter.

'What do you think you're doing?' said Musk. 'That's *my fan* you've just ruined.'

'What's an old fan?' said Baoyu. 'Open up the fan box and get yourself another.'

'If that's your attitude,' said Musk, 'we might as well carry Out the whole boxful and let her tear away to her heart's content.'

'All right. Go and get it,' said Baoyu.

'And be born a beggar in my next life?' said Musk. 'No thank you I She hasn't broken her arm. Let her go and get it herself.'

Skybright stretched back on the bed, smiling complacently. 'I'm rather tired just now. I think I shall tear some more tomorrow.'

Baoyu laughed.

'The ancients used to say that for one smile of a beautiful woman a thousand taels are well spent. For a few old fans it's cheap at the price!'

He called to Aroma, who had just finished changing into clean clothes, to come outside and join them. Little Melilot came and cleared away the broken bits of fan, and everyone sat for a while and enjoyed the cool.

(7)Chapter 40

Lady Jia holds two feasts in one day in the Prospect Garden

And Faithful makes four calls on three dominoes in the Painted Chamber

A woman-servant now entered carrying one of the lunch onboxes and stood in the middle of the room holding it while a maid removed the lid. There were two dishes inside. Li Wan took out one of them and set it down on Grandmother Jia's table. The second, a bowl of pigeon's eggs (deliberately chosen for their mirth-provoking possibilities) was taken out by Xifeng and set down in front of Grannie Liu.

"Please!" said Grandmother Jia, waving her chopsticks at the food as a polite indication that they should begin. At once Grannie Liu leaped to her feet and, in ringing tones, recited the following grace:

"My name it is Liu,
I'm a trencherman true;
I can eat a whole sow,
with her little pigs too."

Having concluded, she puffed out both her cheeks and stared in front of her with an expression of great determination.

There was a moment of awestruck silence; then, as it dawned on them that they really had heard what they thought they had heard, the whole company, both masters and servants, burst out into roars of laughter.

Shi Xiangyun, unable to contain herself, spat out a whole mouthful of rice.

Lin Daiyu, made breathless by laughter, collapsed on the table, uttering weak "Aiyos".

Baoyu rolled over, convulsed, on to his grandmother's bosom.

Grandmother Jia, exclaiming helplessly "Oh, my heart!" "Oh, my child!", clung tightly to her heaving grandson.

Lady Wang pointed an accusing finger at Xifeng, but laughter had deprived her of speech.

Aunt Xue exploded a mouthful of tea over Tan-chun's skirt.

Tanchun planted a bowlful of rice on the person of Ying-chun.

Xichun got up from the table and going over to her nurse, took her by the hand and asked her to massage her stomach.

The servants were all doubled up. Some had to go outside where they could squat down and laugh with abandon. Those who could control themselves sufficiently helped the casualties to mop up or change their clothes.

Only Xifeng and Faithful remained straight-faced throughout this outburst, politely urging Grannie Liu to begin. Manipulating the unwieldy chopsticks with considerable difficulty, the old woman prepared to do so.

"Even your hens here are special," she remarked. "Such pretty little eggs they lay! I must see if I can't get one of these under my belt!"

Under the impact of these remarks the company's composure, which it had only just recovered, once more broke down. Grandmother Jia, abandoning any attempt at self-control, was now actually weeping with laughter. Amber, who feared a seizure, pounded her energetically on the back.

"That wicked devil Feng is behind this," said Grandmother Jia. "Don't believe a thing she tells you!"

"They cost a silver tael apiece," said Xifeng, as Grannie Liu continued to praise the diminutive hen's eggs. "You should eat them quickly, while they're still hot, They won't be so nice when they're cold."

Grannie Liu obediently held out her chopsticks and tried to take hold of one, but the egg eluded her. After chasing it several times round the inside of the bowl, she did at last succeed in getting a grip on it. But as she craned forward with open mouth to reach it, it slipped through the chopsticks and rolled on to the floor. At once she laid down the chopsticks, and would have gone down on hands and knees to pick it up, but before she could do so one of the servants had retrieved it and carried it off for disposal.

"That's a tael of silver gone," Grannie Liu said regretfully, "and we didn't even hear the clink!"

The others had by now lost all interest in eating, absorbed by the entertaining antics of their guest.

(8)Chapter 62

A tipsy Xiangyun sleeps on a peony-petal pillow

And a grateful Caltrop unfastens her pomegranate skirt

They were interrupted by a giggling young maid - "Miss Yun must have been feeling drunk and gone out for some air. She's lying on the granite bench behind the rockery, fast asleep."

"Let's be quiet and not waken her," the others said amidst laughter, and followed her outside to have a look.

They found Xiang-yun where the maid had said, on a large stone bench in a hidden corner of the rockery, dead to the world. She was covered all over from head to foot with crimson petals from the peony bushes which grew round about; the fan which had slipped from her hand and lay on the ground beside her was half buried in petals; and heaped-up peony petals wrapped in a white silk handkerchief made an improvised pillow for her head. Over and around this petalled monstrosity convocation of bees and butterflies was hovering distractedly. It was a sight that the cousins found both touching and comical. They made haste to rouse her and lifted her up into a half-sitting position on the bench. But Xiang-yun was still playing drinking games in her sleep and proceeded to recite the words of an imaginary forfeit, though her eyes were tightly closed.

'One. "The spring water being sweet, the wine is good." Two. "Pour me its liquid amber in a jade cup." Three. We'll drink till we see "The moon above the plum-tree bough". Four. Then, as we're "Rolling Home". Five. It will be "A good time to meet a friend."

They shook her, laughing.

'Wake up! Wake up! Come and have something to eat. Lying on the damp stone like this you'll make yourself ill.'

Xiang-yun... uplifted slowly then those orbs serene and saw the faces of the cousins bending over her. Then she looked downwards and saw her own body and the place where she had been lying. She could remember escaping from the noise to rest for a few moments somewhere where it was cool and quiet. Evidently the wine from all those sconces she had been made to drink must have got the better of her and caused her to drop off. Ashamed to have been discovered in such a predicament, she struggled hastily to her feet and accompanied the others back to the summerhouse, where she rinsed her mouth out with water and drank two very strong cups of tea. Tan-chun made one of the girls fetch a piece of 'hangover rock' for her to suck. By the time she had sucked the rock for a bit and taken a few mouthfuls of hot, sour soup, she was feeling almost herself again.

(9)Chapter 97

Lin Daiyu burns her poems to signal the end of her heart's folly

And Xue Baochai leaves home to take part in a solemn rite

Daiyu looked into the lamp, then closed her eyes and sat in

silence. Another fit of breathlessness. Then:"Make up the fire in the brazier."

Thinking she wanted it for the extra warmth, Nightingale protested:"You should lie down, Miss, and have another cover on. And the fumes from the brazier might be bad for you."

Daiyu shook her head, and Snowgoose reluctantly made up the brazier, placing it on its stand on the floor. Daiyu made a motion with her hand, indicating that she wanted it moved up onto the bed. Snowgoose lifted it and placed it there, temporarily using the floor-stand, -while she went out to fetch the special stand they used on the bed. Daiyu, far from resting back in the warmth, now inclined her body slightly forward-Nightingale had to support her with both hands as she did so. Daiyu took the handkerchiefs in one hand. Staring into the flames and nodding thoughtfully to herself, she dropped them into the brazier. Nightingale was horrified, but much as she would have liked to snatch them from the flames, she did not dare move her hands and leave Daiyu unsupported. Snowgoose was out of the room, fetching the brazier-stand, and by now the handkerchiefs were all ablaze.

"Miss!" cried Nightingale. "What are you doing?"

As if she had not heard, Daiyu reached over for her manuscripts, glanced at them and let them fall again onto the bed. Nightingale, anxious lest she burn these too, leaned up against Daiyu and freeing one hand, reached out with it to take hold of them. But before she could do so, Daiyu had picked them up again and dropped them in the flames. The brazier was out of Nightingale's reach, and there was nothing she could do but look on helplessly.

Just at that moment Snowgoose came in with the stand. She saw Daiyu drop something into the fire, and without knowing what it was, rushed forward to try and save it. The manuscripts had caught at once and were already ablaze. Heedless of - the danger to her hands, Snowgoose reached into the flames and pulled out what she could, throwing the paper on the floor and stamping frantically on it. But the fire had done its work, and only a few charred fragments remained. Daiyu closed her eyes and slumped back, almost causing Nightingale to topple over with her. Nightingale, her heart thumping in great agitation, called Snowgoose over to help her settle Daiyu down again. It was too late now to send for anyone. And yet, what if Daiyu should die during the night, and the only people there were Snowgoose, herself and the one or two other junior maids in the Naiad's House? They passed a restless night.

(10)Chapter 120

Zhen Shiyin expounds the Nature of Passion and Illusion

And Jia Yucun concludes the Dream of Golden Days

On the day when his boat reached the post-station at Piling, there was a sudden cold tarn in the weather and it began to snow. He moored in a quiet, lonely stretch of the canal and sent his servants ashore to deliver a few visiting-cards and to apologize to his friends in the locality, saying that since his boat was due to set off again at any moment he would not be able to call on them in person or entertain them aboard. Only one page-boy remained to wait on him while he sat in the cabin writing a letter home (to be sent on ahead by land). When he came to write about Baoyu, he paused for a moment and looked up. There, up on deck, standing in the very entrance to his cabin and silhouetted dimly against the snow, was the figure of a man with shaven head and bare feet, wrapped in a large cape made of crimson felt. The figure knelt down and bowed to Jia Zheng, who did not recognize the features and hurried out on deck, intending to raise him up and ask him his name. The man bowed four times, and now stood upright, pressing his palms together in monkish greeting. Jia Zheng was about to reciprocate with a respectful bow of the head when he looked into the man's eyes and with a sudden shock recognized him as Baoyu.

"Are you not my son?" he asked.

The man was silent and an expression that seemed to contain both joy and sorrow played on his face. Jia Zheng asked again:"If you are Baoyu, why are you dressed like this? And what brings you to this place?"

Before Baoyu could reply two other men appeared on the deck, a Buddhist monk and a Taoist, and holding him between them they said:"Come, your earthly karma is complete. Tarry no longer."

The three of them mounted the bank and strode off into the snow. Jia Zheng went chasing after them along the slippery track, but although he could spy them ahead of him, somehow they always remained just out of reach. He could hear all three of them singing some sort of a song:

On Green sickness Peak, I dwell; In the Cosmic Void I

roam.

Who will pass over?

Who will go with me?

Who will explore?

The supremely ineffable vastly mysterious wilderness to which I return!

Jia Zheng listened to the song and continued to follow them until they rounded the slope of a small hill and suddenly vanished from sight. He was weak and out of breath by now with the exertion of the chase, and greatly mystified by what he had seen. Looking back he saw his page-boy, hurrying up behind him.

"Did you see those three men just now?" he questioned him.

"Yes, sir, I did," replied the page. "I saw you following them, so I came too. Then they disappeared and I could see no one but you."

Jia Zheng wanted to continue, but all he could see before him was a vast expanse of white, with not a soul anywhere. He knew there was more to this strange occurrence than he could understand, and reluctantly he turned back and began to retrace his steps.

参考文献

[1] David Hawkes. The Story of the Stone [M]. London: Penguin Classics, 1980.

[2] Martin Palmer. The Romance of the Three Kingdoms [M]. London: Penguin Books, 2018.

[3] Sidney Shapiro. Outlaws of the Marsh [M]. Beijing: Foreign Languages Press, 2018.

[4] W. J. F. Jenner. Journey to the West [M]. Beijing: Foreign Languages Press, 2020.

[5] 曹雪芹，高鹗 . 红楼梦 [M]. 李全华，标点 . 长沙：岳麓书社，1987.

[6] 司马迁 . Selections from Records of the Historian[M]. 杨宪益，戴乃迭，译 . 北京：外文出版社，2007.

[7] 王丽 . 名家讲《史记》[M]. 李莉，译 . 北京：五洲传播出版社，2017.

[8] Thus Spoke the Master [M]. 许渊冲，译 . 北京：五洲传播出版社，2012.

[9] Laws Divine and Human [M]. 许渊冲，译 . 北京：五洲传播出版社，2012.

[10] 闫红 . 燕燕于飞：美得窒息的诗经（英汉对照）[M]. 许渊冲，译 . 武汉：长江文艺出版社，2020.

[11] 荀况 . 荀子选译（汉英对照）[M] . 吴思远，译 . 桂林：广西师范大学出版社，2017.